BEING MODERN IN IRAN

The CERI Series in Comparative Politics and International Studies
Series editors: JEAN-FRANÇOIS BAYART AND CHRISTOPHE JAFFRELOT

This series consists of translations of noteworthy publications in the social sciences emanating from the foremost French research centre in international studies, the Paris-based Centre d'Etudes et de Recherches Internationales (CERI), part of Sciences Po and associated with the CNRS (Centre National de la Recherche Scientifique)

The focus of the series is the transformation of politics and society by transnational and domestic factors — globalisation, migration, and the post-bipolar balance of power on the one hand, and ethnicity and religion on the other. States are more permeable to external influence than ever before and this phenomenon is accelerating processes of social and political change the world over. In seeking to understand and interpret these transformations, this series give priority to social trends from below as much as the interventions of state and non-state actors.

Founded in 1952, CERI has forty full-time fellows drawn from different disciplines conducting research on comparative political analysis, international relations, regionalism, transnational flows, political sociology, political economy and on individual states.

FARIBA ADELKHAH

Being Modern in Iran

translated from the French by
JONATHAN DERRICK

HURST & COMPANY, LONDON

in association with the
Centre d'Etudes et de Recherches Internationales
Paris

First published as *Être moderne en Iran*
by Karthala, Paris (© 1998)

First published in the United Kingdom by
C. Hurst & Co. (Publishers) Ltd.,
38 King Street, London WC2E 8JZ
English translation and updating © C. Hurst & Co. (Publishers) Ltd., 1999
All rights reserved.
Printed in Malaysia

ISBNs
1-85065-516-2 (*cased*)
1-85065-518-9 (*paperback*)

For Hossein Toussi

CONTENTS

ACKNOWLEDGMENTS

My thanks go to the Centre d'Etudes et de Recherches Internationales of the French Fondation Nationale des Sciences Politiques, and particularly to its successive Directors, Jean-Luc Domenach and Jean-François Bayart, for the warmth of their welcome and support worthy of a *javânmard* which they gave me. Similarly to Rachel Bouyssou, CERI's head of publications, for her unsparing efforts to come to my help when needed, as an incomparable editor. For the English edition, the translator Jonathan Derrick has proved a most helpful and friendly collaborator.

My fieldwork was made very pleasant thanks to the logistics and friendly support given by Remy Boucharlat, Director of the Institut Français de Recherche in Iran.

Lastly, my fondest thoughts go to Said Farimani, Agha Jean, Mansoureh Khorram, Roland Marchal and Christine Meyer for standing by me.

Paris, Spring 1999   F.A.

PREFACE TO THE ENGLISH EDITION

In May 1997 the victory in Iran's presidential elections of Mohammad Khatami (the outsider of the Left and the advocate of reform) over Nategh Nuri, the speaker of parliament who had been considered the favourite, seemed to confirm that the Islamic regime installed after the 1979 Revolution was being eroded, and 'opened up'. A number of observers saw this as supporting a theory of a new era of 'post-Islamism' for Iran and for the Muslim world more generally. But in fact it may be asked whether this is not a 'second wind' for the Islamic Republic.

It should be stressed first of all that Mohammad Khatami is himself a man of the system. He is not, strictly speaking, a product of 'civil society' as was said too often in the aftermath of his surprise victory. His political career is very different from that of someone like Vaclav Havel in the Czech Republic, for example. Certainly, in his speeches and actions, he has known how to express in words and actions the expectations of wide sections of the population regarding freedoms and the rule of law, and to take advantage of them.. But there is no indication that those aspirations were in themselves in contradiction with the revolutionary heritage of 1978-79, however much coercion there may have been in the political running of the state in practice.

More fundamentally, it would be very difficult to define Islamism precisely and distinguish what is 'pre-Islamic' or 'post-Islamic'. Islamism, as a political and social phenomenon, has never been something rigid, at least not in the context of Iranian society. It has, in particular, inspired numerous ideological debates and has never given rise to a special mode of production, nor even to a specific, original form of political economy comparable to what Soviet Socialism possibly was. In other words, Islamism has always remained in gear with the dynamics of social change, including those of globalisation. That is why it puts on such a different appearance from one country or historical situation to another.

In the case of Iran the historic break due to the Revolution did not have to do with the Islamist movement alone (the Liberals, Marxists and nationalists played a not negligible role in popular mobilisation) and it did not wipe out all the achievements of the old regime. Even where the situation of women was concerned, militant Islamic women turned to their own account the defence of some clauses of the Civil Code which both the conservatives among the clergy and the revolutionaries could have challenged. In addition the Republic had to cope with developments that had nothing particularly Islamic about them and which the Shah's regime had also had to deal with, especially the regionalist pressures of the Kurds, Azeris, Turkmens and Arabs and the Iraqi military threat. And the Republic now has a long history of twenty years, which is often forgotten.

So it is best to distinguish various phases in that history. After the first months of post-revolutionary euphoria and freedom the increased strength of the movements for local autonomy, the terrorism of radical Islamist groups such as Forghan and the People's Mujahidin, and above all the war imposed by Saddam Hussein's aggression led to a hardening of the regime, culminating in a real 'Terror' and a so-called 'Cultural Revolution'. Intervention by Imam Khomeyni put an end to that in 1983; this involved imposing the principle of *velâyat-e faqih* (the guardianship of the Islamic jurist) on the clergy and the political class. The regime remained all the more centralised and authoritarian because the conflict with Iraq made the organisation of a war economy necessary. However, the factional struggle between political tendencies, so intense that it led to the Islamic Republican Party's decision to wind itself up in 1985, foreshadowed the emergence of true Islamic pluralism, consecrated by the accession to power of Ali Khamenei (as Leader of the Revolution) and Hashemi Rafsanjani (as President of the Republic) after the cease-fire of 1988 and the death of Imam Khomeyni in June 1989. The political and economic liberalisation carried out by the new team during the following decade made it possible to speak of 'Thermidor in Iran'. But it should be recalled that that historical metaphor (referring to the French Revolution) denotes a professionalising of the revolutionary class, much more than 'moderation' of that class or questioning of the heritage of revolution; in France in 1794-1815, the Directory and Empire gave institutional form and a new political expression to the revolutionary changes, they secured the transition from the age of 'revolutionary passion' to that of 'revolutionary reason', to use the actual terms employed today in Iran.

In this situation the election of Mohammad Khatami as President of the Republic, preceded not only by an intense election campaign but also by a quite unprecedented turnout in the parliamentary elections of 1996, indicated not the exhaustion of the regime but a reshaping of it. This of course does not exclude conflicts within it. Immediately after the presidential election the factional struggle resumed with vigour, and the outcome remains uncertain. One of Mohammad Khatami's principal supporters, the highly dynamic Mayor of Tehran Gholamhossein Karbaschi, was tried for embezzlement and sentenced to five years' imprisonment in July 1998 by a judicial system still in conservative hands. Similarly his Minister of the Interior, Abdullah Nuri, has been forced out of office by parliament, and several newspapers sympathetic to refom have been closed down. But a decisive contest has not yet been engaged, if only because Gholamhossein Karbaschi has appealed and the Leader of the Revolution, reputed to be close to the conservatives, has several times expressed his support for Mohammad Khatami's policies, even on the very delicate questions of relations with the United States and the resumption of diplomatic relations with Britain in spite of Imam Khomeyni's *fatwa* condemning Salman Rushdie to death. The regime, whose nature is thoroughly collegial, is proving capable of keeping its leading people at its side even when they are in disgrace; the Islamic Left, driven out of parliament from 1992 to 1996, has continued to be represented in other institutional positions and to inspire an influential section of the press; and Hashemi Rafsanjani, who was not able to seek re-election for another presidential term in 1997, has been appointed Chairman of the Expediency Council, and in that position remains one of the key personalities in the Republic.

In practice the stability of institutions is ensured by power sharing between the Leader of the Revolution, the President, parliament and the Expediency Council, at the price, it is true, of some tendency to immobility due to the inevitable compromises among the various political tendencies. That certainly does not mean that the regime is not changing at all. The turns taken by the factional struggle in the last few years show the contrary, and the intensity of the current debate on *velâyat-e faqih*, and the revision of the Constitution in 1989, suggest that the Republic is definitely going through constructive change. But the 'Thermidor' political class knows how to face challenges to defend its revolutionary heritage and, as a connected consideration, its privileges; Gholamhossein Karbaschi, while waiting for the result of his appeal, and while voicing his criticisms of the Constitution Guardianship Council for its methods of selecting candidates, did not hesitate to ask voters, at a press conference in October 1998, to turn out in force for elections to the Assembly of Experts and so to save 'the honour of the system'.

All this means that the problem is not to determine whether the Republic is 'less' Islamist or 'post-Islamist', but to make out the lines of force in what seems to be a second wind for it, based on the renewed legitimacy accorded by the massive turnout of voters in the 1997 presidential elections (including the diaspora, which was something new) and Mohammad Khatami's undeniable popularity. The changes in the regime seem, in particular, to be inseparable from a whole series of social dynamics which it has encouraged or must come to terms with. Among them should be mentioned, in particular, the population movements set in motion by the war with Iraq; urbanisation (61 per cent of the population lives in towns); the spread of literacy, especially among women (74 per cent); the increased numbers of students, and the increasingly youthful population due to high growth rate until the early 1990s; the beginning of demographic transition due to a spectacular decline in the fertility rate; the development of the informal economy, encouraged by women's entry into the labour market; and more generally, the effects of the economic crisis.

Essentially, there are four dimensions to this reshaping of the Islamic Republic. In the first place, the bureaucratising and above all the rationalising of social life have made considerable progress over twenty years. No sphere of society is free of this trend, religion least of all. The organisation of the clergy, theological instruction, and collection of religious taxes have become particularly institutionalised. The believer's relationship with his faith is all the more transformed because the faith is now transmitted through modern means of communication. Thus religious practices such as pilgrimages or charitable deeds are contributing to the emergence of a public space which is largely religious but also a factor in new socio-political trends. The best known illustration of this is probably the following attracted by the philosopher and theologian Abdolkarim Soroush. After being involved in the Islamisation of the cultural sphere in the early 1980s, he philosophised about the historically-related nature of religion and the role of the Subject in it. In that way he became the intellectual Leader of the Islamic Left which renounced the charms of direct action in favour of a critical and constitutionalist conception of the Islamic Republic and *velâyat-e faqih*, and he remains close to the positions upheld by Ayatollah Montazeri - Imam Khomeyni's former heir apparent fallen from favour, more or less under house arrest in Qom, now an avowed opponent of the Leader of the Revolution, but one of the most respected religious dignitaries in the country.

Such interaction between the political and religious fields is also found on the right wing of the political chessboard. The debate among conservatives, expressed through the variety of publications and theological schools, is no less keen, and has led some of them, if not to back Mohammad Khatami, at least to start fresh approaches; the attempt by Ahmad Tavakkoli to start the daily *Farda* in 1998, the hesitation showed by members of the Association of Lecturers at the Qom Theological College during the presidential election campaign, and the compromises between the right-wing majority in parliament and President Khatami show that this political tendency is also undergoing a transformation.

Whatever may be the case for these strictly political expressions, it seems that the Islamic Republic, in contrast to the Soviet and Maoist regimes, has ensured recognition of the social by the political - in that way it has never been totalitarian - and has thus contributed to its strength. The private sphere of the family, the religious domain, and the economic structures have continued in the direction of modernisation and diversification; this has given some consistency, or some plausibility, to the regular theme of civil society to which Mohammad Khatami has been giving prominence since 1997. There is also clear convergence between his insistence on the need to create a state based on the rule of law and the increasing tendency of players in society to resort to legal rules and the judicial system to settle their family, economic property and other conflicts.

In addition, the fortunes of the factional struggle among the various tendencies in the political seraglio are more and more dependent on how it is echoed in the public arena. In 1998, for example, the Karbaschi case showed that judicial rulings were now the object of debate in the media and on the public highway, and thus could be contested. Some officials of the Tehran urban authority have complained in the press of ill treatment that they have endured in prison, and parliament has been considering the case. In April the imprisonment of Gholamhossein Karbaschi led to demonstrations by his supporters, and in June and July the broadcast coverage of his trial was as popular viewing as the World Cup football match reports. Similarly, in September and October, the methods of selection of candidates for the Assembly of Experts opened up a constitutional discussion on the role of that institution and above all on the very principle of clearance of candidates by the Constitution Guardianship Council, while at the same time reviving the debate on the idea of *velâyat-e faqih*. More tragically, the murders of intellectuals and legal opposition figures such as Mr. and Mrs. Forouhar aroused numerous criticisms and questions in the newspapers and more street demonstrations; both reactions contributed to the unveiling of the truth and suspicion fell on the security services, even the higher authorities of the Ministry of Intelligence. We are very far from being able to talk of true democratisation of the regime, as is proved by these dramatic events and also by the attacks by the Ansar-e Hezbollah against their political opponents, including ministers, as on 4 September, as well as the circumstances of the death sentence on Morteza Firouzi, editor of *Iran News*, the release of Faraj Sarkouhi, editor of the magazine *Adineh*, and the temporary detention of the staff of the daily *Tous*. But the progress of pluralism and of 'public use of reason' are undeniable, and even seem irreversible.

Secondly, the political field has - paradoxically - continued to become differentiated from the religious field since the creation of the Islamic Republic. That Republic is based on a dual legitimacy, democratic and religious. This duality is reflected in the heart of the political structures. The twenty-odd consultations of the people since the Revolution, the debate between 'constitutionalists' and 'transcendentalists' on the *velâyat-e faqih* question, and the reservations expressed by a good many of the clergy about excessive politicisation of the religious field have encouraged the latter's dissociation from the state. Political events of recent years provide numerous illustrations of this change. In the winter of 1994-95, Ali Khamenei, the Leader of the Revolution, did not succeed in getting his primacy as a 'source of emulation' accepted after the death of several Grand Ayatollahs, while on the other hand Ayatollah Montazeri has retained his religious following despite the worsening of his relations with the regime. More recently, the Constitution Guardianship Council only approved one candidature for the Assembly of Experts in Qom Province, which showed once again how much the holy city has distanced itself from the Republic's religious ideology. And at the highest level of the state the complementarity of the roles of the Leader of the Revolution - embodiment of the regime's religious and revolutionary legitimacy - and the President of the Republic, responsible for governmental affairs, expresses this tendency towards divergence of the two fields well; it characterised Ali Khamenei's relations with Hashemi Rafsanjani before, and seems to have continued in his relations with Mohammad Khatami.

Thirdly, the Islamic Republic has maintained the centralisation of Iran which it inherited from the old regime. However, it has also presided over increasing differentiation within the national space. Major regional centres are asserting themselves, such as Mashhad, Shiraz, Isfahan and Tabriz. In addition, the war of 1980-88, the opening of the northern frontier following the collapse of the Soviet Union, the large-scale Afghan and Iraqi immigration, and the increase in trade – legal and other – with the Gulf have completed the redrawing of Iran's human and economic geography. The Republic's second wind owes a good deal to this dynamism of the provinces which recurs in all social and cultural domains. The increasing importance of some places of pilgrimage and the Free Zones on the Gulf contributes to the improvement of ties among the regions, through the large increase in multi-directional trade among them. It also underlies the extraordinary mobilisation of charitable activity all over Iranian society, which is now being reflected in major investment in infrastructure. So everything indicates that the Islamic Republic is not lacking in solid support twenty years after its foundation. Its capacity for adaptation - sometimes in spite of itself and without its knowledge - should not be underestimated, especially because it has acquired authentic representative institutions, guaranteeing a minimum level of interaction between the state and society, whatever role coercion may have played within it. Meanwhile the exiled opposition seems out of touch with the realities of the country and does not offer – far from it in fact – an alternative solution.

The main challenge facing the regime now is an economic one: the collapse in oil prices and the world recession make structural adjustment urgent while the built-in immobility of the collective leadership seems incapable of getting it started. The deterioration in living conditions has already led to fairly numerous riots since 1992. But until there is proof to the contrary, these displays of social discontent are not political in nature. Twenty years after the Revolution, the Islamic Republic is continuing basically along the same course.

That basic course does not amount simply to a pitiless struggle between conservatives or radicals and moderates, as is too often suggested. Paradoxically, Mohammad Khatami's strength may come from what is often presented as his weakness or his failure. To explain: in such a differentiated society as Iran's is today, there is no longer room for a man of destiny, and

Mohammad Khatami could not be the demiurge or Messiah of greater openness that some people hoped to see. On the other hand he is presiding over negotiations, discussions and permanent compromises not only among the various elements in his majority following - essentially the Islamic Left and the Reconstructors - but also, and more especially, with the Right: even if his *de facto* policy is marginalising categories of players intimately linked with the development of the Republic since the Revolution, such as, for example, the many cadres emerging from the circle of ex-servicemen. In this way Mohammad Khatami is asserting his independence from the forces that brought him to power, as has been shown by the creation of the Islamic Iran Participation Front - just as Hashemi Rafsanjani cut the Right-wing umbilical cord by founding the Reconstructors. From this point of view Gholamhossein Karbaschi's disgrace may not only be bad news for the President. But the essential point is the consolidation of a system whose principal forces are still represented in the institutions or at the very least in political or civil society, and which is at the same time showing adaptability to social changes. In other words, whether the Khatami experiment succeeds - or how far it goes, at least - does not depend on defeat of the conservatives, but on the compromise that the reformers make with them. If this theory is correct, Iran's political transition would be comparable, *mutatis mutandis*, with the democratisation agreements that have prevailed in Latin America.

Anyway, this work explores the interaction between the institutionalisation of the Islamic Republic and changes in Iranian society, with stress on continual adaptation of an ethos or life style, that of the 'man of integrity'. That ethos serves in many respects as a warning against political or religious determinism which characterises most analyses of Iranian society. This approach makes it possible to grasp the changes in the regime, and thus in Islamism in its Iranian version - going beyond a narrow analysis of the factional struggle which seeks to reduce it to a sort of Muslim Western with the 'good guys' (the 'moderates') fighting the 'bad guys' (the radicals or conservatives) and the former being doomed to be victims or martyrs at the latter's hands.

A POLITICAL EARTHQUAKE

In May 1997 Iran's voters astonished the world and maybe astonished themselves even more by electing Mohammad Khatami as President by a comfortable majority. The right-wing candidate Ali-Akbar Nategh Nuri, Speaker of Iran's Parliament, was generally thought certain to win; this regular political event seemed likely to be, once again, a non-event. Yet the candidate who had appeared as an outsider and had only declared himself at a late stage won hands down, thanks to massive and cheerful mobilisation of his supporters, starting with women, young people and even children who at times gave the election a carnival atmosphere.

Some months later, on 29 November, similar scenes of joy were observed all over Iran to celebrate the national football team's qualification for the World Cup. And when the players, on their return to Tehran, were taken by helicopter from the airport to the Azadi (Freedom) stadium, even women broke through security cordons to take part in the ecstatic welcome for the heroes of the hour.

These were certainly disturbing mass reactions. Disturbing, firstly, for the authorities, who did not necessarily like to see such popular mobilisation, alien to their ideas and to their experience until then. Disturbing, also, for most observers, who had been quick to describe the system as authoritarian or totalitarian, their vision being obscured by the analysis of real or supposed power relations among the various factions; they were used to noting points scored by the Leader of the Revolution, Ali Khamenei, or the outgoing President of the Republic, Hashemi Rafsanjani, in what was seen as an implacable rivalry. Anyone who reminded people that the Islamic Republic of Iran had more to it than a simple system of control and repression, that it had to deal (however unwillingly) with a real human society, was until recently accused of showing reprehensible tolerance towards religious fanaticism, and providing moral support for a hateful regime.

The high turnout in the last presidential election and the enthusiasm of the citizen-soccer-fans brought fully to light processes that had been discernible for several years, even if it was not always a good idea to take account of them. There has been, for a start, the creation of a real public space, if not a civil society. Evidence of this can be found in the rationalising and bureaucratising of more and more features of daily life; the craze for sport among all categories of people; modernisation of the religious sphere; development of private enterprise; the birth of urban culture; social activism among women; the stress on individual autonomy and, at the same time, on respect for legal and other regulations.

1

It would be wrong to veer today to the opposite extreme and glorify the resistance or victory of society after consigning Islamist domination to the Devil. On closer look, one sees that the welcoming ceremony for the soccer team at the Azadi stadium was organised by the authorities, and the mullahs and the Revolutionary Guards were not the last to join in dancing in the streets to celebrate the qualifying match result; and that Mohammad Khatami is himself a man of the system. A member of the clergy, he was a leading participant in the 1979 Revolution. After that he continuously held responsible political positions until Parliament, considering him too liberal, forced him to resign as Minister of Culture and Islamic Guidance in 1992. Mohammad Khatami then began some years in the wilderness, working as Director of the National Library. So he is not really a product of 'civil society'. But he has known how to express in his speeches and actions the expectations of large sections of the people for liberalisation, greater openness, and perhaps even a state based on the rule of law, and turn them to his advantage. In this way he is a living synthesis between the institutions forged in the fire of the 1979 Revolution and forces at work in society which Hashemi Rafsanjani had already been trying, with some success, to bring together since 1989.

The events of 1997, and what they revealed about Iranian society, have importance going far beyond the Islamic Republic itself. They raise in acute form a much more general problem that directly concerns the Western world – its media as well as its political and academic circles: how far Islam is able to invent a form of modern living that is compatible with democracy, capitalism and the ordinary working of the international system. That question is at the heart of debates about immigration, terrorism, the Algerian civil war, the future of Bosnia, Turkey's relations with the European Union, the emergence of the Mediterranean Basin as an entity, the future of India, Malaysia and Indonesia, the talk of a 'clash of civilisations', etc. Indeed, the study of Islam has become a real industry, with colloquia, seminars, lectures, chairs and institutes, periodical publications, websites, and, inevitably, its own star actors. Iran has a very special place in this study as it is the only example of Islamism arising from a true revolutionary mass movement which is now institutionalised, rather on the lines of Thermidor 1794 in the French Revolution.[1]

But what is modernity, if not some relation to real life in all its complexity and diversity? Much of the literature on globalisation and the world village is repetitive and verbose as it fails to make allowance for the great bulk of facts and human beings with all their actions and quirks. To be modern in Iran, or in any other society, is to reinvent its difference, to use a phrase now made famous by a post-modern anthropologist.[2] That is also how one 'makes sense' in the modern world. Plunging into the

1.   F. Adelkhah, J.-F. Bayart and O. Roy, *Thermidor en Iran*, Brussels, Editions Complexe, 1993.
2.   James Clifford, *The Predicament of Culture. Twentieth Century Ethnography, Literature and Art*, Cambridge (MA), Harvard University Press, 1985, p. 15.

labyrinth of Iranian society means returning to some of the universal questions of our time.

Twenty years after the 1979 Revolution the Islamic Republic of Iran remains a subject of misunderstanding, passion and polemic. It remains little known because of the difficulties of access for researchers and journalists. The aim of this work is to provide renewed analyses based on fieldwork carried out from the beginning of the 1990s. But in addition, the aim is to ask questions about interaction between social transformations and political changes, underlying the invention of modernity. Most available works lay emphasis on the big break with the past due to the Revolution and depict the Republic's Islamic character as the decisive factor in its social reality. This means that the religious dimension is systematically given most attention but without being properly understood with all its variations. Yet many aspects of the new regime show – sometimes very much against the regime's inclinations – continuity with the Pahlavi Empire.[3] Consideration of that aspect – which can be compared with Alexis de Tocqueville's study of France in *L'Ancien Régime et la Révolution* – deserves to be pursued more thoroughly, and refined and narrowed down. It should not lead to a simplistic interpretation on the lines of *plus ça change, plus c'est la même chose*. The real problem is not so much emphasising aspects of continuity, even when they are obvious, but putting them in the new context where they are to be found, and assessing properly the strength of social dynamics.

Those dynamics follow their own momentum and logic which the wielders of power have never been able to bring under control, being in fact not always aware of them. The Islamic Republic, in addition, has gone through major changes, especially those following the cease-fire with Iraq (1988) and the death of Imam Khomeyni (1989). Such political changes can simply express changes in society, or else draw strength from them or reinforce them. But we see no one-way or automatic cause and effect link between those two sorts of phenomenon. Our intention is to explore the role of new developments in society within a regime which, decidedly, can no longer be discussed only in terms of the problems of interpreting the Revolution and its origins.[4]

We must, however, avoid a naive interpretation of these changes, such as has been made following Mohammad Khatami's election. There is not an 'odious' backward and repressive regime on one side and, on the other, 'kindly' civil society representing progress and freedom. We cannot imagine an essential dichotomy between the state and society as if they were identifiable objects, refining them in the imagination into worst and best – a

3. J.-F. Bayart, 'Les trajectoires de la République en Iran et en Turquie: un essai de lecture tocquevillienne', in G. Salamé (ed.), *Démocraties sans démocrates*, Paris, Fayard, 1993, pp. 373-97.
4. Anoushiravan Ehteshami goes so far as to speak of the 'Iranian Second Republic' (*After Khomeini. The Iranian Second Republic*, London and New York, Routledge, 1995).

totalitarian regime on one side, and on the other, a society confronted with the simple choice between 'resistance' or acceptance (as if totalitarianism only appealed to a society whose freedom has somehow gone wrong). The problem is not so much the real impossibility of tracing a clearly defined frontier between the two spheres as the difficulty of even conceiving them, even defining them as autonomous in relation to the period which concerns us in this book. It is better to consider the overlapping space, the common ground between the two.[5]

For our part, we shall be analysing the relationship between social and political changes through the differing 'life styles' respected by Iranians today. Such different personalities as Gholamhossein Karbaschi, the Mayor of Tehran; Teyyeb Haj Rezai, the leader of the fruit and vegetable market in the 1950s; the athlete Takhti, 1956 Olympic gold medallist; Ayatollah Khomeyni; and Mehdi Bazargan, founder of the national liberation movement – all, in their different ways, epitomise the ethic of the *javânmard*, the 'man of integrity'. This seems to be a constant of Iranian culture; Henri Corbin devoted a long commentary to it in his published translation of a Persian book, the 'Treatise on the Knight-Companions'.[6] However, the very diversity of the personalities claiming more or less explicitly to follow that ideal, and of the contexts in which they have emerged, suggests two things: such a lifestyle is inseparable from material considerations and, far from being an invariable that can alone account for behaviour, it is a dynamic combination within which individual activities and social changes are discernible. The ethic of the *javânmard* cannot be understood only as a traditional legacy, but rather as a permanent improvisation according to a given mode in the musical sense. Through studying it one can understand more clearly the emergence of 'the individuality of eminence'[7] with a certain charisma; the affirmation of social qualities that can be turned into political qualities; the importance of gifts in Iranian society; the changes in, and especially the institutionalising of, the idea of trust that is at the heart of practices involving gifts; and, in addition, the operation of the economic networks of the bazaar. The *javânmard* ethic, similarly, cannot just be seen as an expression of Islamic ideas, though it does not necessarily go against them. It is another expression of the autonomy of society in relation to the ideology of the regime and, to some extent, to religious orthodoxy.

5. This means that we take a different view from Farhad Khosrokhavar: 'The Islamist State sees itself as the incarnation of the Community. It encloses society with its chains, stifles it, tries to break the autonomy which, until just recently, was still allowing it to escape from the totalitarian state. '*Anthropologie de la révolution iranienne. Le rêve impossible*, Paris, L'Harmattan, 1997.

6. H. Corbin, *Traité des compagnons-chevaliers*. Tehran and Paris, Département d'Iranologie de l'Institut Franco-Iranien de Recherche, Librairie d'Amérique et d'Orient, Adrien-Maisonneuve, 1973.

7. M. Mines, *Public Faces, Private Voices. Community and Individuality in South India*, Berkeley, University of California Press, 1994.

But the *javânmard* ethic has to come to terms with another moral requirement which has been constantly in the course of definition since the 1960s, if not earlier: that of the 'social being' (*âdam-e ejtemâ'i*) who is characterised by his commitment to others, extending into the public arena, on the basis of redefinition of his relationships with others and with his own people. Through this interaction between other people and his own, the 'social being' cares at the same time about being visible in the public arena and maintaining respectability in his private life. In particular, the Islamic thinkers who have marked the revolutionary generation – Shariati, Sadr, Motahhari, Bazargan, Taleghani and Khomeyni – placed the 'responsible individual', the rational person, at the centre of their thinking. They criticised the traditionalist view that saw the faith as 'servile obedience', seeing in it rather a principle of freedom and reason. Even before taking a stance in relation to political affairs, they formed part of a movement for change in the religious field, going back to the great debates of the nineteenth century and, more recently, to the reforms introduced by Ayatollah Borujerdi and the arguments that followed his death in 1961. This rationalising process, and more particularly a process of bureaucratisation of Shia Islam, has continued under the Islamic Republic, though not without conflicts that have been revealed in turn by the institutionalising of *Velâyat-e faqih* (the guardianship of the Islamic jurist), the centralising of religious taxes, and since 1992 the succession to the major clerical dignitaries (the 'sources of emulation', *marja'-e taqlid*). Above all, its impact appears in relation to the religious practices of the believers, such as participation in new forms of religious gathering, ritualising of a ceremony for the 'age of obligation' for children, reform of Islamic education on formal schooling lines, and use of new media in dealing with religious matters: written, computer and audio-visual. This change in religious practice, besides reflecting various individual approaches, also has an economic dimension: a very blatant one in development of the network of Islamic banks and charitable institutions, in the management of *vaqf* (religious property), and in the fixing of charges for services performed by the clergy. A process of commercialising of the religious arena can even be seen.

At the same time Iranian society does not escape the general process of globalisation, even though its involvement is of a special sort because of the nature of its regime, hostile to 'cultural aggression'; its adherence to 'the age of the umma', fundamentally distinct from the 'age of the global village';[8] the special features of the Iranian emigrant communities; and the strength of its identity derived from its own civilisation. Its involvement in the international arena is fairly paradoxical. On the one hand, Iran is forging ever closer links with countries of the region (Central Asia, Turkey, Pakistan and India, the Gulf emirates), and is steadily re-forging its distinct identity. On the other hand, it remains a pariah in the world community, while the United States is seeking

8. Z. Laidi (ed.), *Le temps mondial*, Brussels, Complexe, 1997.

to isolate it still further. The relationship between Iranian society and the outside world remains potentially quite a confrontational one, as was shown by the debate on satellite dishes in the winter of 1994-95. But the logic of trade relations which are expanding apace, the invasion of new communication technology, and the expansion of closer relations with the diaspora – especially the Iranian communities in the United States, Turkey and Japan – probably make Iran's entry into the 'age of the global village' irreversible.

However, globalisation certainly does not just mean one-way influence of the outside world upon Iranian society. That influence is received in a dynamic and inventive way, related to the situation in Iranian society. Thus voyages to other countries, transmission of Japanese and Western television broadcasts, use of consumer goods, the fashion for sports such as football, tennis, riding and body-building, and the emergence of a real import-export enterprise culture are all blended with indigenous processes of social innovation, in family and business matters for example. The affirmation of the 'social being' ethic, the renegotiation of relations between the private and public spheres, the creation of a unified national space – all, to a great extent, pass through the globalisation process, but they retain autonomy in relation to the international system and also in relation to the regime. The individualising process operates partly through borrowing from foreign appearances or behaviour; this is evident from examination of changes in funeral rites, the press, and the increasing number of manuals dealing with 'caring for oneself' in the fields of food, health and beauty, and in consumption practices in daily life.

While we had no desire to consider society and the state as opposed to each other, our research has made it possible for us to establish the autonomy of what pertains to society within the Islamic Republic, and to bring out some of its points of interaction with the political field. Starting with the study of a 'life style', that of the *javânmard* (Chapters 1 and 2), we note that this is associated with a strategic skill in giving and receiving that has been institutionalised over the past decades, especially through charitable organisations and financial networks (Chapter 3); thus the modern *javânmard* has become a social being. We also note how, as a result, this form of open-handedness[9] is contributing to the formation of a true public space. That public space is specifically political, especially because of the vitality of information media and the holding of undoubtedly competitive elections, even if they are not strictly speaking democratic (Chapter 4). But it is also a product of the bureaucratising, rationalising and commercialising of the religious sphere (Chapter 5). At stake in all these developments is Iranian society's entry into the modern world – if that is taken to mean some

---

9. P. Veyne, *Le pain et le cirque, Sociologie historique d'un pluralisme politique*, Paris, Le Seuil, 1976, p. 9. Translator's note: The French word used by Veyne and the present author, *évergétisme*, has no close English equivalent but the sense is sufficiently conveyed by 'open-handedness', which we have adopted generally while sometimes using the term 'public generosity'. Historians of the ancient world, such as Veyne and Peter Brown, use *évergétisme* to describe an individual's liberality in giving to the community.

sort of critical relationship between the private and public spheres and, today, to involve self-reflexivity (Chapter 6). From this viewpoint the social being follows self-oriented practices that come under the heading of 'bio-politics',[10] and he joins in creation of the public space not only through the exercise of his critical faculties, by the 'public use of reason',[11] but also by physical behaviour and acts of production and consumption.[12]

The dynamics of the religious sphere contribute to this change in a confused and often contradictory fashion. As far as Iran in the last two decades is concerned, the conclusion drawn by Olivier Roy, that there has been a 'failure of political Islam',[13] needs to be qualified. However, that does not necessarily mean agreeing with conclusions like that of François Burgat,[14] suggesting an unquestionable modernity in Islamism, or that of Olivier Carré who speaks of the potential for secularism in Islam.[15] Each of these three approaches, backed by solid arguments, deserves to be reexamined in the light of the social realities of an Islamist regime that has no equivalent, since it is the fruit of a formidable Revolution and has now become institutionalised, even routine. Because of this the problems of interpretation concerning political Islam in Iran are inevitably different from those regarding the new Islamist opposition movements, such as those studied at a very early stage by Gilles Kepel in Egypt,[16] or even an Islamic parliamentary party, such as Refah in Turkey; for it is more diffused in Iran, it merges with society at large. Other specific features of the situation which we take into consideration derive from Iran's particular regional environment, bordering the Gulf and Central Asia; the historic weight of Shia Islam and its clerical organisation; and an ethnic and cultural diversity more under control than in most states of the Middle East. In all these respects Iran is clearly distinct from the other 'Islamist' examples with which it is often compared, or which are even said to be inspired by it.

Our aim is not to provide a comprehensive vision of a society of more than 60 million people, comprising about ten major linguistic or ethno-religious groups; that would be impossible. Nor do we intend either to start a prosecution against the regime, or to sing its praises; rather, we want to reformulate the terms of the debate. The debate has, through becoming specialised, tended in practice to concentrate on the one tree of political Islam, at the risk of missing the charms of a forest rich in other varied features.

10. M. Foucault, *Histoire de la sexualité*, I: *La volonté de savoir*. Paris, Gallimard, 1976, p. 188; cf. A. Giddens, *Modernity and Self-Identity*, Stanford University Press, 1991.
11. J. Habermas, *L'Espace public*, Paris, Payot, 1993.
12. A. Appadurai and C.A. Breckenridge, 'Public Modernity in India', in C.A. Breckenridge (ed.), *Consuming Modernity*, Minneapolis, University of Minneapolis Press, 1995, pp. 1-23.
13. O. Roy, *L'echec de l'Islam politique*, Paris, Seuil, 1992.
14. F. Burgat, *L'islamisme en face*, Paris, La Découverte, 1995.
15. O. Carré, *L'islam laïque ou le retour à la grande tradition*, Paris, Armand Colin, 1993.
16. G. Kepel, *Le Prophète et le Pharaon. Les mouvements islamistes dans l'Egypte contemporaine*, Paris, La Découverte, 1984.

It may be that our analysis of the way in which Iranians are fashioning their daily life, and thus inventing their modern life (or a form of modernity that is their own), will arouse criticisms, and will be overtaken by other on-the-spot research. That is no problem: it is precisely one of the aims we seek in what follows. In any case the unique nature of the social experiment which Iran has been going through for the past twenty years deserves something better than invective or conventional ideological discussion. It offers a precious opportunity to reconsider some of the fundamental questions faced by citizens of our time.

1

WHEN TAXES BLOOM IN TEHRAN

Gobineau, in a celebrated passage about nineteenth-century Iran, said that the Persian state did not exist in reality, that the individual was everything: 'The state? How could it exist, when nobody cares about it?' In his view the Persian people were 'incapable of political loyalty and devotion' – 'Full of adoration for the country itself, they do not believe in any means of running it'. At the most one could note that 'policing of the cities is quite effective' – 'You do not hear any noises at night, there is no public disorder'. That is because 'ever since ancient times' cities of that part of Asia 'have known and practised an excellent system of security, consisting of posting night-watchmen in every street'. But for the rest, 'with everyone looting without shame or scruple, and extracting as much as they can from public funds, there is in fact very little administration, or none at all'. Above all, 'a part of the population never pays taxes, either because excessive privileges with no justification except long-established custom have given legitimacy to a claim for exemption, or because such a claim has through dishonest measures been approved by royal authority, or else simply because taxpayers, not in the mood to pay, drive away the collectors or refuse to let them in.' [1]

That French diplomat's words have an amazingly contemporary ring. It is common knowledge that order is maintained in the streets of Tehran today by the vigilance of the Revolutionary Guards, the *bassij* and other *Komiteh* who patrol the streets. But Iranians are still not paying taxes! In 1990 the International Monetary Fund noted that the ratio of tax revenue to gross national product had fallen from 6 per cent in the first half of the 1980s to 3 per cent in 1989. Certainly that decline could be explained partly by a restrictive incomes policy, curbs on imports, the inelasticity of most indirect taxes, and the ravages of war. But the IMF report also blamed the weaknesses of the tax administration and the large number of exemptions: 'It is believed that effective tax collection hardly amounts to half of what can legitimately be expected'.

The Iranian government itself agrees; it has expressed the hope of increasing the ratio of tax revenue to GDP to 8.4 per cent by simplifying income tax, improving collection and reducing the range of exemptions.[2] It

1.   J.A. de Gobineau, *Trois ans en Asie (1855-1858)*, Paris, A.M. Metailie, 1980, p. 298.
2.   IMF, *Islamic Republic of Iran: Article IV Consultation prepared by the Staff Representative for the 1990 Consultation with the Islamic Republic of Iran*, Washington DC, 7 May 1990, mimeo, p. 15; Planning and Budget Organisation, 'Economic Report 1371 (1992)', Tehran, 1372/1993, pp. 34 and 38.

has pointed the finger unambiguously at the people responsible for tax evasion: the bazaar merchants, whose contribution does not exceed that of salaried employees,[3] despite their power and the vast profits they have been making since the Revolution.[4] This explanation is too simple. The bazaar traders have ties, especially family ties, with members of the political class or the clergy. Besides, the great quasi-public foundations inherited from the imperial regime or created since the Revolution, and their offshoots, are not the least of the beneficiaries of a lax system of tax enforcement, on the pretext that they are engaged in charitable work, even though Hashemi Rafsanjani's government set out to discipline them; and despite the currency reform of March 1993 they continue to make use of the different exchange rates to get around their tax obligations. To this must be added an array of organisations – from the Islamic schools approved by Qom to the Islamic Propaganda Organisation, the Supreme Council of the Cultural Revolution, the University Crusade and the Revolutionary Guards – which enjoy similar exemptions.

In reality the Islamic Republic, in that respect as in others, shows historical continuity. A constant feature of the imperial era under the Safavids, the Qajars and the Pahlavis was lighter tax enforcement than that imposed by the state in Europe.[5] In Iran the taxation question is, now as in the past, above all a question of exemption (*mo'âfiyat-e mâliyâti*). It is striking to note, comparing archives of the beginning of the century with contemporary statements, that in the eyes of both the taxpayer and the authorities acts of public generosity or open-handedness merit exemptions; contributions for a religious ceremony, the building of a school, or the running of a sports hall are given as reasons for paying less in taxes.

Iranians' proverbial lack of enthusiasm for their tax obligations illustrates the distance perceived between the state (*dolat*) and the nation (*mellat*) – the 'indifference' which means 'that it is of little importance to the Persians to know who governs them, and they have no preference or hostility to anyone; with this qualification, however – that they never like those currently in power'.[7] However, one must guard against seeing such distrust between the people (*mardom*) and the regime (*rezghim*) as something physical; one should not speak of a 'permanent state of mind' like Gobineau. Such feelings represent historical consciousness rather than atavistic reactions. The *bâzâris* of today are convinced, rightly or wrongly, that they

3. According to the statistical yearbook, the contribution to tax revenue of salaried staff and civil servants of the private and public sectors together amounted to 231 billion rials in 1991, while that of all the guilds for the same year was 221 billion rials (*Markaz-e âmâr-e Irân, Sâlnâmeh âmari*, 1372 (1993), p. 576).
4. *Resalat*, 25.3.1373 (1994). The newspaper *Keyhan*, on 9.5.1373 (1994), promised rewards for denouncing tax evaders.
5. S.A. Arjomand, *The Turban for the Crown*, Oxford, OUP, 1989.
6. We wish to record our thanks to the National Archives Centre, which has since 1992 been publishing a journal of good documentary quality, and which kindly made these documents, of great aesthetic and historical value, available to us.
7. J.A. de Gobineau, op. cit., p. 212.

fulfilled their tax obligations under Mossadegh; you often hear people saying, 'We thought the government belonged to us, so we paid our taxes'. Similarly, the Islamic Republic went through a period of grace for tax payment just after the Revolution, before the classic distance between state and society[8] returned – illustrated today by the very numerous press notices summoning taxpayers before the tax authorities.

Giving Islamic Legitimacy to Taxation

Iranians' relaxed attitude to paying taxes should therefore not be seen as the expression of a timeless political culture, but rather as the fruit of definite political processes. The current regime has been through an intense debate which, paradoxically, has possibly contributed to the legitimising of centralised state authority. It has had to fight on two fronts: on one side, to persuade the clergy, which had never ceased to contest the imperial regime's right to levy taxes, of the lawfulness of state taxes as well as religious ones; on the other, to make state tax collection effective in the disturbed situation created by revolution and war, while still claiming to speak for the common people and the dispossessed who were being asked to pay up.

Article 51 of the 1979 Constitution lays down that 'No form of tax will be enforced unless it conforms to the law. Conditions for tax exemptions and reductions will be defined by law.' This summary wording contrasts with more detailed articles which, quoting verses from the Koran, deal with the highly controversial issues of the position of women, *velâyat-e faqih* and interest (*rebâ*). However, the text applying that constitutional provision, approved by the Revolutionary Council in March of the same year, made it clear that the taxation question was just as contentious, and that the concise wording adopted by the framers of the Constitution was intended to conceal their confusion. There was an appeal for the people's participation, an appeal to their national and social duty (*farizeh melli va ejtemâ'i* – the religious term *farizeh* being preferred to *vazifeh*, but referring to secular concepts of the nation and society). There was a specific mention of the 1967 taxation law which was confirmed as remaining in force; taxpayers were asked to pay in accordance with, and within the limits of, their own assessments (*sic!*); for the biggest ones, three months were allowed to pay their taxes, and they were offered a 20 per cent rebate if they complied with this (*sic!*); a conciliation commission was set up to deal with taxation disputes.[9]

This somewhat confused text calls for three comments. The legitimacy of state taxation was upheld once for all by a Council consisting largely of religious dignitaries, despite the stiff resistance of a large proportion of the clergy;[10] state continuity was formally reaffirmed by the reference to the

---

8. F. Adelkhah, J.-F. Bayart and O. Roy, *Thermidor en Iran*, Brussels, Complexe, 1993.
9. F. Ghorbani, *Madjmou'eh kâmel-e qavânin bâ âkharin eslâhât 1371*, Tehran, Ferdowsi, undated, pp. 29-31.
10 S.M. Beheshti, *Eqtesâd-e eslâmi*, Tehran, Daftar-e nashr-e farhang-e eslâmi, 1362 (1983).

1967 law; and taxpayers' reluctance to pay, a source of dispute, was openly mentioned, and accepted as being a matter for negotiation and compromise rather than repression.

Not until 1988 was a law on direct taxation enacted on the initiative of the Moussavi government. The Guardianship Council did not express an opinion during the ten day period laid down in the Constitution, and the law came into force after one month. What was most remarkable was to see the major religious leaders, throughout that period, falling over each other to defend the separate legitimacy of state taxes as compared with Islamic taxes *stricto sensu*. 'For a Muslim, paying taxes is a part of his contact with the eternal, of his consciousness of responsibility', said Imam Khomeyni. 'Tax payment prevents accumulation of wealth', Ayatollah Montazeri declared, and that, coming from a revolutionary who aspired to serve the dispossessed (*mostaz'afin*), was a positive point. 'One of the duties of the Islamic government is to determine taxes', said Ayatollah Khamenei – today the Leader of the Revolution – on the same lines. 'The most holy of administrative and state systems is that which is founded on taxation', added Ayatollah Ardebili, for long head of Justice. 'Those who do not pay their taxes are like those who do not pay their *khoms*; their property is illicit, because property or wealth that evades tax payment does not belong to the owner but to the people, the martyrs, the wretched rural dwellers', Hashemi Rafsanjani exclaimed. He then echoed a statement by Ayatollah Beheshti: 'Establishing an equitable taxation system to respond to the needs of the Islamic Republic's programmes is in perfect harmony with the principles of Islamic order.'

These eloquent statements, quoted from a series of brochures published in the autumn of 1986 by the Ministry of the Economy and the Treasury,[11] mark a complete change from the numerous religious edicts which, for more than a century, denied legitimacy to state taxation – starting with Sheikh Fazlollah Nuri's stance during the Constitutional Revolution of 1905-09[12] and Imam Khomeyni's *fatwa* calling on traders to pay no more taxes to an impious government.[13] The leaders of the Revolution naturally invoke the

11. Ministry of the Economy and Treasury Public Relations Office, *Az mâliyât cheh midânim*, 4 volumes, 1986-1988.
12. 'Under constitutionalism, the inhabitants of this country will pay taxes at the rate of 90 per cent. Money will be extorted from them bit by bit under a thousand pretexts. The city council, for example, will find a hundred ways to take your money from you. Every governor will have the right, under the Fundamental Law, to levy two contributions per year. And the new Minister of Justice will extract even more from you' (Ayatollah Sheikh Fazlollah Nuri, 1908-1909).
13. On Ayatollah Sheikh Fazlollah Nuri's stance during the Constitutional Revolution cf. V. Martin, *Islam and Modernism. The Iranian Revolution of 1906*, New York, Syracuse University Press, 1989. On his side Imam Khomeyni, following the Ulema considered to be Constitutionalists at the beginning of the century, only wanted to weaken an impious government (*Velâyat-e faqih*, Tehran, Amirkabir, 1360 (1981). He acknowledged - reluctantly forced to do so, one can be sure - the lawfulness of two sorts of tax: the 'primary tax' for financing of Koranic schools was distinct, in his view, from a 'secondary tax' whose amount must vary in accordance with the state's needs (*Keyhan*, 29.4.1372 (1993); *Rahnemudhâye eqtesâdi dar bayânât-e Emâm*, vol. 3, 1366 (1987), pp. 136-7).

Islamic character of their regime to justify the obligation to pay taxes. But they are also able to quote in support texts by certain religious leaders such as Ayatollahs Sadr, Taleghani, Beheshti and Motahhari, who argued in favour of taxation. In this way they follow the tradition of the great reformers of the nineteenth century such as Naraghi (d. 1829) and Naimi (d. 1936) and the generation of Islamist thinkers who, in the 1940s, were calmly contemplating the creation of a state religious affairs authority, to make up for the inadequacy of contributions from the faithful and to profit from state resources.[14] Religious tax collection itself is continuing to undergo bureaucratisation, as we shall see in a later chapter.

The 'Rentier State' and Taxation in Iran

It is clear, then, that the recurring phenomenon of light tax enforcement in Iran should not conceal the complexity of the debates and the scale of the changes under way. The facts confirm that the break due to the Revolution was not complete and that the Islamic Republic, in many respects, is continuing the centralising and rationalising work of previous regimes.[15] The mistake would be to see this continuity as a linear and conscious process, when in reality change springs from disparate and often local practices, at various points in a society in the midst of thoroughgoing change. From this viewpoint the principal theories concerning the relationship between taxation and state building, which have been the focus of Middle East specialists' attention in recent years, probably need to be qualified and supplemented. Some authors have stated, on the basis of the historical experience of western Europe, that direct taxation has been directly correlated with the principle of political representation, while on the other hand indirect taxation or oil rent has favoured authoritarian government. One of the main exponents of this theory, Giacomo Luciani, recently brought it up to date to take account of the fall in oil prices: 'Even in countries where a tax revenue crisis was proclaimed long ago, the government follows a policy of adapting to reduced rent rather than accepting the need to alter the economic foundation of the State – precisely to avoid changing the institutional system.'[16]

That comment, made with reference to Arab states, has an obvious relevance to Iran. While the Rafsanjani government started economic reforms to respond to the needs of reconstruction and make up for the decline in oil revenue, many observers doubted its determination or its ability to carry the reform through by bringing under effective control the numerous channels for tax evasion enjoyed by the regime's big speculators

---

14. *Ain-e eslâm*, 56, 1324 (1945).
15. J.-F. Bayart, 'Les trajectoires de la République en Iran et en Turquie: un essai de lecture tocquevillienne', in G. Salamé (ed.), *Démocratie sans démocrates*, Paris, Fayard, 1994, pp. 373-96.
16. G. Luciani, 'Rente pétrolière, crise de l'Etat et démocratisation', in G. Salamé, op. cit., p. 201.

– smuggling, the Free Zones outlets, the multiple exchange rates, and public generosity activities legally exempt from taxes.[17] Although non-oil exports have been increasing for several years and the government is committed to increasing its tax revenue, there is a long way to go before Iran leaves the suspect category of 'rentier states' to join the more respectable one of 'producing states'. However, that does not mean that Homayoun Katouzian's analyses of 'oil despotism' are wholly applicable to the Islamic Republic.[18] Iran has a relative social and even political pluralism, evidenced by the variety of the written press, regular elections with some measure of competition, differentiated powers for the regions, and a real growth of autonomy for social and economic forces.[19] In fact the relationship between authoritarianism and taxation is more complicated. It is never one of simple cause and effect, Giacomo Luciani explains.[20] As John Waterbury puts it, 'There have to be several intermediate variables between the levels and the forms of tax enforcement and the requirements of responsibility; before we can be specific about those variables, we can only have an intuitive and often inaccurate idea of the dynamics of the situation.'[21]

One of those 'intermediate variables' can now be explored. In the winter of 1989-90, while the new President of the Republic, Hashemi Rafsanjani, was starting on his policy of economic recovery and reform, Gholamhossein Karbaschi was appointed Mayor of Tehran. He had already made a name for himself in his earlier job as Prefect of Isfahan, by improving the city's appearance for the greater enjoyment of its inhabitants; the banks of the Zayandeh Roud had been tidied up and monuments restored, the parks had become more lively, and everyone agreed that Isfahan had finally become once again 'half of the world' (*nesf-e jahân*), to use the classic description. With this reputation preceding him, Mr. Karbaschi settled down immediately to the task of restoring to Tehran the splendour of a capital city.

This was no small challenge. The urban area had by then 10 million inhabitants and was on the verge of choking up; in addition its population, now more youthful, was longing for change after eight years of war, impoverishment and ideological drabness.[22] The decisive and efficient new mayor, immediately greeted by a concert of praise from public opinion and

---

17. On the tax exemptions for public generosity activities cf. F. Ghorbani, op. cit., p. 99. According to the Chairman of the parliamentary Planning and Budget Committee, Hojatoleslam Dorri Najafabadi, in an interview with the daily *Keyhan* of 8.12.1373 (1995), tax revenues for the year 1993-94 amounted only to 5,700 billion rials compared with the forecast of 7,800 billion.
18. M.H. Katouzian, *The Economy of Modern Iran. Despotism and Pseudo-Modernism 1926-1979*, London, Macmillan, 1980, Chapter 12.
19. F. Adelkhah et al., op. cit.
20. G. Luciani, op. cit., p. 205.
21. J. Waterbury, 'Une démocratie sans démocrates? Le potentiel de libéralisation politique au Moyen-Orient', in G. Salamé, op. cit., p. 105.
22. B. Hourcade and Y. Richard (eds.), *Téhéran au-dessous du volcan*, Paris, Autrement, 1991.

secular intellectuals and by a special issue of the fortnightly *Gardoun*,[23] brought about numerous improvements, and today the transformation of the capital is striking. But that policy has been at a price: creation of new taxes and increases in local taxation. Mr. Karbaschi, who is very popular, is also very much under attack; he has, for example, become the favourite target of the satirical weekly *Gol Agha*. We intend here to look at this municipal debate to study what is arguably the growth of a public space, or even of the idea of citizenship.

In Iran the relationship between taxation on one side and, on the other, the reform of society and the state for the sake of saving the nation is an old one; it was, notably, dominant during the Constitutional Revolution.[24] But development of taxation does not lead automatically to growth of a public space. The two processes are connected, but not necessarily in a simple cause-and-effect way. The operation of the taxation system is an essential element in political consciousness, especially in the way in which power is perceived. But in that respect public statements and laws in force are perhaps less important, in the roles played by people involved, than the existence or non-existence of a visible and direct relationship between money collected and public achievements recorded. From that point of view the debate between 'state control' and 'liberal' viewpoints, which has dominated political life since the Revolution, has been to a large extent divorced from the real issues at stake: the Left's hopes of limiting accumulation by the richest through taxation and various forms of economic regulation did not win the day, and neither did the charity-oriented ideas of the conservative Right, since social inequality has continued to grow since the Revolution.

However, Mr. Karbaschi is an adept at public presentation of tax collection, through bringing the taxpayer closer to the fruits of his contributions. One of his first operations, in the spring of 1990, was to call on the people of Tehran to put pots of flowers on the pavement, in front of their houses or at their workplaces, to brighten up the capital. This plan, announced repeatedly by the city council, was supported by a true verbal barrage from the most popular radio broadcast – *Salâm Sobh Bekheyr*, 'morning greetings', presented every day between 7 and 8 a.m. by Atash Afrouz – and was thoroughly prepared by the city's technical departments. It was wildly successful. Spurred on by the prospect of winning prizes, the people responded to the call on a massive scale, and for several days the only topic of conversation was 'the Mayor's flowers'. Not that people were taken in: it was clear that Mr. Karbaschi was aiming at the most visible and easiest target, and that Tehran's fate was not bound up with pots of flowers – 'one bud does not make spring'; in addition, the spectacular nature of his initiative could annoy as well as attract people, like all political gimmicks,

23. *Gardoun*, no. 13-14, 1370 (1991).
24. V. Martin, op. cit.; S.M.H. Naini, *Hokumat az nazar-e eslâm*, Tehran, Sherkat-e sahamiye enteshar, undated.

and did not indicate the existence or otherwise of a proper urban development plan. Even so, his method was in impressive contrast with the state's accustomed ways; at the opposite pole from the prevailing Messianic ideology, Mr. Karbaschi related to the most intimate preoccupations of the people under his jurisdiction – gardening is a true cult in Iran – and he acted in a less *maktabi* (doctrinaire) style than the apparatchiks of the regime, although he wore their beard and collar and was himself a former student of the religious schools, a *talabeh*. In particular, he has worked unceasingly to speed up the rate of municipal development: not only are more and more projects being completed, the works are being hastened as much as possible to limit the inconvenience to people in the neighbourhood; such vigorously implemented projects, called 'lightning operations' (*'amaliyât-e zarbati*), are like a symbol of the city hall's determination to make the use of taxpayers' money immediately tangible.

The language used by the municipality also reveals its concern to get closer to the people. Its newspaper is called 'Fellow-Citizen' (*Hamshahri*), a term which Mr. Karbaschi has propagated more than anyone, but which nonetheless reflects the spirit of the times. It expresses the feeling of a belonging to the city (*shahr*), which certainly existed before but had some difficulty in prevailing over communal sentiments such as regional (*velâyat*), tribal (*qowm*) or district (*mahalleh*) feelings. In a certain way Mr. Karbaschi is seeking to replace the 'geography of nostalgia' of old Tehran by a 'geography of desire'.[25]

Similarly one of the municipal taxes, *khod-yâri* ('self-help'), explicitly takes up the idea of self-help, putting it in monetary form; this has produced amused reactions – is it really necessary for money to be taken from you for you to help yourself? But Mr. Karbaschi is not bothered by such objections; like his city councillors, when he gets off the radio he rushes to appear on the television screens, and while he may have the skill of a *javânmard* – as we shall see later – he certainly does not always have the discretion expected of such a person!

The case of Tehran helps us to understand better that bureaucratisation, of which taxation is one element, does not only mean the centre grinding down the periphery. It can take place in the periphery, which thus contributes to legitimising it. Of course Tehran is the capital of the country and in a way belongs to the centre of the state. But it should be recalled that Mr. Karbaschi fought his first campaign in Isfahan and is widely imitated today by provincial city authorities. Emulation among regional capitals has encouraged the adoption of bureaucratic modernisation of city dwellers' space. There is a true interaction between the reforming will of mayors and the expectations – confused and contradictory as they may still be – of the people they govern.

25. To adopt the very good expression used by Paul Zumthor about the Middle Ages: *La Mesure du monde*, Paris, Le Seuil, 1993.

The killing of doves in Qom provides an interesting example of this. The authorities' call for their slaughter in 1994 aroused some emotion in the Western press, always ready to denounce the Mullahs' fanaticism: after obligatory veiling of women, stoning of adulterous women to death, and the ban (at least in theory) on satellite dishes, now came a massacre of innocent birds! It is hard to believe that those birds were agents of the 'cultural aggression' denounced by the Leader of the Revolution, Ali Khamenei – the head of the judiciary, Ayatollah Yazdi, in fact came to their defence, calling the Qom city council's order irresponsible. So it is necessary to examine why that strange decision was taken.

In Iran one cannot talk of doves without thinking of a particular group of people, the *kaftar-bâz* (pigeon-fanciers). Those people were already under some suspicion in the Shah's time. The *kaftar-bâz* is a solitary man who devotes his life to his doves: he feeds them, looks after them, makes them fly and lovingly watches them return. He has hardly any time left to carry on proper professional activity; he saves up his slender resources to buy rare species which will allow him to show up well in competitions, betting contests and gambling on the bird market. In addition the *kaftar-bâz* is often unmarried. When the moment finally comes to marry he must sacrifice his brood of doves by selling it. That does not prevent him from continuing to visit the pigeon market, where the objects of his past obsession are traded, for the pleasure of seeing his friends and admiring rare specimens, keeping his eyes glued to the sky to watch out for doves' free flight, and keeping some of his favourite birds in a cage, on the roof or in the courtyard of his house. In short, the *kaftar-bâz* is a misfit or at least an unusual character.

He is also a lean man with staring eyes. He has the reputation of living in a dream world. Malicious tongues assure everyone that his passive appearance does not come only from waiting daily for his birds to come down from the sky before nightfall to return to their dovecot, but also from imbibing certain toxic substances. Although he is of dubious reputation, without a respectable occupation, and in a world of men only, the pigeon-fancier is a peaceful character, except when his birds are in danger – and that in fact happens quite often.

The difficulties faced by the *kaftar-bâz* start from the very nature of his passion. The flights of his doves are a nuisance for the neighbourhood, which complains that droppings foul the soil, the small water basins in courtyards, clothes hanging out to dry and mattresses waiting for nightfall before being unrolled for summer conviviality. The *kaftar-bâz* is also criticised because, as he stands on the roofs to watch the flight of his birds, he trespasses on the intimacy of inner courtyards. Lastly, people do not much like him being in contact with children, because of the risk of his tempting them to follow him in his madness.

But the dove is also a privileged link with sacred and symbolic things. Iranian film producers, like Ali Khatami in *Toghi*, readily choose the death of a dove as the tragic moment of a story. Doves perched on the minarets and domes of mosques are a sign of continuity between this world and the next. They are a further reminder that the mystery of the mystical is forever rooted in what is prosaic and material. Thus the pigeons of the Imam Reza shrine at Mashhad are forever fed by the offerings of pilgrims. Those offerings are so abundant that they form a real carpet of wheat in the mosque courtyard reserved for the purpose; the guardians – 'servants of Imam Reza' – assiduously gather up whatever is left to repackage it and put it on sale again.

In its context the extermination of the Qom doves reflects not so much bloodthirsty fanaticism on the part of Mullahs for whom tyranny had gone to their heads, as the many aspects of a programme of urban renewal. That programme has aroused the approval of the greatest number, despite the increased tax burden involved, and it has been combined with a struggle against social practices seen as undesirable – gambling, drug-taking – and against superstitions.

A Look Inside the Mayor's Gardens

Our ideas need to be more clearly defined. In addition to macroeconomic and macropolitical analyses of the relationship between taxation and state building, there is room for an anthropologist's angle. Fieldwork in Tehran during the summer of 1994, through interviews and on-the-spot observation, made it possible for us to define more clearly the terms and the range of the urban government debate launched by Mr. Karbaschi's modernisation policy.[26] The Shah set about creating monumental gardens 'in the desert', to reflect the grandeur which he saw as surrounding his dynasty, and did not care about integrating them into an overall town planning vision. In contrast the new Mayor of Tehran – without completely abandoning that tradition, as is evident from the embellishment and opening to the public of the Sad-Abad, Niyavaran and Pirouzi parks, and the restoration of the Javadiyeh slaughterhouses, the former brewery and the Mesgarabad cemetery – has concentrated its efforts above all on creating many smaller green open spaces in the different districts of the capital, for fairly basic 'public health' reasons.[27] The various squares are generally laid out between houses, quite often on plots of land confiscated or abandoned during the Revolution, and especially at the centre of crossroads that have been systematically planted with trees. Besides the inevitable municipal authority flowers, the district public gardens have been provided with benches, children's play areas, and

26. Research carried out in the spring of 1994 among 100 people, through generalised interviews, especially in the western districts of Tehran (Pirouzi, Nirouye Havai, Tehran Pars).
27. Our thanks to Mrs. Nasrine Faghih, architect and town planner, for her help in establishing this point. See her report, produced at the request of the Mayor of Tehran, on 'Urban improvement of the capital and its future', Tehran, 1370 (1991), mimeo.

water basins with fountains. At nightfall lighting in the national colours (green, white and red) plays on the vegetation and fountains; it contributes greatly to the attraction of these places in a climate where the first hours of the evening are the most pleasant moments and are particularly good for relaxation. In addition there are news-stands and especially refreshment stalls offering their services.

The new municipal gardens have generated various everyday habits. People visit them in family groups, which is after all fairly traditional, but also in various special groups – of women, young people, retired people, soldiers, etc. – who are able to go there independently without arousing curiosity. The parks are thus a factor for social differentiation and autonomous conduct for individuals, as we shall see later. The inhabitants of the localities make use of the new public gardens in numerous ways: they go there to rest, to sleep, to have picnics, to look after their children, to chat, to play sports, to follow artistic shows, to revise for their examinations, to read newspapers on display, to watch open air films, to pray, to do shopping, to go after girls, or just to pass by. Most of these ways of making use of the open spaces involve new ways of living. The public parks are the principal places for practicing fashionable sports – aerobics and jogging in the early morning, table tennis and badminton in the afternoon – and eating pizzas, sandwiches and hamburgers. Craftsmen's stalls are also found there, for embroidery, basket making, lute making, woodwork, stonework, etc.; these illustrate well some of the new consumption habits of city dwellers, and confirm that, in Iran as elsewhere, commercialisation involves an '*imaginaire* of the authentic and special object'.[28] The parks are the setting for social innovation, though maybe at the expense of 'inventing tradition'; but they do not exclude old habits, which have even acquired some new legitimacy – people play chess and draughts there, they unroll their carpets and pray.

For all these reasons the public gardens are the setting both for social reconciliation and for at least potential conflict. They provide – better than the mosques, religious meetings, good-bye parties and birthday parties – for coexistence among different classes of society and their favourite consumption and leisure practices. Next to the young couple tucking into a pizza bought from the fast food dealer at the crossroads is a *sonnati* (traditional, 'authentic') family eating *shâmi-kabâb* prepared at home; and the father will move to one side to pray while his grandchildren play ball games.

But at the same time the public parks are the scene for social practices so varied that they can become contradictory and rival, and thus a cause for conflict. For example, despite the prying eyes of the neighbourhood, the watch kept by the local authorities and the vigilance of the Revolutionary

28. J.-P. Warnier, *Le paradoxe de la marchandise authentique. Imaginaire et consommation de masse*, Paris, L'Harmattan,1994.

Guards, they are places for meeting and flirting by the ever growing ranks of the young, who do not always submit to the austere moral code demanded by the regime. Of course this does not stop the district *bassij* from calling for collective prayers in the same parks. We should not see in these brief glimpses the expression of some Manichean confrontation between totalitarian authority and a frightened populace; for several years past the *bassij* have been ordered to act in a non-coercive way in this regard, and they compete above all with the mosque's space;[29] in any case their intervention is not so frequent, and one can spend hours in the parks without seeing them appear. However, it is always a possibility, one that is constantly mentioned by people using the parks, especially by the young who dread it but who also show their social standing by such hostility or concern. It is after nightfall, when – as we have seen – the parks are most popular, that the tensions near the surface are most visible. The public parks are scenes of reconciliation and conflict, or, as Pierre Sansot put it, of 'alliance and tension'; they really are public spaces in the fullest sense.[30]

The interviews we conducted during the summer of 1994 confirmed this point but also allowed us to establish it more precisely. The people we interviewed spoke without reticence on the subject. First of all, they immediately identified the Mayor of Tehran. That may seem unremarkable, even obvious, to a Western reader. But Mr. Karbaschi is the first municipal office holder to be in the public eye in this way, at least since the 1960s (Mr. Shahrestani had real popularity at that time, and it was that which cost him his position). Mr. Karbaschi's action aroused immediate comments from the people interviewed. They spontaneously linked it with the policy to improve open spaces, which aroused unreserved satisfaction. The parks give the city its character of a great modern 'European' (*orupâ'i*) city; that opinion corresponds to the city authority's own – already, at the end of the last century, the Qajar administration took Paris as its model,[31] and today Mr. Karbaschi, who readily visits the great capital cities of the world while others devote themselves to international Islamic conferences, cites Bonn and Tokyo as examples to follow in addition to Paris.[32]

When asked what constitutes modernity in a city, people gave answers both spontaneous and remarkably rich in detail. Behind the most obvious signs of modernity – parks, big tree-lined avenues helping the flow of traffic, cleanliness, public benches, lighting, etc. – processes of redrawing of public and private spaces can be made out. Traditionally the individual homes or small blocks of flats which make up most of the housing inTehran have had courtyards turned into gardens (*bâqcheh*, literally 'small garden'). The

29. F. Adelkhah, 'Voiler pour mieux mobiliser', *Cemoti*, 17, 1994, pp. 293-8.
30. P. Sansot, *Jardins publics*. Paris, Payot, 1993, p. 54.
31. M. Mahboubi Ardakani, *Tarikh-e moassessât-e tamaddoniye jadid dar Iran*, vol. II, Tehran, Enteshârât-e dâneshgâh-e tehrân, 1376 (1977), p. 133.
32. Interview, Mr. Jamali Bahri, head of the Public and International Relations office of the Tehran central municipality, spring 1994.

people we spoke to tended to see the new municipal parks and gardens as an extension of the courtyard gardens of their homes – and that, it will be recalled, was the idea behind the 1990 operation in which Tehran's citizens were called upon to decorate their doorsteps with flowers. The feeling of intimacy produced by the green open spaces was emphasised. Those spaces have become *de facto* extensions of family space, made inevitable by the housing shortage in the present situation of inflation and economic crisis; people take their children there and meet there to relax. As this has become a regular habit, and as the public gardens are nearby, many have the feeling that it is 'like home'. But it may be worth noting that the municipal authority's gardeners are good at encouraging such a feeling; the green open spaces are cleverly divided into numerous *bâqcheh*, well suited, if not to flirtation, at least to meetings, conversation and picnics.

Besides the feeling of intimacy produced by the parks there has been individualising of their use. The public gardens aim to satisfy the individual needs of precise categories of people: mothers who are offered play areas for their children, retired people who find a haven of peace, students who do their revision under the shade of trees, lovers who re-enact the favourite scenario of the region's film producers – a fountain, flowers, tears and reconciliation! The public in the parks is heterogeneous; Mr. Karbaschi has well understood this, and facilities are provided to try to respond to varied expectations. In short, the parks back up the individualising process that characterises Iranian society.

As well as this feeling of familiarity, the municipal parks provide the people of a district with a way to widen their social space. For example, they make it possible for women to go out in a completely lawful way, and also in a quite distinctive way: nothing is more respectable, but nothing is more modern either, than taking the children for a walk in the park – and from that viewpoint the public gardens are places of particular importance for the 'social being' (*âdam-e ejtemâ'i*) or the person of integrity (*âdam-e hesâbi*).[33] The city authority provides furnishing that reveals very well the way the park legitimises modern ways. While it is possible to lay out a traditional carpet to sit down or eat together as a family, it is more fashionable to sit on the Mayor's multi-coloured benches, if only to preserve the crease of one's trousers or the neat appearance of one's Islamic robe. Similarly, old people no longer hesitate to occupy benches for hours on end to make conversation or just to enjoy the peace and quiet of the place. The city authority is beginning to install benches in a circle to make conversation easier and tables to discourage picnic parties from invading the lawns.

It is not only at the district level that the green open spaces contribute to broadening the city dwellers' social life. You can escape there to wait for relatives whom you wanted to visit but who were not at home; a retired man can take a bus across the city to spend the afternoon in a park that he

---

33. F. Adelkhah *et al.*, op. cit., pp. 65-7.

particularly likes. In a less tangible fashion, but no less real to judge by our interviews, the policy of improving the appearance of the capital is encouraging a feeling of Tehran identity transcending barriers of area and of sex, age and social class. It opens up a field for consensus or at least neutral feeling among the city dwellers. Admiring flowers, trees and fountains in Iran is a bit like talking about the weather in France: there is a code that allows someone to start a conversation costing nothing and unrelated to any particular social group – religious, political, sexual or professional. Since almost all the Iranian urban centres follow similar town planning policies, it could even be that public parks are helping to unify society on a national scale and encouraging a feeling of national identity.

The value attached to green open spaces is not due only to the amenities they provide. The language used by people that we interviewed evokes more particularly the spiritual – so to speak – qualities of the parks. Besides being the Koranic symbol for paradise, they are described as places of 'reviving the spirits' (*ruhiyeh*) and 'peace and quiet' (*ârâmesh*); they 'bring joy to the heart' (*del-e âdam shâd misheh*), and the flowers are endowed with a 'mystical virtue' (*khâsiyat-e 'erfâni*). People who do not like flowers are seen as lacking 'inspiration' (*zoq*) or 'taste' (*saliqeh*). In 1992 Mr. Karbaschi himself made this comment at the opening of the first Tehran flower show: 'Arranging flowers and trees expresses our turning towards the culture of beauty, the culture of aesthetics, the culture of fullness. We want to rise above today's economic and material problems. It is an effort on our part to turn society's thoughts to the spiritual dimension of life.'[34] In this way he sought to answer his detractors who reproached him for paying more attention to non-essentials than to essentials. But the parks do not in fact seem to be experienced as a useless luxury. They appeal to imaginary concepts, deeply rooted in people's minds, of the 'oasis of fertility' (*âbâdi*), as opposed to the idea of ruin (*kharâbeh, virâneh*) or aridity (*khoshki*). People readily declare that Mr. Karbaschi has 'made the city fertile' (*shahro âbâd kardan*), or even done so to 'the country' (*mamlekat*), but that the Mullahs have 'ruined' the country (*kharâb kardand*).

These views invite two comments. In the first place, parks link spirituality with material plant life, and that is indeed what gives them strength, as the basic principle of life is to ally spirit with matter – *bâten* (inner reality) with *zâher* (appearance). In that way parks are an antidote to corruption (*fesâd*), which arises precisely from separation of the internal order (*bâten*) and the external order (*zâher*). And as they, representing the principle of fertility, are opposed to 'ruin', so they are also the antithesis of 'poverty' (*faqr*), the mother of all vices.

Secondly, parks succeed in bringing together the pre-Islamic heritage and Koranic tradition. The Mayor and the press constantly refer to both

---

34. *Golnameh*, 1, 1371 (1992), p. 15.

backgrounds, quoting equally readily the Hadith of the Prophet and the poems of Hafez, sometimes mentioning Socrates and Western admirers of Persian gardens. Green open spaces are a setting for coexistence between the Islamic Republic's ideology and national culture (*maktabi* and *melli* respectively), and even between both of them and something universal: flowers have no country or religion. It is well known that the current holders of power are less and less hesitant to identify themselves with expressions of Iranian identity given prominence by the laity. Mr. Rafsanjani paid an official visit to the ruins of Persepolis, and Mr. Karbaschi considers that of the speeches by Ayatollah Khamenei, one of the most 'imbued with spirituality' ('*erfâni*) over the past fifteen years was dedicated to the importance of flowers in the poetry of Hafez.[35]

It is certainly clear to see how municipal policy relates to other sensibilities besides a modernisation concerned only with the city's world standing. Mr. Karbaschi has been at the point where spirituality (*ma'âd*) and material things (*ma'âsh*) converge, and at a precise historical moment, that of the reconstruction of the country after a ruinous war. So he has in practice been opening up a space for all sorts of practices which, as we have seen, involve reshaping the private and public spheres. In an unprecedented way his parks allow the people of Tehran to live their spirituality, their inner lives every day and in public. In addition, this ancestral and mystical dialogue between man and flower is now carried on collectively. It governs social habits, norms and behaviour, no longer just individual ones. This expansion of the space in which life is lived, this reshaping of the private and public spheres, finds expression in the new distribution of flowers. Some flowers, once reserved for the *bâqcheh* of interior courtyards – violets, pansies, geraniums and roses, for example – now adorn the streets of the capital. On the other hand certain plants, such as varieties of fir and cactus, are moving more and more from the public parks to the family *bâqcheh*. This traffic in plant life expresses better than any words the support Tehran's people give to their Mayor's actions. But we should not conclude that these have completely unanimous backing. They also arouse tensions and even antagonisms, which should now be examined more closely.

Parks as Scenes of Conflict

The municipal parks are also the setting for antisocial behaviour that arouses disapproval from people who use them; they can even inspire more or less violent acts of vandalism. It is not uncommon for street lamps to be smashed, flowers uprooted or trampled, or litter left behind after picnics. Such behaviour is severely criticised by the public using the parks; they readily attribute it to 'lack of culture' on the part of Iranians, especially of

35. *Golnameh*, 1, 1371 (1992), p. 16.

those living in the south of the capital. Open warfare has been declared between the Mayor and the hooligans. According to one woman who deplores the regular decline in the state of her boulevard's lampposts, but who is pleased at the determination of the municipal authority to go on repairing them, Mr. Karbaschi makes a point of being more patient than the vandals, and counts on them getting tired of it. But he also seeks to be a teacher, and wants to wage many more campaigns of enlightenment, especially in the schools.[36] While waiting for these efforts to bring results, it is possible to see numerous petty frictions among the park users, ranging from a condescending attitude towards behaviour considered vulgar, or children's annoyance at grandparents' attitude, to the reprimands which young men chatting up the girls get from outraged mothers.

Above all, the merits of Mr. Karbaschi's policy can be contested. He is accused of continuing to give priority to the north of the city – the parks there are seen as more numerous and better laid out than those in the south. Refuse collection is still very defective during the main rainy season in the most populous parts of the capital. The period of economic crisis seems to some ill chosen for a preoccupation with flowers. 'The Mayor should have concentrated attention on the flowers of our *bâten*, the flowers of our soul (*golhâye junemun*), instead of the flowers of the *zâher*, and given jobs to young people so that they can marry', as one comment has it. The city authority's generosity over plant life contrasts with demands that people restrict water and electricity consumption. Less well-off families can also feel frustrated at being unable to satisfy children's requests when they go to the parks where money is now king.

That is the rub, in fact: Mr. Karbaschi's policy costs a good deal and, as we have seen, it has been accompanied by increased tax pressure. Not only are local taxes heavier than before, but the various services provided by the municipal authority have increasingly to be paid for. Taking the motorway to Qom, building an extra floor on to one's house, putting up an illuminated sign in front of one's shop, placing a footbridge between a shop and the street crossing over a newly dug open drain, cutting down a tree in one's private garden or (still more) a tree in the public highway, rearranging the space of one's flat, driving in the centre of Tehran between 6.30 a.m. and 5 p.m., having a private parking space when one does not even have a car – all these are pretexts, among others, for payment of a fee to the municipality. It goes without saying that a number of Tehran's citizens, especially traders, are fairly exasperated by this fiscal or quasi-fiscal harassment, which they tend to see as arbitrary. Indeed the city authority sometimes shows the same zeal in forcing recalcitrants to pay up as in carrying out public works: a shopkeeper who refuses to pay his local taxes immediately sees his shop boarded up, hence the large number of disputes before the courts between the municipal service departments and citizens.

36. *Golnameh*, 6, 1371 (1992), p. 13.

At the cutting edge of the criticisms of Mr. Karbaschi's actions seem to be institutions and networks which feel that the municipal authority is competing with them, and which in any case contest the authority's ideological direction or its style, perhaps just because it is becoming a rival centre of power or interferes with property speculators.[37] In particular the Ministry of the Interior, the Resalati parliamentary group, the newspapers and foundations linked with that group (such as the daily *Resalat*, the Organisation of Islamic Banks, the Chamber of Commerce), satirical publications and – at least until 1996 – the Islamic Left (through the daily *Salam*) have expressed open disapproval, following the example of Movahhedi Savodji who condemned in the Majles the '80 taxes' demanded by the city authorities.[38] The readers' letters columns – which, it is true, are said to be commonly invented by editorial staff in accordance with their own political opinions – seem to reveal definite discontent among the public, which goes together with the real popularity of Mr. Karbaschi.

On the one hand there is criticism of the burden of municipal taxes which today exceeds that of taxes payable to the state, and which is blamed for the high rate of inflation. For example, the determination shown by the Tehran municipality in struggling against itinerant traders, piling pressure on them for breaches of regulations, contributes – in the view of Mr. Karbaschi's detractors – to the rise in prices of fruit and vegetables, just as the new municipal tax policy leads retail traders to put up their prices. On the other hand, the modernising actions of the city authorities are getting dangerously friendly with 'cultural aggression' which some leading figures in the regime denounce unceasingly. One deputy, writing in *Resalat*, attacked the style of a newly completed building, saying it recalled 'a church' and was 'without any link with the urban context, or with Iran's national and religious culture';[39] while *Keyhan*, which was already outraged that such a modern building could be called the 'White House', today calls the Cultural Centre (*Farhang-sarâ* in Persian) in Bahman the *Farang-sarâ* (the foreigners' dwelling). As for the municipal authority's publications, they show too many footballers wearing shorts and too many underclad wrestlers to be entirely respectable. Generally speaking, the voluntarist modernisation embodied in Mr. Karbaschi involves some waste – is it really reasonable to plant narcissi along the motorway, and are all the successive construction sites always justified? – and it is in many ways contrary to the religious and revolutionary ethic of belt-tightening which is fitting for the *mostaz'afin*, especially at a time of crisis.

37. On the extent of property speculation in the 1960s, see the pioneering work by P. Vieille, *Marché des terrains et société urbaine. Recherche sur la ville de Téhéran*, Paris, Anthropos, 1970. It goes without saying that the Revolution has in no way brought an end to speculation, especially by the big foundations. In fact it can be suggested that these networks of interests are among the main opponents of Mr. Karbaschi's policies.
38. *Resalat*, 19.2.1373 (1994).
39. Ibid.

It is difficult to interpret these divisions in strictly political or institutional terms. Often it is simply conflicts of interest, inherent in the world of factional conflict, that explain the position of this or that group, and those positions are not always obviously coherent. The Leader of the Revolution, who has taken the lead in the crusade against 'cultural aggression' since the summer of 1992, has never criticised Mr. Karbaschi. And the Mayor, who in theory comes under the Minister of the Interior, was until 1997 in open opposition to the policies of Mr. Besharati, especially on the questions of building high-rise blocks, urban renewal, and the defence of taxpayers up against the arbitrary power of the municipality. There were even press notices in which the central government urged motorists not to put money in the city's parking meters![40] But behind these often quite confused antagonisms lie the fundamental issues of state centralisation, bureaucratisation and the emergence of a public space.

On one side some traditional networks want to preserve their freedom of action and their tax exemption, which they describe as their liberty but which in fact is akin to a monopoly, involving regulation of the world of the guilds (*asnâf*) with which the state must constantly come to terms. On the other side Mr. Karbaschi plans to rationalise this liberty of the city dweller – whether trader, landlord or tenant – through the tax system. His action widens the social space of Tehran's citizens, but assumes that they will always pay the price for its enjoyment. The city authority now seems determined to take over the essential part of the prerogatives formerly held by the guilds by setting up the Refâh (welfare) chain of stores. But the process is still incomplete and such a transfer of material resources and administrative powers is meeting resistance, even if it involves some liberation from the subtle constraints of sociability in the bazaar. Flower selling has given rise to just such a conflict; in his parks, on the public highway, and around hospitals Mr. Karbaschi has opened kiosks whose keepers sell at a profit flowers bought from the municipal greenhouses, to the great annoyance of traditional dealers and horticulturists. In addition he decided to organise in 1994 – as we have seen – a flower show rivalling that of the producers' guild, linking the flower theme with sport and moving the event to the big stadium in the east of the city. Professionals who believed that their skill had been usurped and not recognised for its true worth succeeded in wrecking the municipality's show by boycotting it and organising their own flower show a week earlier, at the usual site of the annual show, and did so with the backing of the Export Promotion Organisation.[41]

40. *Keyhan*, 14.10.1374 (1996).
41. By the organisers' own admission, the producers' flower show was not as brilliant as had been expected, for lack of means. While the general public hardly thought the identity of the producers of the two rival shows mattered, and rather saw the public and private initiatives as complementing each other, a number of visitors were disappointed by the municipal show and spoke of it as 'a mess' (personal information, May 1994).

However this contest between the guilds and Mr. Karbaschi is resolved, the Mayor does not emerge simply as the agent of state centralisation. At the same time as he tries to impose his hegemony over traditional trading networks through the tax system, he is taking care to obtain more autonomy from the central government through the increase in his own resources, encroaching on the state's prerogatives and slipping away from its hold. So it is quite logical, and at any rate revealing, that *Hamshahri* is campaigning for the election of municipal councils (*shorâhâ-ye eslâmi-ye shahr*) which would have the power to choose the city office holders. Although less spectacular than the restoration of multi-party politics – which is also being suggested by some political leaders – such a change from current practice would be of considerable importance. Even the word used, *shorâ*, fits in with the Revolution's political vocabulary. Although the style is very different, Mr. Karbaschi's administrative actions show continuity with the revolutionary movement of 1978-79 which, through mass demonstrations, laid the foundations for a first public space.

However, the city which is thus asserting its existence vis-à-vis the state and the guilds is not a monad; it is rather a differentiated grouping of more or less autonomous districts, with distinct personalities, and a setting for social practices which – as we have seen – vary according to the people involved. In this sense 'the Worshipful Mayor's' Tehran has some features recalling the 'democratic city' analysed by Max Weber, 'divided not according to guilds, but along the lines of territorial districts, which, formally speaking, were mostly rural districts'.[42] With its runaway expansion after the Revolution, due to an influx from rural areas but also to liberalisation of land tenure policy and speculation, the capital has absorbed a number of towns in its periphery, which are thus becoming new spaces for urban integration and identification. The public parks, watered every day by local taxes, are an essential element of consensus, conflict and movement within the 'democratic city'. They are helping it gradually to win pre-eminence over the old city of the guilds, and they may be proclaiming the birth of a new idea of citizenship.

John Waterbury, it will be recalled, wrote that 'there have to be several intermediate variables between levels and forms of taxation and the requirements of responsibility'. The modernisation of Tehran and the increased tax pressure that goes with it seem to illustrate that necessity to bring analysis of actual social practices into discussion of the 'rentier state'. Mr. Karbaschi's action has opened up contact with the various districts that make up the capital, and facilitated unprecedented movement among them. The city air makes the inhabitants – especially those coming from the countryside – 'social' people: in Persian *âdam*, in the sense in which one speaks of *âdam-e ejtemâ'i*, the social being. In this sense the development of Islamic Iran is no different from that discerned by Serif Mardin in

42. M. Weber, *La Ville*, Paris, Aubier Montaigne, 1982, p. 179.

Kemalist Turkey.[43] In Tehran the public parks are an important force backing
up this social change, and we have seen how they are now a burden on the
city finances on their own. But a similar analysis could have been made of
public transport or sporting events, cultural foundations or youth centres,
which are other preferred areas for the operation of the municipal voluntarist
outlook.

A key to all these changes is the still very uncertain struggle over the
creation of a true public space. Mr. Karbaschi's policies give the city its
dynamic unity among the various districts. They organise complementarity
and movement between north and south, and are making progress towards
overcoming discrimination according to sex, age, social status and religious
or secular labels. Even more than the schools, reserved by definition to the
young, and the mosques, valued by the devout, the space being opened up to
the city dwellers is truly 'public' in the sense in which the word is used by
P. Sansot:[44] 'No-one risks being charged' for entering it. Of course all that
does not exclude either tensions or the revival of some forms of
discrimination – or even prosecutions of those breaking the so-called Islamic
rules of the new space. However, those conflicts themselves help the
emergence of a public space as a field of inequality, power and self-
enrichment, but also, above all, of rights. The basic notion of *haq*, which as
P. Vieille and F. Khosrokhavar have shown greatly influenced demands
made in the Revolution, remains at the centre of the debate between city
dwellers and the Mayor in the newspapers and over the radio.[45] Criticising
Mr. Karbaschi means not only raging at a *dolati* authority which one can do
nothing about, it means above all demanding one's rights as regards public
transport, cleanliness in one's district, green open spaces: in short, it means
demanding to be considered as a full citizen. In this sense tax collection is
as much an opening for negotiations as a mark of arbitrary assertion of
power or of the distance between the state and the nation.

The formation of a public space, however, should not be seen as a linear
process. There is no reason to assume that it will lead to democratisation of
the regime in due form. And it is interesting to note that the vast majority of
the people we interviewed ruled out the possibility of Mr. Karbaschi being
elected President of the Republic. 'That would mean he would not longer
work for us', people said in answer to our question; a link between
competence in city administration and that required for governing the state
did not appear obvious to the people we talked with.

In addition, the process of rationalising the Tehran municipality and
giving it a tax-based administration continues to be mixed up with the
actions of one man who is immensely popular, however much he is

43. S. Mardin, 'Religion and Secularism in Turkey', in A. Kazancigil and E. Ozbudun (eds.),
    Atatürk: Founder of a Modern State, London, Hurst, 1981, pp. 191-221.
44. P. Sansot, op. cit., p. 49.
45. P. Vieille and F. Khosrokhavar, *Le Discours populaire de la révolution iranienne*, Paris,
    Contemporanéité, 2 vols., 1990.

criticised. Mr. Karbaschi is seen less as an administrator than as a hero, though maybe a technocratic hero, whose position on the national political chessboard is not well defined – although he is known to be backed by Hashemi Rafsanjani and Mohammad Khatami – and who, while he holds a position of power, is no less close for that to the people for whom he is a mediator. The people using the parks declare, 'May God pardon his parents' sins!' or 'May light shine upon the tomb of his parents!' – expressions that indicate familiarity and sympathy towards the person referred to. In addition the city is constantly buzzing with rumours of amazing adventures said to have befallen the Mayor, ranging from kidnapping to various attacks to imprisonment, in the best vein of traditional gossip.

This is because Mr. Karbaschi, modern person though he is, is seen in terms of society's conception of the *javânmard*, the man of integrity (or would-be man of integrity). The relationship between taxation and the public space is perceived through an ethos which, while deeply rooted in Iran's history, is neither a fixed cultural phenomenon nor an obstacle to social change. The bureaucratising and rationalising process under the Islamic Republic must be placed in that context.

2

THE MAN OF INTEGRITY: A MATTER OF STYLE

In an avenue in the well-to-do centre of Tehran can be seen a showroom for luxury cars imported from Europe or Japan. Its owner, whom we shall call Ali, resells new vehicles which individuals entrust to him on their return from a stay overseas or a business trip to Dubai. Ali asserts that the cars are left with him on sale or return, but it is more likely that he has bought at least the ones displayed in his showroom. In the same way a carpet dealer will always maintain – if only to stave off the taxman's curiosity – that the samples in his shop do not belong to him. Ali is therefore a middleman (*vâseteh, dallâl*). He deals in a consumer product which is among the most valued, 18 years after the Islamic Revolution. One of the regime's leading institutions, the Foundation for the Disinherited, showed awareness of this in 1992 when it announced its intention to build a Mercedes Benz assembly plant – which inevitably aroused some criticisms in the newspapers and quite a few smiles among the public. As a middleman, Ali is an active operator in the 'second economy' which has mushroomed in the past ten years or so because of the black market in foreign currency.[1] This 'second economy' is not strictly speaking an 'informal sector' to be distinguished completely from the official economy. Most of the regime's economic institutions are involved in it, especially the major foundations, the Revolutionary Guards and the network of Islamic banks, which are in fact very active in the importing of foreign cars. Ali sees this as competition which he comes near to calling unfair because of the political support it enjoys. However, it would be interesting to know whether he does not deal in some cars imported by those networks himself; in that case his annoyance would be due to his downgrading – he finds himself now at the end of the chain, and sees his power (but not necessarily his profits) reduced accordingly.

Today, anyway, his business has 'ignited', as it is put in Persian by analogy with a fire (*kâr-o bâresh gerefteh*). It is solid, one might even say it is imperishable, or it is in gold (*sekkeh*, literally 'in coins'). Ali is seen as a

---

1. H. Pesaran, 'The Iranian foreign exchange and the black market for dollars', Geneva, November 1990, mimeo; H. Amirahmadi, *Revolution and Economic Transition. The Iranian Experience*, Albany, State University of New York Press, 1990; B. Hourcade and F. Khosrokhavar, 'La bourgeoisie iranienne ou le contrôle de l'appareil de spéculation', *Revue Tiers Monde*, XXXI (124), October-December 1990, pp. 877-98.

man of property (*dârâ*), he has money at his disposal (*puldâr*), he is a rich man (*servatmand*), he is well situated (*vaz'esh khubeh*). However, it would be wrong to concentrate on the material aspect. The way he is seen also includes more symbolic elements. Ali is also a *sarshenâs*, an expression with a double meaning: first, he knows many people, and secondly, he is recognised by a truly unlimited circle of friends and contacts. He can go into a bank, to the police, to the middle of the bazaar, to the Revolutionary Guards, or into a travel agency without any risk of people not knowing who he is. But it is not only wealth that constitutes his basic quality. It is hope (*omid*), pride (*eftekhâr*), the way those near to him are in his shadow (*sâyeh-e sar*). 'Haj Agha', says one of his brothers, at the risk of committing an anachronism, 'is like Imam Ali, he scores 20 out of 20 in everything.' 'Ali always answers a call for help (*faryâd-ras*),' adds one of his sisters, who has eventually taken to giving him that nickname. 'Haj Agha sows good around him,' a colleague adds. Ali imposes himself, sometimes without wishing to do so, by a constant presence – linked to his wealth, of course, but above all to the use he makes of it, his behaviour, his style of living.

Ali is 'a good customer' (*khosh hesâb*) in the view of people we interviewed who have business dealings with him. One might almost say he is 'straight up', but the Persian expression is not slangy. Ali inspires confidence (*e'temâd*), you can rely on him and his word (*rush*, or *ru harfesh hesâb mikonand*). But he is also a philanthropist (*ensân-dust no-dust*), he has a good heart (*delsuz*). In him correct professional conduct goes with upright feelings and a temperament imbued with humanity. All these qualities are expressed through the material assistance that he brings to anyone deserving it in concentric circles, including his more or less close family, his employees, his neighbours. This ranges from a personal gift at family ceremonies to religious donations, especially during the month of Moharram. But there too, Ali's generosity is not confined to material or quantifiable things. There is above all a gamut of qualities which make up a 'life style' as defined by Max Weber.

In former days people would have said Ali was a *javânmard*, to stress his following of a social ethic centred on selflessness. They would also have recognised him as possessing fully the quality of a man (*mardânegi*), referring to his courage, honour, modesty, humility and rectitude.[2] In our research we heard these last expressions used only twice to describe Ali, by a man of over 70. So such words seem to refer to the past and to apply to a time now gone. However, the situation is probably more complex. One of the people we interviewed said rather crudely, 'Today you are a *javânmard* if you succeed in bringing home a kilo of meat.' He meant that the acts of

2. Similarly Paul Veyne says of Roman public benefactors (*évergètes*) that 'their quality as men who were fully men imposed on them a duty to be sensitive to all human ideals...they considered themselves the ideal human type' (*Le pain et le cirque. Sociologie historique d'un pluralisme politique*, Paris, Le Seuil, 1976, p. 17).

the most praiseworthy of men were now reduced to that trifling act. But behind the apparent cynicism of those words is the idea of giving and sacrifice that it represents – more precisely, the overwork, tiredness and skill that make it possible to buy a product whose price has now shot up because of runaway inflation. The economic crisis seems to be reducing the field of action for the *javânmard*; 'The best thing one can say about a colleague is that he is "a reliable customer". One can readily do without him being a real *javânmard*', said a dealer in audiovisual material. The ambitions of a *javânmard* have been narrowed down: 'He is one of the people who bring in daily bread, who ensure daily life goes on', people say. His generosity has withdrawn inside the confines of his family, who now exhaust the essential portion of his strength.

But to go on from there, to believe that this ethic has disappeared, as Taeschner[3] forecast more than thirty years ago – that, for us, is going too far. Paradoxically, the shrinking of the *javânmard*'s field of action widens the social categories that can identify with his values. The social practice of giving remains a basic part of daily life, in economic activity and, naturally, in the religious sphere. It is thus a true 'total social fact', which should allow us to 'discern the essential, the movement of the whole, the living aspect, the fleeting instant where society takes, where men take sentimental consciousness of themselves and their situation regarding each other.'[4]

And, as we have seen, the Mayor of Tehran, who is so popular and at the same time so controversial, is also seen as being a *javânmard*. He has such a person's ambivalence, for example when he acts as an intermediary between official action and the expectations of citizens, or between rich and poor, or among the various districts of the city, or between the national-secular agenda and the Islamic one, while also seeking to circumvent all other sorts of intermediaries, such as the guilds specialising in the flower, fruit, vegetable and motor trades. Is the figure of a true *javânmard*, with his impressive appearance, not opposed to the despised figure of the *dallâl* (intermediary)? Mr. Karbaschi also has the man of integrity's practical skill, his 'back' (*posht*), both through his relations with the highest state authorities and through his popularity among the people he administers. On the positive side, he takes from the rich to give to the poor, to fertilise his city and make it a real Gulistan; he is the skilful forger of modernity whose only tools are tar and flowers. But on the negative side he is seen by people interviewed by us as a 'roughneck' (*gardan koloft*), a 'bully' (*qoldor*), never sparing with threats, who 'chops up' taxpayers, 'extorts' from the people of the city, acts as a 'bulldozer' and behaves like a 'zero kilometres' character (i.e. a vulgar one). Mr. Karbaschi is seen as a *bâjgir*: he uses his position to

3. F. Taeschner, 'Fotowwat in Islamic countries and its emergence in Iran and neighbouring countries in particular' [in Persian], *Revue de la faculté de lettres de Téhéran*, 2, 1335 (1956-57), pp. 76-94.
4. M. Mauss, *Sociologie et anthropologie*, Paris, PUF, 1983, p. 275.

fleece his fellow citizens, although nobody can say that he makes any profit for himself except his prestige and influence.

Javânmardi as a Package

The word *javânmardi*, which thus defines an existential ethic – that is a life style – comes from the idea of youth (*javân*, young; *mard*, man). It is the Persian translation of the Arabic word *futuwwa* (pronounced *fotowwat* in Persian), which in turn comes from the root *fati* (young). Those who act in accordance with this code of ethics are called *javânmardi* or *fati*. They are distinguished by two essential traits: the spirit of generosity (*sekhâvat*) and courage (*shojâ'at*).[5] But those terms have a richer meaning; their use has encouraged three sorts of debate.

The first is about the historical origin of *fotowwat*. Some authors speak of a direct relationship between *fotowwat* and Islam; others speak of the specific influence of Shia Islam in the development of this ethic. Some see the relationship between *fotowwat* and Sufism as organic, with the two phenomena merging with each other at certain historical periods. This idea is qualified by those who see *fotowwat* as a branch of Sufism, whose primary function would be to make its founding principles more accessible. Someone like Ibn Taymiyya is more critical; he identifies *fotowwat* as an attempt at innovation in Islam (*bed'at*), which he rejects out of hand. Lastly, Massignon and Hamid see *fotowwat* as a pre-Islamic principle and consider it important as such.

A second controversy is about the *fati* social and community customs. One theory sees *fati* as groups of men with no fixed profession, doing any work they can find, ready to live by robbery if necessary; they are therefore bandits, *'ayyâr* in Persian. A second theory suggests the *fati* have a form of social organisation which recalls precisely the corporative practices of the guilds. Between these two extreme theories there are other interpretations which mention the ban on *fati* practicing certain trades such as public baths attendant, hunter, butcher, state official or middleman (in the exact sense in which our car dealer, Ali, is a *vâseteh* or *dallâl*). Contrary to what one might think, thieves are not excluded from the *fati* circle and can even acquire a good reputation in the world of *fotowwat*.

Then there is a third and rather special source of disagreement. It is known that the *fati* joined in a number of rebellions throughout Iran's history. But were they playing a political role in the strict sense, proclaiming a struggle against despotism, even a struggle for democracy? Or was it a case of a movement to assert identity, a national resistance movement against Arab occupation? Or, on the contrary, just a social

5. See Henry Corbin's analytical introduction to *Traité des compagnons-chevaliers*, Tehran/Paris, Département d'Iranologie de l'Institut Franco-Iranien de Recherche, Librairie d'Amérique et d'Orient, Adrien-Maisonneuve, 1973.

protest movement against tax collectors, even a simple form of 'social banditry'?[6]

It is not our intention to settle these questions. What interests us here is the permanent adaptation to modern times, in the contemporary political and economic context, of a historical ethic. To study this we have to abandon any anachronistic idea of *fotowwat*, such as is found in the writings of a philosopher like Henry Corbin or a historian like Bastani-Parizi. That ethic does not exist in a timeless form, nor separately from all material considerations; it does not appear as a principle predetermined by history, but as an existential ethic. As such it has taken very varied forms according to the social groups and historical contexts where it has developed.

The history of *javânmardi* is punctuated with personalities whose life stories, largely mythical, are unceasingly brought forward as a reference and in order to give a modern meaning to this set of ideals. Among them can be mentioned at random:

– Abraham, who went to the extreme in his faith and was ready to sacrifice his son to divine justice;
– Joseph, one of the twelve sons of Jacob, who never revealed his brothers' criminal act against him;
– Imam Ali, for his humility, courage and thirst for justice;
– Yaqub-e Leys, founder of the Saffar dynasty in the ninth century, who fought with determination against the Arabs after they extended the power of their Caliphate over the whole of Iran;
– Puriyaye-vali, traditional wrestler living in the fourteenth century, for his lessons in humility;
– Sattar Khan, hero of the revolutionary constitutionalist movement at the beginning of this century, for his fight for justice;
– Teyyeb, leader of the Tehran fruit and vegetable market, who upheld justice-truth (*haq*) at the cost of his life, and to whom we shall be returning at length;

6.   On these approaches to *fotowwat* see F. Taeschner, op. cit.; Ibn Asir, *Akhbâr-e iran az alkâmel-e ebn-e Asir*, tr. Bastani Parizi, Tehran, Donyâ-e ketâb, 1365 (1986); Ibn Batuta, *Safar nâmeh*, tr. Mohammad-Ali Movahhed, Tehran, Bongâh-e ketâb, 1348 (1969); Vâ'ez Kâshefi Sabzevâri, *Fotowwat nâmeh soltâni*, Tehran, Bonyâd-e farhang-e iran, 1350 (1971); Dr. Mohammad Riyâz Khân, 'Sharh-e ahvâl va âsâr-e mir seyyed 'ali hamedâni', thesis, Tehran (Faculty of Arts, University of Tehran), 1347 (1968); Kâzem Kâzemeyni, *naqsh-e pahlavâni va nehzat-e 'ayyâri dar târikh-e ejtemâ'i va hayât-e siyâsi-e mellat-e irân*, Tehran, Châp-khâneh bânk-e melli, 1343 (1964); Bastan-Parizi, *Yaqub-e leys*, Tehran, Negâh, 1344 (1965); *Târikh-e sistan*, unknown author, Tehran, Peyk-e irân, 1366 (1987); Hamid Hamid, *Zendegi, ruzegâr va andisheh-e puriyâ-ye vali*, Tehran Sâhel, 1353 (1974); Mortezâ Sarraf, 'javânmardân', in *Armaqân*, nos. 2, 4, 5, 6 and 7, 1350 (1971); W.N. Floor, 'The political role of the Lutis in Iran', in M.E. Bonine and N.R. Keddie (eds.), *Modern Iran: The Dialectics of Continuity and Change*, Albany, State University of New York Press, 1981, pp. 83-93; C. Cahen, 'Y a-t-il eu des corporations professionnelles dans le monde musulman classique?' in A.H. Hourani and S.M. Stern (eds.), *The Islamic City: A Colloquium*, Philadelphia, University of Pennsylvania Press, 1970, pp. 51-64; L. Massignon, 'Les corps de métiers et la cité islamique', *Revue Internationale de Sociologie*, 1920, vol. 28, pp. 73-88.

– Takhti, traditional wrestler and Iran's first gold medallist at the Melbourne Olympic Games in 1956, whom we shall also look at again in a later chapter.

This list could be lengthened. However, these names are not really the result of an arbitrary choice on our part. They assert themselves in written and oral history, as well as in circles going well beyond that of the specialists in *fotowwat*. This rather quaint list underlines, as well as the richness and deep roots in society of the *javânmard*'s acts, the extraordinary diversity of the historical contexts in which that ethic can express itself, and the great variety of the individuals who have expressed it. Between the courage of Imam Ali, mingled with Islamic fervour, and the struggle against Arab domination by Yaqub-e Leys, between the secularising justice advocated by Sattar Khan during the Constitutional Revolution and Abraham's Hebrew justice – what a world of difference!

So a list of heroes of *fotowwat* does not make it possible to fit its field of action into a narrow normative framework. A little anecdote defines the commitment of the *fati*. How will he react if, when sitting down by the street, he sees a man running past with sword in hand who makes him promise to say nothing to the people pursuing him? The action of the true *fati* must be to move: then, if questioned, he can say he has seen nobody 'since he has been sitting there'.[7] It is clear that the *javânmard* ethic is very much tied in with the fundamental distinction between appearance (*zâher*) and inner reality (*bâten*), which is said to be basic to the Iranian world view: pureness of heart is more important than overt acts. For example, the *hejâb-e zâher*, as an article of clothing, is only important for women through respect for *hejâb-e bâten*, that is, the whole range of values to which they must adhere to be fully women, to be considered 'the ideal of humanity', as P. Veyne put it. It is partly because of the same logic that the Iranian who practises open-handedness owes it to himself to keep a low profile.

We now need to examine how this set of values is related to, and contributes towards, modern economic and political life on the contemporary social scene. The figure of Teyyeb, a highly ambiguous one, will help us answer the questions.

Teyyeb: A Very Ambiguous Hero

Teyyeb Haj Rezai was born in 1912 in Tehran, to a father who supplied fuel to butchers' shops. According to his son, he graduated from the Tehran military academy and went to prison for murder during the reign of Reza Shah. After his release he seems to have been recruited for the fruit and vegetable market by Arbab Zeyn-ol Abedin, a childless man and one of the biggest dealers in that market. Teyyeb rapidly advanced to become the principal manager of the market. He contributed, with Shaban Jafari, to the

---

7. Onsor-ol Ma'ali Keykâvus ebn-Eskandar, *Gozideh-e qâbus nâmeh*, Tehran, Amir-Kabir, 1368 (1989), pp. 308-9.

organisation of demonstrations in support of Mossadegh's nationalist government. But after the religious leaders dissociated themselves from Mossadegh, the two men let themselves be bought by the CIA and the supporters of restoration of monarchical power. Shaban Jafari entered court circles and, thanks to backing from there, opened a 'house of strength' (*zur-khâneh*), a place for practising a form of traditional wrestling, where people claimed to follow *javânmardi*; at the same time he organised the supporters of the national football team. Later he emigrated to the United States after the 1979 Revolution.

As for Teyyeb, he stayed at the fruit and vegetable market, where his influence kept growing, especially because of the monopoly of banana imports that he secured. In 1963 the Shah's government accused him of having organised Âshurâ processions that turned into riots in support of Ayatollah Khomeyni, when the latter was arrested for opposing the 'white revolution'. When the prosecutor called on him to declare that he had been paid by the Ayatollah, he refused and was executed. Ayatollah Khoi, the most eminent figure in the Shia hierarchy, with whom Ayatollah Khomeyni found refuge at Najaf in Iraq, conferred posthumously on Teyyeb the honour of '*Horr*' (free man), from the name of the person who went over from Yazid's camp to Hussein's at the battle of Karbala. Ayatollah Khomeyni, for his part, hardly made any public homage to him after 1979, although one of his sons was appointed to head the Oil Products Marketing Association.[8]

Teyyeb's death marked the culmination of his *javânmard* life, not because he saved the life of a man who was to change the course of history of that region of the world fifteen years later, but more simply because he refused to testify in favour of the unjust and false (*nâ-haq*) instead of the just (*haq*). This episode is more important than all other aspects of his life because those ideas basic to the *javânmard* ethic were at stake.

However, well before his execution, Teyyeb showed complete adherence to that ethic by his generosity (the giving hand, *dast-e bedeh*) and the constant help he gave to the needy. 'Four hundred families received their winter coal every year from Teyyeb'; 'He went in person to distribute meals to the people working in the brickworks in the south of Tehran'; 'Long after his death you would still see unaccompanied women – that is, poor women – asking after him near his scales, at one of the main gates of the market' – such sentences are repeated constantly by people who approached him or heard about him. They emphasise how he was a man of open-handed character. His son, today an engineer with a diploma from an Italian university, says on that point: 'Being heir to such a father is not very easy at all. People expect the same things from me as from him, and I cannot refuse

8.   Our information on Teyyeb's life story comes essentially from our private conversations with his friends and members of his family. We should also refer to the remarkable research work by Jamshid Sedâghat Nejâd, partially published under the title 'Teyyeb, qaddâreh-bandi dar kenâr-e tâqut va bar 'alayh-e ân', in *Asiyâ-ye javân*, 1, 3, 4, 5, 1358 (1979).

anything when I see the difficulties in which people are struggling to live.'

But it was not only the poor and the deprived who were touched in this way by Teyyeb's actions: 'Teyyeb paid the bill for all the customers in the restaurant where he entered.' And he was not a man to taste his meal alone, as the following story – probably apocryphal – shows. At the end of a march organised on Teyyeb's initiative and attended by thousands of people to protest a decision by the Mayor of Tehran prohibiting him from keeping his sheep at the fruit and vegetable market, our hero was received by the Prime Minister. After a long argument, he invited Teyyeb to have lunch with him. Teyyeb refused because he had to attend to his own guests who were waiting at the gate of the government building for his return. The Prime Minister, very affably, assured him that the guests would be served by the ministry guards. The story goes on that while Teyyeb's followers ate their fill, the barracks went without a good meal! The act of eating, it seems, was a moment of necessary communion in Teyyeb's eyes. This fitted in with the ethic of the *javânmard*, for whom 'holding a table-cloth' (*sofreh dâri*) is a fundamental principle. But it must be emphasised that Teyyeb's public activities did not lead him to neglect his family: 'Teyyeb took his midday and evening meals with his family almost every day', one of his closest companions recalls.

In short Teyyeb had a sense of family, of sharing, of giving and of justice, qualities crowned by the courage (*shojâ'at*) which he proved by sacrificing his life, in refusing to utter the words which an all-powerful government wanted to put in his mouth. Those are the essential characteristics of a *javânmard*, updated to fit the second half of the twentieth century. But a personality such as Teyyeb, involved in important and controversial episodes in the history of modern Iran, does not always arouse comments as approving as those just recalled. He was also the focus of contradictory, even antithetical accounts. Historians and intellectuals, in particular, generally criticise Teyyeb in a fairly sharp way. It is especially remarkable that the Iranian Left has not adopted this figure so celebrated in popular accounts, as it has not pardoned him for his role in the overthrow of Mossadegh, a way of life considered immoral, and his refusal to respect the most elementary rules of a state governed by law. Among intellectuals it is above all the film producers who have given this sort of hero some recognition, for example in *Qeysar*, a masterpiece by Kimiyai. It is possible even to speak of a real cinematic school, 'Jahelism', portraying such colourful personalities who dominated urban neighbourhoods before the great wave of urbanisation in the 1960s, and who liked similarly to pose as *javânmard*.

Teyyeb's ambivalent role is not at all exceptional. It is typical of most life stories of *javânmard*. Everything depends – to use the expression coined by Jean-Pierre Warnier[9] on which gate we use to enter their life

---

9. J.-P. Warnier, *L'esprit d'entreprise au Cameroun*, Paris, Karthala, 1993.

stories: on the courtyard side or the garden side? Such double entrances are essential to understand better the subtleties of the many sides to a life like Teyyeb's.

On the 'garden side' we have Teyyeb's spirit of generosity, which may be emphasised in a qualified way, but which is unanimously recalled among both his supporters and his opponents, even though debate continues about the resources lying behind it. 'Where did the money he distributed so generously come from?' some people ask. Others emphasise his prodigality that stopped him from building up a large fortune as he gave away so much, and dismiss the question of the origin of his money as niggardly and baseless probing. On the 'courtyard side' is the darker side of the man, often involving the use of force. Courage can be another word for blind obstinacy, authoritarianism, despotism and atavistic attachment to an outdated way of life. It is interesting to note that the expressions used to describe Teyyeb are almost identical when coming from his supporters and his critics; only the way in which they are uttered can make it possible to discern the nuance of positive or negative meaning. Thus Teyyeb is often called a 'roughneck' (*gardan koloft*), a 'wielder of the knife' (*châqu kesh*), and a host of other terms (*mashdi, dâsh-mashdi, luti...*) that denote both the quality of a neighbourhood leader and that of a *javânmard*. The meaning conveyed by such words changes according to the context in which they are used. While Teyyeb's use of force divides opinion, it is in spite of everything a reminder of a past era which can be recalled in a more or less nostalgic way. The past is recalled as a time when 'roughnecks' imposed their law in the streets. But that law could be the law of generosity and lavish giving, or the law of protection rackets and cellars where the disobedient were punished.

However, Teyyeb's ambivalent role, inherent in the *javânmard* personality, cannot be dissociated from the formidable social changes that Iran underwent during his lifetime. As a historical personality Teyyeb is on the borderline or, indeed, at the fulcrum. As we have seen, he applied the ancestral ethic of *fotowwat*, but at the same time he stood out in his modern chic appearance, his numerous suits. Teyyeb's period was that which saw the beginning of the urban explosion and the extension of Tehran beyond the limits of its twelve gates. His principal base, the fruit and vegetable market, must be recalled as it was then.

The Fruit and Vegetable Market: Inventing Tradition

It was in the second half of the last century that the Prime Minister Amin os-Soltan, so it is said, donated one of his properties to help Tehran enjoy its status as the capital by getting supplies of fruit and vegetables from other regions of the country. The fruit and vegetable market, an extension of the bazaar geographically, is distinguished from it by being in almost daily use – durable goods are not sold there – and by its name: it is called the *meydun* (the square). In addition its management turned out over the years to be more difficult than that of the bazaar.[10]

This fruit and vegetable market is a very important place for the people of Tehran. While they can do without meat, they hardly ever cut back on consumption of vegetables and fruit, which are indispensable elements in the endless game of reciprocal visiting (*raft-o amâd*) within the extended family, according to the principle of daily sociability which requires that every respectable home must keep its door, even its 'tablecloth', open. Probably this importance of vegetables and fruit in the diet of Tehran's citizens was even greater in the 1950s than today, because consumption of meat and rice was reserved for feast days. This means that considerable sums of money changed hands in the fruit and vegetable market – especially as that place, by its central position, also became the nodal point of trading networks that extended over the principal parts of the country, some goods being immediately forwarded to other cities. Conflicts, sometimes bloody, broke out among the 'roughnecks' who tried to control the business. In addition that market was the place where three categories of vendors interacted, all under pressure from the perishable character of the fruit and vegetables: the producers, the middlemen and the traders, including itinerant traders. Negotiations were often rough. The harshness of the place was further emphasised by its lack of hygiene, rubbish and droppings of draught animals, mud and dust. The *meydun* never became a place where people could go in a family group to do the shopping.

The market middleman (*meyduni*) is linked in common accounts with other sorts of traders. He is said for example to be a 'hat-snatcher' (a con-man) from morning to night. He is a fraudster who hides his game from everyone – except from God, who forgives him for nothing and makes him drink the cup of punishment. 'The *meyduni*'s family is diabetic because they eat so much that they have no right to have,' said one of the people I interviewed; he spoke of the fruit and vegetable market with some nostalgia, as he had worked with others as a strong-arm man for Teyyeb, but he had parted company with him voluntarily to spare his children the unpleasant side of that environment. Indeed the *meydun* has a bad reputation.

It was precisely to manage this difficult place that Arbab Zeyn-ol Abedin, after the war, called on Teyyeb, who had made a name for himself for his authority among the lorry drivers of Kermanshah. Our roughneck hero did not let him down, and asserted his pre-eminence over the whole market in a short time. But his success – establishing *his* order, rather than order – was due essentially to two facts that contributed to his reputation. Firstly, his courage (*shojâ'at*). Teyyeb had shown this in Kermanshah when, in a café, he vigorously called to order a group of lorry drivers at a table who

---

10. It should be noted in addition that Tehran's demographic growth made it necessary to open several branches of the *meydun* in the rest of the city, and that the mayors of the capital tried several times to move it, before achieving this in 1995.

were praising the British too loudly. He quickly confirmed his reputation within the market where his worst enemies and rivals ended up by becoming their friends. Teyyeb was respected for his practical skill (*tar-dasti*), for his cunning in conflicts with his enemies, whatever their social rank might be; he dealt equally readily with a colleague and with the future head of the Savak, Nasiri, whom he apparently slapped in public. Teyyeb also had business sense (*vâred bud*). On his appointment to the *meydun* he imposed a tax on all goods entering or leaving it. Only the poorest, with whom Teyyeb claimed to identify, were exempted from payment. Later, as we have seen, he obtained from the Shah the banana importing concession, with complete exemption from customs duty. It was that which allowed him to become rich, but without amassing a fortune as he did so much to ensure that the people around him benefited from his income. Lastly he owned scales at one of the principal gates of the market, and by controlling measurement of weight in that way he obtained decisive power to dominate the *meydun*.

Courage, however, is only an individual quality. It only has value if it acquires a collective dimension. Teyyeb in fact had support from numerous followers. He had a 'back' (*posht*), in the sense of support, backing. First of all he had the support of his family, especially his brothers. Teyyeb's father was a polygamist without equal: he seems to have contracted more than thirty temporary marriages, while respecting his four legitimate wives. His family was thus especially numerous. But only three of his brothers backed him up in the market: Taher, Ali Akbar and Masih. Besides this immediate support there was also the help received from a number of cousins and from all those who were linked to him by blood or by marriage. Teyyeb also had help from his 'small boys' (*nocheh*) who often acted as his bodyguards, and for whom he was a real model to emulate. After this second circle of supporters came a final group composed of people that could be mobilised at his call, recruited among all the trades in the bazaar and especially among the workers at the brickworks. The social variations among Teyyeb's supporters were obvious. In his movement, soldiers, lawyers, big landlords, clerks, traders, strong-arm men and workers marched together. It is precisely for that reason that Teyyeb can be said to have 'had a back' (*posht dâsht*).

These alliances had many varied origins. But it is certain that Teyyeb's own open-handedness played a major role in the social setting that grew up around him. Giving was one of the conditions for that influence. But it must be noted that the giving varied considerably according to its character, the recipients, the context in which it occurred, and the feelings underlying it. The idea of giving is an all-purpose concept which often raises as many problems as it solves. What comparison can there be between gifts in kind that one distributes in front of the homes of the needy during religious festivals, paying customers' bills in restaurants in the south of the city, and the welcome around the family table-cloth for the person entering one's home? It is even more difficult to bridge the gap between those gifts and the 'gift' which Teyyeb and some of his disciples presented to the Shah, on the occasion of the Crown Prince's birth, by lifting up his car, to the great annoyance of the courtiers; and the gift which our hero offered to a cabaret dancing girl by heating her tea over a pile of banknotes!

Teyyeb's public-spirited conduct, in its extraordinary variations, confirmed that he was a transitional character bridging the gap between different worlds. Fond of the good things of life, he frequented cafés, gambling establishments, drug-taking dens – in fact places far removed from the ethic of a *javânmard* even though they may not be so far removed from his actual life. Yet Teyyeb kept well away from those places during the three months of solemn religious mourning (Moharram, Safar and Ramazan). Then he devoted himself solely to pious activities suited to that period: distribution of meals, organisation of *takiyeh* (places reserved for commemoration of the saints for a certain period), and various processions. In those processions he continually fascinated those around him by wearing the largest *'alâmat* (emblem made of a blend of metals) of the time – which, according to legend, no one could use after his death – and walking at the tail end of the procession to show his humility. According to some of our interviews women took advantage of such occasions to see Teyyeb and sometimes paid someone who could point out quickest the figure of that man who aroused admiration and fear by his forename alone.

Teyyeb was constantly passing from one world to another without making a definitive choice. He did not make the Pilgrimage to Mecca, which is often a way for men with life stories just like his to ask for pardon and renew their allegiance to God. That made it possible for him to run his two lives in tandem without incurring serious reproach from those around him. Teyyeb's matrimonial history also shows how he belonged to two worlds and refused to make a choice between them. His first marriage was entirely traditional: he married the daughter of a leading gentleman of the bazaar, a highly respected butcher. But as his second, and last, wife he married Fakhr os-Sadat, who was well known to the cabaret-goers of the capital. This must not be misunderstood: such marriages could at that time be highly respected, and even treated like a Pilgrimage to Mecca, by taking his future wife away from her profession, Teyyeb purified her and gave other people a supreme example of self-denial, so much so that nobody – except his enemies – dared ever again to speak of her except with respect and humility. That woman, whom Teyyeb loved passionately as his will proved, made an impression in her own right and was honoured by history for her virtue, her maturity, and the care she devoted to the upbringing of her children. 'If Teyyeb's children have never been mixed up in politics, it is really thanks to their mother, a highly competent woman', said someone close to them. By an irony of fate, or mere chance, it was the children of that second wife, and not of the first, who were best able to pay respect to the memory and reputation of their father by doing higher studies and holding important posts.

Javânmardi and Contemporary Life

To sum up: the various sequences of the life of Teyyeb as a *javânmard*, which we have been recalling, suggest that he drew on four major categories of conduct: giving, a 'back' in the sense of a circle of contacts, practical ability involving skill, and purifying acts. These values are still respected today, as shown in expressions in current use.

A person's importance is always measured by the standard of his open-handedness: 'He is Hatam-e Tai', people readily say of a generous person, referring to a legendary Arab figure. He is also said to have a 'giving hand' (*dast-e bedeh*). It is understood that religious leaders are greedy characters, that they have grasping hands (*dast-e begir*) and have wide pockets under their '*aba*: 'pockets the size of a bank' (*jîb chon bank*), a new expression which conveys not only a criticism of the present regime but also an allusion to its turning towards Asian countries, as the 'Chinese' sound of the expression suggests; the *hoseynieh* – religious centres that are used for various celebrations – are nicknamed 'houses of beggars' (*gedâ-khuneh*). Other expressions are drawn in an equally obvious way from the *javânmardi* set of values: 'the man with an open heart and hand' (*dast-o del bâz*), to describe a man who gives with modesty; 'the man with no good in him' (*âdam bi kheyr*), a phrase used to condemn someone who is incapable of serving others; 'the man with full eyes and mouth' (*cheshm-o del sir*) to designate a man who shares without keeping anything. As all this shows, giving is involved at all moments of life, from birth to death via marriage, and is present also at events marking modern life, such as buying a house, returning from a non-religious journey, celebration of a birthday.

The idea of 'back' is also topical. We recall that our car dealer, Ali, has the reputation of being a *sarshenâs* (a head that knows and is known). As such he is involved in a set of contacts, he 'has a back'. That phrase 'having a back' is often used to describe solidarity among a group of individuals, and to indicate the interdependence of roles and interests within it. There are also the phrases *posht-e ham budan* or *posht-e ham râ dâshtan*, 'to be one behind the other' or 'giving their backs to each other'. *Posht garmi dashtan*, 'to have something to warm the back', means one is not without backing. When speaking of a large crowd, for example describing the demonstrations of the revolutionary period, one can speak of a crowd going 'back to back' (*posht be posht*). At a moment of departure God is called upon to be both a back and a protection for the person of whom one is taking leave (*khodâ posht-o panâhet*). And to assert one's independence one may say: 'Nobody will scratch my back except my own finger-nail' (*kas nakhârad posht-e man joz nâkhon-e angosht-e man*).

These terms have a particular application when one has to assert some social distinction, or a field of sociability with strategic matters at stake: on the occasion of marriages where the number of cars is counted rather than the number of guests, or funerals where the procession following the coffin has to be of considerable size to guarantee Paradise for the dead person, or religious meetings where the hostess feels pride in her family's regular practice of the faith. The 'back' denotes, besides solidarity, the idea of the 'untouchability' of a person, a particularly ambivalent quality. The reason why Teyyeb was sentenced to death was that he had a 'back' which worried a government threatened by more and more serious popular demonstrations. But when Ayatollah Montazeri was excluded from power in 1989, it was because his 'back' was too narrow and fragile. People say that the Mayor of Tehran has a 'hot back' because he arouses as much enthusiasm as hostility. In the network of interest-free loan funds, whose presence is evident in the bazaar, people speak of *shenâs* (acquaintance) or *shenâs-e khânevâdeh* (family acquaintance); we shall see in the next chapter that one single connection of this sort is enough for a loan to be agreed. So everywhere there is talk about 'back' – even though the system of *parti* (arranging favours) has used more modern terminology since the last years of the old regime, in matters concerning the administration.[11] The symbolism of the 'back' can even relate to the basics of life: a person who is knocked down physically, but also socially, is said to have his 'back on the ground'.

In the area of 'practical skill', one of Teyyeb's most important fields of action, private fighting, has been steadily circumscribed. The supremacy of the law over private settling of accounts between individuals has been asserted. Reza Shah was very firmly opposed to the former ways, and radical measures calmed down those inclined to reach for the dagger. But the transfer of power to his son, Mohammad Reza Shah, put an end to the calm and brought the traditional 'men of order' back onto the social scene. That was probably due partly to the arrival of the Allies in Iran during the Second World War and the weakening of the central government which benefited local elites, always ready to recruit 'roughnecks' as in the Qajar era. We have seen that the nationalisation of oil and the troubles that followed brought those people on stage again. As a social category the figure of the justice-loving brigand, the knife-wielder (*châqu kesh*), seems to have disappeared for good with Teyyeb amid the general changes in society, although some individuals or groups ensure that something remains of it and even renew contact with that category of people, as we shall see later. It is therefore in the fields of calligraphy, games and sports that the idea of 'strength in action' as an element in a person's life style remains relevant; nowadays an Iranian can show his agility and skill in activities other than street brawls, such as football and chess.

But in trading, the *bâzâri*, today as yesterday, has to show the same know-how: he must be bold, 'have a heart' (*jigar dâshteh bâsheh*), not look

11. J.A. Bill, *The Politics of Iran. Groups, Classes and Modernization*, Columbus, Charles E. Merrill Publishing, 1972, p. 104 ff.; W.O. Beeman, *Language, Status and Power in Iran*, Bloomington, Indiana University Press, 1986, p. 44 ff.; A. Nasseri, *The Ecology of Staffing in the Government of Iran*, Beirut, American University, 1964, p. 64 ff.

too closely at the risk he is taking. A new vocabulary has been developed to deal with this. The *bâzâri* is described as a wolf (*gorg*), which does not necessarily mean that he wants to act to others' detriment, even if they inevitably suffer the consequences of his acts. He will find it easier to find business partners if he 'knows how to go about it'. It must be stressed that in the present state of the Iranian economy – dominated by speculation, playing on contacts (*pârti bâzi*), distortions in exchange rates and the informal sector – what the traders say about risk is not just pretentious language. A *bâzâri* said on this subject: 'The bazaar is a permanent battle against risk. Of course, when you are young and starting up, the risks are high and can go as far as bankruptcy. But when you have acquired a solid foundation for your business, risk becomes a game, a hobby. Today, if I did not take any risks, I would stay where I am for all my life. That is not desirable, and I prefer to opt for risk which will certainly cost me some sleepless nights but will make me get ahead.' This almost epic view of business is characteristic of Iranian traders' way of operating, which is by 'attacks' rather than following a strategic plan.

Finally, purifying acts are largely mixed up with self-denial and are therefore partly included in acts of giving. Rejection of adultery and paedophilia is a constant theme in the *javânmard* ethic. But the spectre of those acts seems to haunt the accounts given, for they continue to be referred to by hints accompanied by apologies for touching on such improper subjects. In truth, references to this subject are so obsessive that one cannot avoid thinking they relate to some degree of practice. Anyway, every normally constituted individual should have eyes as pure as the heart (*cheshm-o del pâk*), whatever his occupation may be.

Marriage with a prostitute to save her, following the example of Teyyeb, is no longer favoured. Since the Revolution and especially since the war, it is the widows of 'martyrs' whom one may take pride in saving, following calls made by leading figures in the regime. What matters here is protecting the dead man's family, his wife and children, and staving off the spectre of 'corruption' which is said to hang over any household left without a head. Thus a senior politician may be asked by his wife to take as a second wife the widow of her brother killed in battle. Polygamy, which was very badly regarded under the old regime and in the first years of the Republic, and which according to rumour caused several ministers to lose their posts, is tending to acquire a certain legitimacy again in this particular case. While it is claimed to be in accordance with Islam and the ideals of the Revolution, the concern to save a family suddenly deprived of its head comes from the ethic of the *javânmard*. In any case, can one really talk of polygamy in this sort of situation? The precedents of the Prophet and his son-in-law Ali are cited: several of their wives were old, and they married them to help them; in doing so they behaved like perfect *javanmârd*. But a reasonable comment is that in the case of the wives of 'martyrs', one should rather talk of *javânzan*: it is above all the woman (*zan*) who shows self-denial in accepting the arrival of a co-wife, and it goes without saying that the stability of those unions is sometimes precarious.

The expression commonly used, *az khod gozashtegi*, literally means that you 'do without yourself' or 'efface yourself'. The *javânmard's* purity of heart (*cheshm-o del pâk*), which is part of the *bâten* side of life, is shown in the externalised practice of giving which, being a material action, belongs to the *zâher* category, but is conceived as above all giving of oneself: 'the man with full eyes and mouth' (*cheshm-o del sir*) is not overwhelmed by the good things of this world, he can give up his interests, he willingly 'does without' his wealth by letting others benefit by it. These include members of his immediate family of course, but also the anonymous mass of the poor and disinherited (*mostaz'afin*). In Iran, giving is an act for every day. A great number of collecting-boxes of all sizes have been set up on the public highway, in bazaars, in government offices and in shops, for alms given by passers-by. It is not uncommon to see miniature collecting boxes in private homes, and schools distribute them to children as money-boxes at the New Year.

As a 'life style', the *javânmard* ethos is above all building and assertion of the self. But by definition it assumes overcoming of the self. The game is naturally very ambiguous: it is difficult to avoid ostentation where discretion is concerned. Even if the giver pretends not to make himself known – and that, it will be recalled, is the first rule of open-handedness – everybody knows his name. The *javânmard* derives his quality precisely from that reputation, and in that way the expression 'individuality of eminence' suggested by Mattison Mines to describe the leading citizens of Madras seems to us to be just as applicable to Iranian benefactors. Similarly the first wife who persuades her husband to marry a 'martyr's' widow, and covers the new wife with kindnesses, is only stressing her own generosity more. In the last resort her self-denial is a way of retaining control of a situation which would otherwise slip out of her hands: would not her man have married again anyway, or else embarked on a temporary union?

The ethos of the *javânmard* allows him to get on the stage and build his life doing exemplary deeds to win attention from others and also to acquire self-respect himself. There is a certain theatrical side, or an element of putting on good appearances, to this conception of life. The first wife, by her generosity, turns the suffering of a victim into virtuous heroism. Resorting to the self-denial agenda can also act as a joker in the pack: it allows the woman to take the initiative again, and gives her moral credit which frees her from a number of social rules. At the same time she does not fail to make people uneasy because everyone is surprised that she can act in that way. Basically, the *javânmard*, while arousing recognition and admiration, also provokes perplexity by his unpredictable, rash and sublime side. Because of this he is at the meeting point of conformism – to the extent that he is the best embodiment of society's values – and anti-conformism, in so far as he takes those values to extremes.

Javânmardi as a Modern Political 'Imaginaire'

It remains to be seen how far the set of values called *javânmardi*, omnipresent in everyday language, still provides a working programme for political action in modern Iran. The way in which the personality of Mr. Karbaschi is perceived by public opinion has given us a first indication.* More revealingly, perhaps, the figure of the *javânmard* has risen again in audiovisual productions by the Iranian diaspora in the United States. Hamid Naficy has shown how that diaspora has turned itself into an 'imagined community' (as defined by Benedict Anderson), especially through videoclips. Some of these are on themes dealing with cabarets, settling of scores and city neighbourhoods (*mahalleh*), beloved of the 'roughnecks', even if it means linking them with rap music. It is even easy to discern in one of these recordings the historical figure of Shaban Jafari, alias Shaban the Brainless, who, as we have seen, took part in the overthrow of Mossadegh in 1953, and who went into exile in Los Angeles after the Revolution.[12] The *javânmardi* code thus seems sufficiently flexible to adapt to the experience of emigration and globalisation.

In fact this concept still influences the economic and political organisation of the Islamic Republic. That state has been described as a true 'Republic of the Initiates';[13] it could also be described as the Republic of the Public Benefactors or of the *javânmard*. Observers have stressed that the new regime has not given birth to a party system, not even a one-party system, and that it operates on factional lines. Iranian public opinion itself speaks now of the power of the families (*qodrat-e qowm-o khysh*), just as people spoke of 'the thousand families' at the end of the old regime. This,

---

* *Author's Note to English Edition:* Gholamhossein Karbaschi assumed that *javânmard* style again in 1998 during his brief imprisonment and his trial, with some histrionics involved (Iranians in fact spoke of the 'Karbaschi show' when referring to the televised coverage of his trial, which competed fiercely with the World Cup reports, so that viewers had to jump from one channel to another). After his wife visited him in his cell he uttered through her the words 'I see only beauty', in Arabic, recalling the words of Zeynab on seeing her brother's head cut off by the enemy in the battle of Karbela; he added, 'If my imprisonment ensures the survival of the system [*nezâm*], I am ready to stay here for ever' (*Hamshahri*, 22.1.1377/1998). He declared a little later, facing a throng of journalists on the day of his release, 'People are not my supporters, but supporters of work, effort and reconstruction'; in that way he humbly (!) placed emphasis on the three watchwords of his own party, the Reconstructors (*Hamshahri*, 29.1.1377/1998).

12. H. Naficy, *The Making of Exile Cultures. Iranian Television in Los Angeles*, Minneapolis, University of Minnesota Press, 1993.
13. J.-F. Bayart, 'Entre "dirigistes" et "libéraux": La République islamique' in F. Adelkhah, J.-F. Bayart and O. Roy, *Thermidor en Iran*, Brussels, Complexe, 1993, pp. 15-53.

as one can guess, is another way of asserting the central importance of 'back' or *pârti* as a field of action and human relations.

Fotowwat, as a historical reference and source for a vocabulary, definitely seems to provide the schema for this organisational reality. It is characterised by two aspects which appear to be partly contradictory. On the one hand there is a hierarchical principle particularly strong within the group, expressing itself through a set of command and obedience values. On the other hand, the group has very ill-defined borders, probably because of the individual moral character of *javânmard* actions. It is this duality that is found at the heart of the Islamic Republic's institutions. Let us take for example the word *beyt* (house). It was used previously to describe the entourages of the most eminent personalities of the early days of Islam. But it also seems to have been used more specifically for the meeting places of the *fati*. Before the Revolution the word was applied to the entourages of the 'sources of emulation' (*marja'-e taqlid*); there was Borujerdi's *beyt*, Khoi's *beyt*, etc. From 1979 the idea tended to become politicised: people came very rapidly to speak of Imam Khomeyni's *beyt*, and then they spoke of the *beyt-e rahbar* to describe the household of the Leader of the Revolution, Ali Khamenei.

Similarly the word *hezb* (party), whose use by the *fati* has been noted by Taeschner,[14] has had well known success under the Islamic Republic. Its connotation is more secular, and Islamists have made a point of explaining that there is a *Hezbollah*, a 'party of God'. But the history of that movement clearly shows that it is impossible to define the limits of a *hezb*. The same can be said of the People's Mujahidin Organisation: one of its dissidents has admitted[15] that it never had more than a thousand paid-up militants, but in 1982 hundreds of thousands of Iranians identified with it as determined sympathisers, putting their lives at risk, though without considering themselves full members. Just as it was not necessary to be a full initiate according to the rules to follow the existential ethic of *fotowwat*, so today formal membership is not a condition *sine qua non* for moral or political adherence. In daily life religious activities follow the same logic; the *jaleseh* and *hey'at*, meetings reserved for women and men respectively, are not held in fixed places and do not have precisely defined attendances.

It is striking to see that some of the most eminent politicians of the last twenty years have willingly adopted the style of the *javânmard*, or, more precisely, that public opinion has interpreted their popularity or their historical personality on the basis of *javânmardi* values. Imam Khomeyni himself embodied many of those virtues: lonely courage, the most extreme determination, the simplicity of habits suited to a mystic. One of the best known photographs of him shows him modestly serving tea to his guests. As very numerous slogans recalled, his dearest wish was to fight at the front as

14. F. Taeschner, op. cit.
15. See Y. Khaled and R.X., 'Une expérience de lutte clandestine', *Peuples Méditerranéens*, 29, 1984, pp. 145-64.

a *bassij*, and he saw himself as a caretaker (*farrâsh*) in the service of the people. The words used have a clear meaning: the *bassij*, unlike the Revolutionary Guards or the military, were at the lower end of the hierarchy and provided cannon fodder in the 'human waves' strategy employed against the technologically superior Iraqi army; as for the *farrâsh*, he is the caretaker that everyone has known at school, who opens doors, sweeps the courtyards, lights the oil stoves and serves tea to the teachers.

Imam Khomeyni's style of government did not involve any breach with the *fotowwat* style. When he intervened it was advisedly, for essential arbitration, and he usually let members of his *beyt*, and especially his son, Ahmed, act as spokesmen for his ideas.[16] Hence his was a very special style in which power was exercised between 1979 and 1989. Like a *javânmard*, the Imam was both very present and strangely absent, deliberately keeping his distance from the state – in a way that he would have wished to impose on the clergy just after the Revolution, but had to let them abandon after the wave of attacks organised by the People's Mujahidin in 1981.[17]

Similarly, the tributes paid on the death of Mehdi Bazargan in December 1994 drew largely on the same stock of values. His successor at the head of the National Liberation Movement, Ebrahim Yazdi, spoke of 'his conviction' and his 'honesty': 'He was not only a political activist, persevering and tough, nor only a social reformer, but a sincere teacher with solid political convictions [Mr. Yazdi used the word *moallem* rather than *ostad*, the word for 'schoolteacher' which one would have expected, to illustrate the man's simplicity]. He was a courageous, straightforward and pious man. In social and political affairs he was to the point and subtle...He had overcome the despot who lurks within everyone.'[18] Ezzatollah Sahabi, editor of the *Iran-e farda* magazine, emphasised that Mehdi Bazargan was 'close to the people'; he was 'on equal terms both with humble servants and with influential people'; 'he would give without expecting any return, with completely honesty and no guile'; 'he was in permanent contact with the people without presuming it in his speeches'.[19] Ahmad Shayegan considered that the departed, 'despite his remarkable knowledge of politics, did not play around with it (*siyasat bâz*)'[20] in the sense in which the womaniser plays around with love and distorts it in the process, or the paedophile abuses children for his sole pleasure (*bacheh bâz*). Abdolkarim Soroush, the great dissident philosopher, paid a stirring homage on the theme: 'He was a merchant (*bâzargân*) in name but not in his good qualities.'

16. We thank Christian Bonnot for drawing our attention to this management style on Imam Khomeyni's part.
17. S.A. Arjomand, *Turban for the Crown, the Islamic Revolution in Iran*, New York, Oxford University Press, 1988.
18. *Adineh*, 100, 1374 91995), pp. 74-5.
19. *Adineh*, 100, 1374 91995), pp. 75-6.
20. *Adineh*, 100, 1374 (1995), p. 77.

He was a man who showed the greatest self-denial in his life. Head of the Faculty of Technology, holder of a university chair, enjoying life's comforts and the benefits of a good reputation, he could have obtained more by showing a bit more docility. But when he set foot in political activity he also trod all his privileges underfoot. He earned himself the pain of imprisonment in Tehran and Borazjan. With his comrades and his companions in the struggle, he held out against the Shah's despotism at a time when the mere mention of the Savak's name made people tremble. That was how they gave us a lesson in resistance and continually renewed it, with honesty and firmness, until the Revolution. After that they did not fail to make constructive criticisms of the Revolution, while expressing their support for it. Bazargan's life, the purity of his line of conduct and his actions, his campaigning for dignity and freedom, his love for science, his knowledge of Islam, his self-denial, his generosity, his *javânmardi* teach many lessons to us all and are worthy of the greatest respect.[21]

It is clear that Mehdi Bazargan's qualities, or at least those praised by his contemporaries, coincide with those of a *javânmard*. But this historical figure is a useful reminder that such an ethos is not in itself an obstacle to social or political change. Indeed the leader of the National Liberation Movement reformulated the style of the traditional *fati*: he was an eminent scholar, a learned Muslim, but also an engineer who studied in France, and a layman. He founded a political party which was not without weaknesses as Houchang Chehabi has shown,[22] but which was nevertheless different from a simple gathering of followers (*beyt*) and was a notable example of institutionalising that has so far remained unique in the country's history. Above all he offers a first example of a *javânmard* who was at the same time a social being (*âdam-e ejtemâ'i*): 'He resolved the contradiction between thought and action. There was no hiatus in his declarations and practice between the period before he came to power and the period in power. He had the same attitude in his family circle, in private, and on the political stage, in public bodies, at the university. His interior being (*darun*) and his outward appearance (*birun*) were those of a person of integrity', said Ebrahim Yazdi.[23]

In that respect Mehdi Bazargan was very different from Teyyeb who, as we have seen, led several separate lives in rigid compartments: the fruit and vegetable market sphere and the sphere of companionship did not interfere with that of family life. In this sense the social *javânmard* embodied by Bazargan tended to reduce the ambivalent aspects inherent in the *fotowwat* ethos. In addition there was a change of scale. Although Teyyeb used his fists against lorry drivers who were servile towards the British occupation, he could not pass for a nationalist hero, and for all his fame in the country, he remained associated with a narrowly defined area, the fruit and vegetable market. On the other hand Bazargan was a national figure whose activities were constantly in the *mellat* category.

21. *Kiyan*, vol. 4, no. 23, 1373 (1995), p. 12.
22. H. Chehabi, *Iranian Politics and Religious Modernism. The Liberation Movement of Iran under the Shah and Khomeini*, London, I.B. Tauris, 1990.
23. *Adineh*, 100, 1374 (1995), p. 75.

The *fotowwat* ethos, lastly, is more and more coming to terms with the Weberian bureaucractic ethos. Sociologically, the Revolutionary Guards and the *komiteh* recruited partly from the 'roughnecks' underworld in the early days after the Revolution. But they quickly became institutionalised as police and army formations. Those of their members who did not understand the new rules learned them the hard way: several individuals who continued to commit abuses for personal reasons were dismissed or even arrested. However, in popular belief the commander-in-chief of the Revolutionary Guards, Mohsen Rezai, was supposed to be none other than Teyyeb Haj Rezai's own son. As for Mohsen Rafighdoust, who shared that command until 1988 and who today heads the powerful Foundation for the Disinherited, he is – again according to common rumour – said to have remained the final arbitrator in conflicts in the fruit and vegetable market from which he came himself.

The two categories – the romantic concept of the traditional *javânmard*, built on the hero's unchallenged authority and arbitrary power, and the legal and rational order of bureaucracy – coexist. However, the trend in the Islamic Republic seems to be towards the bureaucratic way. For example, the word *beyt*, household, is increasingly replaced by the word *daftar*, office, or *nahâd*, institution; instead of speaking of the *beyt* of the Leader of the Revolution, people prefer now to refer to the *nahâd* or *daftar-e rahbari* to make it clear that it is an official and indeed constitutional body. Similarly, Parliament regularly discusses the need to set up real parties (*hezb*), which some deputies see as 'the principal components of civil society' which should 'establish legal relationships between the people and the government.'[24]

The real question that arises today – especially in connection wih the Tehran municipality and the election of Mohammad Khatami as President – definitely relates to the compatibility of the *javânmard* ethos with the idea of citizenship. However much power may still be held by the security services set up at the time of the Revolution, however influential social forces quite far removed from any question of democracy – such as the bazaar and the clergy – may still be, things have perhaps advanced more than people think. Deputies favourable to a return to multiparty politics refer to provisions of the Constitution which they want to see fully implemented. No doubt the Islamic Republic is not a state based on the rule of law, but this idea is far from being alien to it, as we shall have the chance to see in the coming chapters.

One may wonder whether Imam Khomeyni did not play a part in this development in a certain way, and quite consciously. He knew from experience how the support of the 'roughnecks' (*luti*) for dynasties in power and clerical leaders had proved fickle throughout history.[25] His reticence

24. Ahmad Kalimipour, Deputy for Zanjan, in parliament, *Keyhan*, 15.4.1373 (1994).
25. W. Floor, 'The Political Role of the Lutis in Iran', in M. Bonine and N.R.Keddie, *Modern Iran, Dialectics of Continuity and Change*, Albany, State University of New York Press, 1981, pp. 83-95.

about paying tribute to Teyyeb and his companions for their sacrifice in 1963, his refusal to have the *luti* play any role except in the *komiteh* and the ranks of the Revolutionary Guards, are evidence not necessarily of democratic aims, but at the very least of a desire to break with the city neighbourhood order dominated by street leaders.

While the neighbourhoods remain spaces for identification within the 'democratic city', they are no longer centres of power strictly speaking, nor even bases that can be sufficient on their own, because of the political changes and the social and economic transformation of urban life. Besides the persistence of certain cultural manifestations, revealed by contemporary vocabulary, the figure of the neighbourhood *javânmard* survives in various sequences of social life. For example, a personality of the south of Tehran close to the powerful underworld of motor mechanics – who, incidentally, have given a good deal of trouble to Mr. Karbaschi in his urban improvement schemes – has been co-opted by the official physical education organisation in the section dealing with *zur-khaneh*, the favourite martial art of the *javânmard*'. In an eastern district of the city a *bâzâri*, in his role as public benefactor, finances a *rozeh* every year shortly before the Âshurâ celebrations, and his reputation and skill are such that nobody thinks of competing with him. But whatever may be the influence of those people, it is exceptional and does not cover the whole social life of their neighbourhoods. Once the month of Moharram is finished our merchant loses his prominent position, and the supremacy of our *javânmard*-mechanic is limited to *zur-khaneh* circles – in fact one may wonder whether that martial art is not changing into a simple sport, a separate activity not connected with other aspects of daily life.

From time to time the press reports trouble with the law incurred by people whose behaviour, considered as criminal, in some ways recalls that of the 'roughnecks' of former days, or is at any rate seen in the same way. The press calls them 'hooligans' (*obâsh* or *arâzel*), and their reputation is unanimously acknowledged by the people of their neighbourhood. In April 1992, not far from the Bahman Cultural Foundation headquarters, a man well known by the name of Abas Kaka was arrested for extortion from the neighbourhood – that, it will be recalled, was the favourite vice of the 'roughnecks' – without anyone understanding what was held against him precisely, except perhaps his power which caused problems for that of the state (or for that of rival gangs?). In July 1994, in the same district, a certain 'poor star' (as he was called), apparently ready with his dagger and eager to deal blows against the 'honour of the people' – meaning, in good Persian, propositioning women and girls, which carries with it consequences for family honour – was found by the guardians of public order with his head shaved, at the scene of his exploits.[26] In the absence of more precise accusations, such as drug taking or trafficking, one cannot avoid thinking

26. *Keyhan*, 11.5.1371 (1992) and 24.5.1373 (1994).

that, by such arrests, the Republic seeks above all to establish its hegemony in populous districts and supplant rival influences.

The flexibility of the *javânmardi* code raises a second question about its future. Iran today has very rapid population growth, accompanied by fast and often uncontrolled expansion of the cities. It is Iran's turn to face the problem of overpopulated, poorly provided for suburbs, whose residents may feel neglected by the state and may face serious problems of housing, employment and transport in their daily lives. Although one cannot rule out the possibility that the riots regularly making an impact on the political scene are partly manipulated by factions in their power struggle – notably those at Mashhad in 1992 and Qazvin in 1994 – they are primarily an expression of social problems in the urban periphery.[27] That seems especially to have been true of the clashes in Islamshahr in March 1995, a mushroom urban growth in the south of Tehran. If the state's inability to control and channel these new forms of urban growth is confirmed, and if the education system continues to let a considerable proportion of the youth slip through its net, a new generation of 'roughnecks' could emerge, with inevitably new style, economic practices and political alliances. For not only have the players in the power game changed – the imperial court has disappeared, the clergy have been transformed – but, in addition, the economy is in crisis for an indefinite period as oil income is no longer sufficient to guarantee growth in a country of 60 million people. Iranian society is now experiencing an almost universal sort of crime, for which the stadiums are a favourite place.

27. A. Bayat, 'Squatters and the State. Back Street Politics in the Islamic Republic', *Middle East Report*, Nov.-Dec. 1994, pp. 10-14.

3

THE ECONOMICS OF BENEFICENCE: GENEROSITY AND BUSINESS ORIENTATION

The bureaucratising and even democratising of the *javânmard* ethos has not been a straightforward process. At every level of society the classical code of *fotowwat* is seen intermingling with that of Weberian rationalisation; this is especially seen in the institutionalising of open-handedness or public generosity.

Under the old regime there were already – even without mentioning the *vaqf* – some charitable institutions supported with funds from the big *bâzâri*s, such as orphanages and hospital departments for diabetics. The Âstân-e Qods, which administered the Imam Reza shrine at Mashhad and had controlled Khorassan province for ages, was a power in its own right, caring for the well-being of pilgrims. The state had its own centre, the Welfare Organisation (*behzisti*), which helped disabled people, orphans and the deprived, while the imperial court had its bodies for good works, especially the Diba Foundation and the Pahlavi Foundation. But since 1979 the Republic has aimed to devote itself as a priority to the disinherited (*mostaz'afin*), and has sought to build a Welfare State by creating many new foundations of its own – such as the Foundation for the Disinherited, the Martyrs' Foundation, the Imam's Relief Committee, the 15th Khordad Foundation, and others – to manage assets confiscated from the *tâquti* (literally 'idolaters', in revolutionary parlance personalities linked with the Shah's regime) to help the poor. More recently, the Welfare Organisation, which had never ceased activity, took a leading position again alongside the Imam's Relief Committee, and was authorised by the government to receive the *zakât* and various other religious donations.

The network of institutions for public generosity has become very diverse, and its relations with the wielders of power and state institutions are all the more complex because not all the institutions have been set up on their initiative. For example, the galaxy of interest-free loan funds dates from before the Revolution and was for long in conflict with the new regime, as we shall see in more detail shortly. Today, the autonomy of these public beneficence institutions seems even to be increasing, especially in the economic and financial domain, because of the economic crisis and the privatisation programme. The state's centralising intentions need therefore to come to terms with the strength of those bodies which should really be called true 'meta-governments' endowed with considerable fiscal and legal privileges. In fact the public beneficence bodies – especially the foundations – are today economic operators of the first rank; they are real holding companies which invest indiscriminately in agriculture and real estate, air transport and insurance, reconstruction of cities destroyed in the war, and import-export trade. As for their field of operations, it now extends beyond the borders of Iran, stretching to other states in the region and even to Africa and some Asian and European states; nor does it neglect the possibilities offered by the offshore financial havens of the Caribbean. This means that the institutions of public generosity – notably the Âstân-e Qods, the Foundation for the Disinherited, the Martyrs Foundation, the 15th Khordad Foundation and the interest-free loans movement – exert direct political influence and contribute to the country's foreign policy orientation. But whatever their role may be in this respect, whatever the implications they have for the definition of sovereignty and 'governance' in Iran, they remain above all beneficent institutions, and it is as such that they need to be understood.

They aim to be at the service of the deprived, in the traditional sense of the term – widows, orphans, the disabled, aged and sick – but also to respond to social needs understood in a broader and more modern way, for example educational needs and even 'development'. Their concerns now include scholarships, building of roads and railways, electricity, and increasingly, youth work and helping the young towards marriage. In this way, the public beneficence institutions are akin to what is called in the West, the social economy, integrated into the market economy but constituting a third sector between capitalist enterprises and state-owned ones, and following (at least officially) a non-profit-making orientation (*qeyr-e entefâ'i*). The underlying theme remains explicitly that of open-handedness, 'good works' (*'amal-e kheyr* or *nikukâri*), which encourages the believer to undertake good on his own initiative and is thus different from the 'ordering of good and prohibition of evil', beloved axiom of the Islamists.[1] But on a closer look several interesting new features can be discerned.

First, terms currently in use tend to come from expressions of national culture, some of them pre-Islamic. The term *nikukâri*, 'good works', employed as a rival to *kheyrieh*, is borrowed from the terminology of Zoroastrianism and is coming into common usage; the state itself organises a 'good deeds week', *hafteh nikukâri*. It would be going too far to say that the question of good works is being disconnected from Islam, but, like the symbolism of flowers, it certainly offers a meeting point between people adhering to religious values and sympathisers with secularism.

1. Popular religious sentiment speaks of 'achieving good' (*'amal-e kheyr*), with the implication that the field of evil will be reduced as a consequence. The believer himself chooses the beneficiaries of his good deeds, in accordance with his spirituality or his personal ideas. It was the politico-religious language of the Revolution and the Republic that brought in the militant idea of the struggle against evil, not without annoying a number of the faithful who saw this as interference in their private lives. Such tensions have been frequent within families and neighbourhoods.

Secondly, 'good deeds'/*nikukâri* are coming to be more and more distinct from 'good deeds'/*kheyrieh*. They imply less a relationship with the next world than involvement in social affairs through personal commitment; they consist less in doing good to enter Paradise, or renouncing one's wealth without a care like a dervish or *fati*, than in helping one's neighbour rationally, without necessarily treating assertion of oneself or one's social distinction as unimportant. Thus charitable action is no longer the attribute of the devout only. It can also be a form of social participation, favoured by women of the middle or upper classes who find in it an opportunity for going out, for social contact, even for showing off. It is increasingly this fashion, definitely a very urban and modern one, that is valued by the senior politicians and their families; for example, one of Hashemi Rafsanjani's daughters heads a charity for people with blood disorders. In this respect, open-handedness recalls in some ways the charity movement in Victorian England; it widens access to the public space and to some extent echoes the idea of the social being (*âdam-e ejtemâ'i*).

Lastly, as we have seen, contemporary open-handedness exists more and more obviously in an institutional framework. The act of purification favoured by the *javânmard* is now mediated through involvement in a bureaucratic-type organisation, whose character is more or less economic, political, religious or associative. Remarriage of widows of martyrs is now the responsibility of an agency, just as in the early days after the Revolution, an Islamic Foundation for Protection and Reform had the task of working among the prostitutes of Shahr-e No, the red-light district of the capital. It is not irrelevant to our theme that one of the main leaders of this last charity was Mohsen Rafighdoust, Chairman of the Foundation for the Disinherited, who, it will be recalled, was a former trader in the fruit and vegetable market.

However, while the Republic has institutionalised open-handedness, it has not abolished the role of individuals and their self-affirmation through such activity. The charitable institutions are networks of personalities, linked with each other by the customary working of the 'back', as well as bureaucratic organisations. Their leading figures are clearly identifiable, even if they like staying in the background to conform to the *javânmard* ethic or for the more prosaic reason of sheltering themselves from the pressure of beggars, and they are frequently found in several networks at the same time. For example, Ali-Naghi Khamoushi, who comes from one of the leading bazaar families of Tehran, is at the same time President of the Chamber of Commerce, Mines and Industry and has senior positions in the Âstân-e Qods, the Islamic Economic Organisation, the Imam's Relief Committee, and the Jame'at-os Sadegh University.

The role of 'eminent personalities' in the public charity sector seems all the more crucial because, in contrast, the cooperative sector – whose inspiration was perhaps more egalitarian or Socialist, and for which the

1979 Constitution seemed to promise a good future alongside the public and private sectors – has not really taken off.[2] This can naturally be explained by other, more political and ideological factors: in the first years of the Republic, the planned-economy and Third-Worldist line embodied by Prime Minister Mir-Hossein Moussavi was subjected to attacks from conservative circles hostile to anything that challenged the sacrosanct principle of property, and the cooperative idea smelt too much of the ideology of agrarian reform to escape that sort of onslaught. But, more fundamentally, the success achieved by the good old formula of pious good works and by its modernisation left hardly any space for other approaches.

We now need to examine the diversity of the public beneficence sector, its own internal dynamics in relation to the government, and the conflicts to which its development has given rise. The Islamic credit networks provide a way to make an initial assessment.

Two Islamic Credit Networks

In October 1990 the Iranian parliament passed, after many hitches, a bill already approved by the Guardianship Council, whose purpose was to struggle more effectively against 'disturbers of the economic order'. Penalties ranged from five years' imprisonment to the death penalty, with illicitly acquired property being confiscated in all cases. In addition, the court was authorised to sentence people convicted of 'economic sabotage' to public flogging.[3]

Who were those 'disturbers' (*ekhlâlgar*)? In the media there were both more allegorical and more precise terms used for them: the language of politicians, deputies and the man in the street was borrowed partly from the negative aspect of the *javânmardi* code of values. So people spoke of 'the corrupt of the earth' (*mofsed-e fel'arz*), 'economic terrorists' (*teroristha-ye eghtesâdi*), 'spongers' (*okhtâpus*) and 'bloodsuckers' (*zâlu-sefat*) – terms drawn from the revolutionary vocabulary – and of 'hat-thieves' (*kolâh-bardâr*), 'roughnecks' (*gardan koloft*), 'market managers' (*meydun-dâr*) and 'middlemen' (*vâseteh* or *dallâl*). In fact these attacks were aimed at two Islamic banking networks: limited partnerships and interest-free loan funds.

The former had an entirely legal and Islamic basis in the form of contract called *mozârebeh*. This contract consists in principle of an agreement between two people of whom one, the *mâlek*, owns cash capital and the other, the *mozârebeh*, some capacities for work. The *mozâreb* commits himself to carrying on commercial activities (*tejârat*) with the help of the *mâlek*'s financial contribution, to the exclusion of any other economic or

---

2. At least until 1996, when it enjoyed a revival, in different forms, as a result of economic liberalisation and the autonomy obtained by new players in the foundations, enterprises, guilds, Islamic schools, city authorities and government departments.
3. *Keyhan*, 19.9.1369 (1990).

social activity. The sharing of profits must, on pain of annulment of the contract, be fixed beforehand on the basis of halves, one-third and two-thirds, one-quarter and three-quarters, etc. The Civil Code mentions *mozârebeh* but gives no indication of the sort of trade that can be practiced within its limits; where there is no written specification, current regulations (*mote'âraf*) are to be applied (article 535). In particular, the *mozâreb* cannot be responsible for loss of capital unless the contract includes a precise clause providing for compensation for the *mâlek* from the *mozâreb*. There are other specific characteristics of *mozârebeh* contracts, but it was essentially these few elements that provided an argument against the limited partnerships.

As for the interest-free loan funds, they were set up to 'fight against *rebâ* and usurers' (*rebâkhâr*, literally 'eaters of *rebâ*') and to help the needy. Such actions provide grounds for hope of a divine reward, according to several texts of the Koran and Hadith. The people running these organisations, and their customers, make a choice in favour of lending money without demanding interest in accordance with Koranic tradition. Hence the generic name of *gharz ol-hasaneh*, 'good loan', is given to describe this sort of loan. That expression is not used either in the Civil Code or in the Constitution which, for its part, uses the word *bahreh* (literally 'interest'), a more recent word commonly used in conventional banking institutions; in the imperial era people spoke of bank loans and bank interest (*vâm-e banki, bahreh banki*). The bazaar uses other terms, *nozul* and *nozulkhâr* (eater of *rebâ*), instead of *bahreh* or *rebâ*. The last term appears only once in the Constitution, in the 49th preamble where the different forms of illicit accumulation of wealth are listed; *rebâ* is listed alongside theft and gambling.

So we start off with two radically different situations. Profit-seeking was an explicit aim of the limited partnerships, while the interest-free loan funds seemed to have no other aim than divine reward. The contracting parties in limited partnerships agreed to share profits, while partners in the interest-free loan funds had the appearance of public benefactors or philanthropists. But this contrast should be qualified. The limited partnerships did not only claim to guarantee profits for their contracting parties; they assured everyone that they were also working to revive production and to build a self-sufficient society under the cover of a revival of Islamic practice. As for the interest-free loan funds, they recalled that it is written by the gates of Paradise that God rewards almsgiving ten times and interest-free lending eighteen times. Their argument was simple: 'When you give you encourage passivity on the part of the person receiving, and he no longer feels any need to find solutions to his problems. When you lend, the person you help cannot remain apathetic, he's got to pay you back.' So the emphasis is on effort and work, which become the component parts of Iranian society's economic ethos.

Each of these two institutions, the interest-free loan funds and the limited partnerships, had its specific course of development.

The limited partnerships were really the fruit of the Revolution and the war, with the attendant shortages; they grew up in a society whose economic structures had been weakened by destruction and speculation. Their founders and customers went through the experience still imbued with the spirit of the 1979 Revolution. Among the leading figures in the limited partnerships were an army colonel, the head of a major driving school, a manufacturer of children's clothes, a dealer in household electrical goods – relatively well-off people – alongside small-scale neighbourhood traders and even a young man of 20 from a very humble family, whose father was a refuse collector.

Media criticisms began in the autumn of 1989 with a headline in *Keyhan*: 'Your money, our work!' For the next six days the same daily published an investigation into the limited partnerships, recounted legal actions against them, and exposed their real activities, in sharp contrast to their declared intentions. They were accused of providing illegally for a fixed interest rate (24 per cent per year as a minimum, up to 48 per cent for some partnerships) and engaging in other activities besides trade.[4] But criticisms were not confined to those legal aspects which hardly affected public opinion. Although it meant forgetting the legal provisions of a *mozârebeh* contract which exclude non-commercial purposes, the critics attacked the speculative character of their commercial activities – essentially middleman trading, *dallâli* – and accused them of neglecting productive activity. In addition, *Keyhan* hinted that the limited partnership managers' way of life did not conform to Islamic ethics – though without going into detail, out of respect for the Republic's moral code. The campaign reached its peak with the appearance on television of three leading figures in the limited partnerships who confessed to the illegal character of their activities, especially of their *dallâli* trading. They added, however, that their primary objective had been to help others and not to rob them, and they said they were in a position to repay people.

Several factors seem to have contributed to the launching of this campaign: the end of the war, a new Public Prosecutor, the number of legal actions against the limited partnerships, and, according to rumour, the flight abroad of the heads of two partnerships. On the other hand one may wonder why the campaign began so late when the first arrests of managers took place in the spring of 1988. In fact a number of shareholders had refused to make their lawsuits public, first because they feared that bringing in the law would decisively damage their prospects of obtaining refunds, secondly because they were afraid of being called 'rebâ-eaters' themselves. According to a magistrate, 'the creditors discovered, when they brought their actions, that they were themselves guilty of usury in the eyes of the law.' Several theology students thus renounced asserting their rights so as to avoid damage to their reputation. More basically, state or parastatal

4. *Keyhan*, 1.8.1368 (1989).

institutions had established financial or commercial links with the limited partnerships: banks, the Saypa vehicle plant, the National Olympic Committee.[5]

In the event, no doubt for the reason just mentioned, the campaign against the limited partnerships came to a halt. They were indeed declared illegal, but their liquidation did not benefit their victims; not only did plaintiffs have to renounce their dividends and deduct them from the capital invested, but the balance of the capital has, until now, only been partially refunded to them.[6] The prosecutor's office seems to have sold off the limited partnerships' assets cheap, especially real estate, with the result that the income from sales did not make it possible to compensate shareholders. It would incidentally be interesting to identify the buyers of those assets: probably people who would be called in other countries 'people in the know'.

According to the literature of the Islamic Economic Organisation, the first interest-free loan fund, the Jâvid Deposit Fund, was opened in Tehran in 1969, in the south of the city in buildings annexed to a mosque. It operated both as a public beneficent institution (*kheyrieh*) and as an interest-free loan fund, and has devoted itself to retaining both functions until today. *Keyhan* started regularly reporting the setting up of interest-free loan funds as from 1974.[7] Other establishments of the same sort were opened in similar conditions in the main urban centres, so that their number had reached about 200 on the eve of the Revolution. These funds were the fruit of the traditional alliance between men of religion and traders of the bazaar. Among their founders were leading figures of the present Republic, such as Mehdi Karroubi, but also prominent people of the time, such as the Mayor of the city of Rey, on the outskirts of the capital.[8] Although their activities were in truth limited, the funds were very much involved in the organisation of the big demonstrations against the monarchy in 1978-79, if some statements by deputies, such as Mr. Sheybani, are to be believed.[9] Notably, some funds financed the printing of leaflets spreading the message of Imam Khomeyni, assistance to the families of political prisoners or strikers, or the social rehabilitation of street-walkers of the Shahr-e No red-light district.

Since 1979 the interest-free loan funds have been broadening their activities and are developing at high speed; from 200 in 1979 their number had increased to nearly 3,000 in 1988. But, in contrast to what had happened before the Revolution, this increase occurred independently of the mosques, at the heart of the bazaar and the urban neighbourhoods, and through

5. *Keyhan*, 14.12 and 16.12.1369 (1991).
6. *Keyhan*, 26.10.1375 (1997); *Keyhan*, 5.6.1375 (1996).
7. *Keyhan*, 29.10.1352 (1974).
8. *Keyhan*, 17.10.1354 (1976).
9. *Keyhan*, 22.2.1366 (1987).

women's as well as men's initiative.[10] The funds also operated beyond the country's borders; an establishment was opened in Lebanon in 1981 thanks to the intervention of Mr. Hashemi Rafsanjani, then Minister of the Interior;[11] other funds were started in India. In addition the University, the country's major enterprises, the foundations set up in the aftermath of the Revolution, and ministries started their own funds.

Such success did not come without resistance or criticisms, whose origin seems to lie in the post-Revolution transformation of the banking system, which was nationalised in 1979. The number of banks fell from 35 to nine, not of course counting the Central Bank.[12] A number of loan funds held shares in the Islamic Economic Bank. So there was a real call to arms against a nationalisation that would have meant serious loss for those funds. In the end the Islamic Economic Bank was exempted from the general rules and changed its name to become the present-day Islamic Economic Organisation (IEO), which up till today has been playing a crucial role in coordinating and supporting almost half the loan funds now operating in Iran. In addition the definition of new *rebâ*-free banking practices implemented in 1983 led to a serious flight of capital invested in commercial banks, to the benefit of the loan funds because these were – and still are – accustomed to giving beneficiaries bonuses in the form of consumer goods, highly valued in the context of war and recession, or journeys to the Holy Places.[13]

In 1980 a debate was launched about the loan funds' functions in the new economic system. There was talk of taking some of the functions delegated by the state away from them and giving them to a conventional bank, the Saderat Bank, which would take responsibility for loans to farmers in particular.[14] They were also criticised for favouring consumption of luxury goods because of the ease with which loans could be obtained from them.[15] But the response was not long delayed. A national congress of interest-free loan funds, sponsored by the IEO, was called the same year at the Refah School, the place that had welcomed the Imam back from his 15 years of exile. The purpose was of course to lay down the legitimacy on which those financial establishments were based, as the congress resolutions show: 'The people running the funds, by setting up cooperatives, industrial centres and agricultural and food projects, by developing stockbreeding, by importing

10. *Keyhan*, 22.5.1375 (1996). On the growth of the loan funds and their impact on the financial system, see the excellent doctoral thesis by Ali Asgari, 'Barresi-e naqsh va asarat-e sandoqha-ye qarz ol-hasaneh dar system-e puli va banki-e keshvar', Tehran, Daneshgah-e tehran, Daneshkadeh-e eqtesad, 1368-69.
11. *Keyhan*, 24.12.1359 (1981).
12. Thierry Coville (ed.), *L'économie de l'Iran islamique. Entre l'Etat et le marché*, Tehran, Institut français de recherche en Iran, 1994.
13. It goes without saying that the commercial banks did not remain idle in the face of this competition, and offered bonuses themselves to compete with the interest-free loan funds.
14. *Keyhan*, 24.2.1359 (1980).
15. *Keyhan*, 19.2.1359 (1980).

only goods for which the country has a pressing need, aim to marginalise all non-Islamic and unjust activities, and all those based on profit alone.'[16]

However, in 1983 the Minister of the Interior, Ali-Akbar Nategh Nuri, decided to close down all interest-free loan funds which did not have official authorisation.[17] What exactly was held against them? Three arguments were put forward. First, they were accused of offering services only to their founders' family and friends – hard luck for people not belonging to that social network! Secondly, there was disapproval of their taste for profit-making, which was not only in contradiction with their initial objective, but also against the law. Lastly, some forms of loan granted by them seemed to encourage speculation. But parliament remained divided, especially as the strongest criticisms were aimed less at the principle of the funds than at the way in which some of them had developed, and especially their institutional organisation under the IEO umbrella. For behind everything there was an increasingly open fear that the funds' economic and financial power might at some time provide the basis for interference in political matters.[18]

A high point in the debate came in 1987 with the trial of a manager of an interest-free loan fund. He was accused of theft and breach of trust.[19] Several other trials followed in 1988. The point was reached when the head of the intelligence services in the Tehran region banned the opening of new interest-free loan funds and the Minister of the Interior demanded that the IEO stop intervening in the affairs of those bodies; according to him the funds affiliated to the IEO hardly ever made loans to the needy, but rather consolidated the holding company's commercial activities.

Under this pressure, the interest-free loan funds marked time and the IEO adopted a low profile, ceasing publication of its magazine for two and a half years. The fund managers still remember today that difficult period when they had to stick together, balance their books and deal with customers panicking because of the trials and wanting to settle their accounts: 'That was a difficult time, but we got through it without suffering much damage, because when people saw we were ready to refund those who so wished, they understood they had been lied to. It is true that some funds had abused the trust the public placed in us, but breach of trust is found everywhere, why suddenly attack only the loan funds?' said one manager. He added, 'The media tried to destroy our reputation, but they failed because our solidarity came into play.'

In 1989 a second national congress of the loan funds, again sponsored by the IEO, brought this troubled period to a close – but without removing all the ambiguities, to judge by the 'dialogue of the deaf' which started between Ali Khamenei, then President, and the Chairman of the IEO. The latter asked

16. *Keyhan*, 20.2.1359 (1980).
17. *Keyhan*, 2.8.1362 (1983).
18. *Keyhan*, 25.11.1366 (1988).
19. *Keyhan*, 24.6.1366 (1987).

his followers to avoid trading and not to go in for speculative activities with 'multiplying' (*jadvali*) loans. The President preferred to insist on the need for the loan funds not to meddle in politics and to follow rules laid down by the Currency and Credit Council; those ideas were not greeted with enthusiasm and were not respected later.[20] In the end the victory of the *resâlati* tendency in the 1992 parliamentary elections confirmed lasting acceptance of the legitimacy of that credit network.

To judge by appearances alone the limited partnerships could be termed 'modern' and the interest-free loan funds 'traditional'. But on closer study such a view needs to be qualified considerably.

Initially it was small-scale and large-scale traders working both in the bazaar district and outside who played the key role in the creation of interest-free loan funds. One of the fundamental characteristics of those funds was, and still is, their collegiate management. Solidarity can go beyond the circle of a fund's founder members (*hey'at-e omanâ*), whose number varies from 20 to 30, and involve members of several interest-free loan funds, especially as it is possible to belong to a number of funds at the same time. Management of a fund is in the hands of a group of seven people who form the management council (*heyat'e modireh*). But while traders have a crucial position in the interest-free loan funds, other social categories are also represented in them: the clergy, senior civil servants, judges, accountants, political leaders.

The way the funds are run reflects Iranian society's corporatist tendency: they tend to bring together members of the same profession. However, there can be more complex groupings of people, often on individuals' initiative. So in one fund there can be jewellers, mechanics and shoemakers, on the basis of personal or family connections. Some of these ventures can be quite voluntarist or artificial, such as a common interest-free loan fund at the *hozeh* and the University.[21] The bazaar is the preferred place where initiatives of that sort can be developed through the *hey'at*, the men's religious associations which are often set up on a regional or professional basis and are the principal mould from which the interest-free loan funds are cast. It is thus clear that the founders of the funds, appealing to a Koranic principle (that of lending without interest) and reviving a traditional practice, are creating a new space for links, transcending but not abolishing older forms of solidarity.

Traditional elements are omnipresent in the interest-free loan funds, beginning with the revival in up-to-date form of former social relationships based on trust, the pledged word and the code of honour. In general the relationships called *hojrehi* or cellular – recalling a code of behaviour, language and set of attitudes among traders and shopkeepers characteristic of the bazaar and some trading circles – are tending to come back. In that

20. *Keyhan*, 1.11.1368 (1990).
21. *Keyhan*, 2.10.1363 (1985).

setting there is very little institutionalising of loan procedures to be seen. A loan can be agreed anywhere, at any time – in a home, in a mosque, on a carpet, in an armchair, in front of a shop or at a cash counter – and often it is enough to fill out a simple form, as long as one knows an influential person in the place. In theory certain conditions can be insisted upon and can seem draconian; this was the favourite theme of critics of the funds at the height of the campaign. Two prerequisites are particularly important: it is necessary to be introduced to a fund by one of its members or by an acceptable intermediary in an arrangement like co-optation and to have a guarantor who deposits a cheque for the amount of the loan to be able to cover possible default in repayment. Except for certain major institutions, however, these conditions are less severe than they seem to be at first sight. In practice one does not apply for a loan from a fund unless one has been introduced there or else holds an account whose balance is equivalent to the loan requested. Most people questioned by us have a more or less close tie with one of the members of the fund where they took out the loan. Often one is told, '*hâj âghâ* so-and-so knows me', 'my father knows *hâj âghâ* X', or 'we were introduced to *hâj âghâ*'.

In practice a *hâj âghâ* has considerably more powers than that of introducing his close relations or friends for them to be given loans according to the rules of the institution; he can, for example, also block all of his account in the service of a person of his choice who can use it in accordance with the principles of interest-free lending. Within those networks the flexibility of social relationships is thus obvious; it varies according to the borrower's 'back', but also that of the person who introduces him to the fund or acts as guarantor. It should be noted also that 'eminent individuals' whose social profile can be quite varied – an Imam of a mosque, a grocer, a teacher, a civil servant – do not advertise themselves as such, out of modesty and prudence. The *hâj âghâ* who recommends a borrower to a fund may hide from him that he is one of the fund's founders; in that way he conforms to the *javânmard* style and spares himself both the annoyances and the financial risks that could come from admission of his real influence. Under these conditions the depositing of a guarantee cheque is essentially a formality which puts institutional veneer over actual practice that is considerably more flexible, though equally demanding.

The interest-free loan funds follow two potentially contradictory principles, and it is a delicate operation to keep the balance between them. On the one hand they are based on mutual confidence between managers and customers which assumes that they know each other personally. On the other hand they have to be able to extend their networks to be financially viable. But in this subtle balancing act, the principle of trust is the most determining factor. As the managers themselves say, those who do not keep to their commitments are rare. However, one should not give an idealised picture. Trust has its limits: the amount of the loan and the repayment details are not negotiable and do not follow simple philanthropic principles. When it provides a loan the fund automatically deducts 1 per cent as management fee and insists on depositing 1 per cent in an account opened in the customer's name. In addition, it expects that the customers will continue to deposit sums into their accounts. Thus a woman of about 60 who had already received one loan and was trying after three years to get another through the agency of the person who introduced her, and had even acted as her guarantor, had her application refused on the pretext that her account book 'had not been working.' She complained, 'These interest-free loan funds only provide money to people who have placed money in their accounts'.

However, the interest-free loan funds care greatly about preserving their Islamic ethics. Generally, the way of dressing and the sort of language used at their counters recall social intercourse of a past age. You never see men wearing ties among either the staff or the leaders and founders. The founders are always very simply dressed as befits their age. They readily take off their shoes to put on slippers. Decoration is austere and there is no separation according to rank; members of the management board work alongside the staff. A plan for uniformity in the interest-free loan funds' premises, made in 1982, led to adoption of neo-traditional Islamic architecture for the façades but did not go further; the idea of improving the settings and functional quality of those premises is still around.

When customers address the staff they always use the word *hâj âghâ*, a term of respect and deference. The founders respond suitably; they do not fail to emphasise the customers' honour and probity which inspired their initiatives. For example, one fund, although situated in a 'modern' setting – at the Ministry of Labour and Social Affairs – has been called the 'Loans of Honour Fund'.[22] The founders of the funds take pleasure in saving the honour of an old woman in distress, an office worker reduced to poverty by inflation, a fashion designer faced with some unforeseen expense. Thus the existence of the interest-free loan funds is founded both on a religious obligation and on a pressing social need which must be heeded by any man of good deeds.

The modern adaptation of the code of honour and effort in Iranian society often borders on rather different preoccupations. The interest-free loan funds' magazine published by the IEO has several sections recalling the memory of the martyrs, Hadiths and Koranic verses justifying interest-free loans, the indispensible elements of ethics in an Islamic society, and the range of activities of this financial sector. However, it also reproduces extracts from politicians' speeches regarding the IEO's field of activity and the country's economic policy more generally; it translates articles in the international press giving information on foreign countries. This wide-ranging coverage seeks to uphold the economic policy advocated by the

---

22. *Keyhan*, 25.5.1360 (1981).

IEO which has come out in favour of complete privatisation and liberalisation of foreign trade.

All this confirms the ambiguous position of the interest-free loan funds in relation to tradition. One of their managers aptly remarked: 'We calculate with an abacus but we sell computers.' But in fact there was some change in 1991. Attempts are now being made to computerise the interest-free loan funds, and, notably, a new Director has been appointed to head the IEO. In contrast to his predecessor, a carpet dealer, he is a company (*sherkat*) executive and does not belong to the category of *hojrehi* mentioned above; although he still does not wear a tie, he refuses to wear slippers at the office and never takes off his jacket whatever the weather. Modernity does not only have advantages!

There is nothing comparable on the limited partnerships side. The company's name would be written on multi-coloured signs or engraved on the outside of the building where it was located and reflected the founder's ambitions: the first names of his children – boys *and girls* – were included, and those were 'modern' rather than *sonnati* (traditional) names. The company's name could also proclaim its purpose: 'House of the Apprentices of Scholarship' (*dânesh âmuz*) for an educational supplies enterprise, or 'Advance Guard of Clothing', 'Tehran Tools', etc. More rarely the company could invoke a moral idea: 'The Truthful', 'The Red Rose', etc. But, in contrast to what has been seen in the interest-free loan funds sector, no reference was ever made to saints or to religious ideas.

Improvement work on the limited partnerships' premises appealed to modernity in all its grandeur: furniture and telephones were the latest models, the secretaries – women, of course – were fashionably dressed, the principal executives wore ties and dressed with care. The office space was divided according to rank; the chairman had his own office, the waiting room had armchairs for customers. In addition, the limited partnerships' offices were often in the modern city centre, and in some cases, in buildings erected specially for them; this showed the founder's unshakeable determination to back his customers' desire for social improvement.

The style of language used in the limited partnerships was also different from that heard at the same time in the interest-free loan funds. The executives were not greeted as *hâj âghâ* but as 'Mr. Engineer' (*Mohandes*), possibly followed by the surname. Management was not collegiate; the board came under the authority of the founder. The trials of Mr. Mahmoudi, Chairman of the Golbiz company, were revealing in this respect: the judges called on him alone to repay the shareholders' liabilities. It was thus laid down that a single person could be liable for considerable sums to several thousand creditors; for example, the boss of the Golshir company had to deal with 5,800 creditors. Whether this form of management is called 'modern' or not, the attraction which it held for the public needs to be understood. It is known that in Tehran 25,000 lawsuits were instituted against about twenty limited partnerships. During our research, we met plaintiffs who had gone as far as selling their own homes to invest in the partnerships. Those companies' customers were extremely varied. They certainly included a large number of office workers, but also academics, teachers, bankers, military men, clerics, all sorts of people with a high level of education.

Statements that we gathered confirm the modernising character of the companies' management, but may perhaps also serve to relativise their personal and centralised character. When asked why they placed their trust in those bodies, people answered, 'Why should we have had doubts, since several *fatwa*s approving them from leading Sources of Emulation, Ayatollahs Araki and Golpayegani, had been published in the press?'; 'If the limited partnerships were going astray, why did the state let them go on, with all the advertising they did, and why did it go on placing organs of the press at their disposal for years?'; 'You would see a photo of the founder together with such-and-such a politician displayed at the entrance'; 'How can a "hat snatcher" have a right to dozens of cheque books?'; 'The company took us one day, about twenty of us, on a visit to its *duq* [yoghurt drink] factory, and to its farm and its livestock herd. With all those investments, I cannot believe, even now that I have lost my home, in the failure of those partnerships'; 'There were so many people in our situation, I even saw a cinema actor one day.'

In view of these comments, it is clear that the image of modernity which the limited partnerships conveyed only had an impact when linked with the state and with the religious sphere, and was embodied in tangible achievements. Contrary to widespread opinion, the flourishing of those companies did not reveal a lack of confidence in the state's institutions and political figures; the latter, in fact, reassured the public, and their presence by the side of the limited partnerships encouraged people to invest in them. However, the impression of the state which one discerns in the statements quoted is not without ambiguity. A number of wronged customers still believe in the efficiency of the limited partnerships and see in their problems with the law an attack on them by the authorities. It is seen as what is called in Persian 'a jewellers' war' (*jang-e zargari*), whose reasons no-one can understand and whose losers will surely be the customers! The outcome of the trials of managers of the limited partnerships who are still at liberty reinforces this opinion.

It is useful to listen to what the founders have to say, though without prejudging their guilt or innocence. In fact only one of them has left the country, apparently to set up a Samsonite suitcase factory; he seems to have sent samples to the court dealing with his case! Generally, the managers of the limited partnerships are not sparing in self-justification: 'For a thousand years the Silk Road supplied Europe and America [*sic*!] with spices; today our garlic powder is sold in foreign companies' wrapping. Why not do it ourselves?';[23] 'I would like to serve Iranian society. Our country needs to export, and for that the collaboration of the whole population is required.'[24]

Even this too brief comparison of two Islamic credit networks, one still operating, the other dormant because it upset some consciences – and, one can be sure, some interests – confirms that the code of open-handedness is capable of adaptation to modern conditions in different institutional forms, possibly conflicting. It also confirms that the figure of the *javânmard*, definitely an ambiguous figure who can be a 'man of good deeds' but also a 'hat-snatcher', can just as easily take on the humble appearance of the *hâj âghâ* or the flashy modern appearance of the 'engineer'. But in their various modes, the Islamic banking networks, which can seem of secondary importance relatively from the macroeconomic viewpoint – at the level of Iran's economic recovery and its reopening to foreign trade – have contributed to major changes in society. Besides being often the only means of survival in the context of hyperinflation and speculation in the country, thanks to the financial income or material advantages which they bring to depositors, they help to put social relations on a cash basis, family relations included. Through them money is finding its exchange value again.

However, these changes do not necessarily challenge older cultural and ethical practices. The interest-free loan funds are special places for re-creation of tradition, in the name of 'business orientation' of family, neighbourhood and bazaar relationships. From this perspective, the failure of the limited partnerships is due less to their modern and individualised management than to their relative isolation in the political and social system. Their customers certainly know that their managers have backing in the bazaar, among the clergy and in the political class, and trust them for that reason. Yet such contacts, while they have made it possible to delay and cushion the scandal of bankruptcy, have not sufficed to prevent it from happening – unlike what happened with the interest-free loan funds, saved from collapse by mobilisation of the bazaar. The crucial role of the bazaar in the functioning of the Islamic Republic is once again confirmed – even if it does not appear as an actor in its own right, homogeneous and distinct from other social forces. Through family alliances, public constitutions and plurality of jobs, there are numerous footbridges connecting the bazaar, the clergy, the political class and the enterprise sector – among them limited and short-lived partnerships.

Open-Handedness as a Social Movement

In the light of these two examples the ethos of public generosity or open-handedness should certainly be understood not as a static 'culture' inherited from the past, but as the product of social relationships with historical roots.

23. *Keyhan*, 4.8.1368 (1989).
24. *Keyhan*, 1.8.1368 (1989).

The re-casting of political roles and the development of the 'second economy' in contemporary Iran, the business practices of our car dealer Ali or of the *bâzâri*, savings and credit procedures in the interest-free loan funds and the limited partnerships – all these certainly owe a good deal to the social code of the *javânmardi*. However, this social *imaginaire* is a historically defined one. From one age to another we see it being constantly altered; it is not an unwavering set of ideas which could suffice to explain everything on its own. Besides, it cannot be dissociated from identifiable groups and places: one cannot, for example, speak of the *javânmardi* independently of the fruit and vegetables market, Ali's so very modern car showroom, Gholamhossein Karbaschi's municipal policies, the political line followed by Mehdi Bazargan, and credit practices by the interest-free loan funds and the limited partnerships. One cannot be satisfied with seeking causal connections between the existential ethic of the *javânmardi* and economic, administrative and social action; it is necessary also to examine the ways, often very material ways, in which that 'life style' is permanently reshaped.

Max Weber's term 'life style' is important as it reminds us that an ethic like *javânmardi* is all-embracing; it inspires not only economic and political activities, but a whole gamut of other behaviour – moral, social and religious – which can be in conflict with those activities. For example, giving is not necessarily a rational use of one's 'back', but a pleasing way of affirming moral qualities; for the giver and the receiver, the way in which giving is done is often more important than the nature of the gift.[25] In reality it is not possible to draw a clear dividing line between the two major classical interpretations of giving. The first of those sees giving as an instrument allowing social actors to obtain concrete advantages – allowing leading citizens to extend their clientage networks, for example. To some extent Mauss accepts this explanation when he says the native American-style potlatch ritual resembles 'a struggle among noblemen to establish a hierarchy among them from which their clan will profit later.'[26] and when he writes, 'Giving is showing one's superiority, being more, higher, a *magister*; accepting without giving in return or without giving more in return, is subordinating oneself, becoming a client and servant, falling lower (*minister*).'[27] The second interpretation contests the utilitarian view, refuses to reduce giving to a purely rational pursuit of advantage and sees in it the expression of 'cultural reason' (as opposed to 'utilitarian reason'), or alternatively of an imaginary concept of society.[28] It explains giving as a

25. V. Zelizer, 'Repenser le marché. La construction sociale du "marché aux bébés" aux États-Unis, 1870-1930', *Actes de la recherche en sciences sociales*, 94, Sep. 1992, pp. 3-26.
26. M. Mauss, *Sociologie et anthropologie*, Paris, PUF, 1983, pp. 152-3.
27. Ibid., pp. 269-70.
28. M. Sahlins, *Au coeur des sociétés. Raison utilitaire et raison culturelle*, Paris, Gallimard, 1990.

'total social fact', political, economic and religious but also involving appearances, with 'feeling' never absent.[29]

In reality both dimensions are present: the *javânmard* ethos is both the pursuit of the properly understood interest of those adhering to it and a social *imaginaire* which gives their life its style, its aesthetic attraction. Besides – a point to which we shall be returning – individualisation is not the same thing as individualism; while the *javânmard* cares about his own self, that does not reduce the extent to which he defines himself in relation to those around him. This is precisely the meaning of the term *sarshenâs*, which describes how the *javânmard* is recognised by a truly unlimited circle of relationships; it is also the meaning of the word 'back' (*posht*) in a metaphorical sense.

The *javânmardi* practised by the social being must therefore be understood in the specific form that is conferred on it by the context: that of an urban and literate society which is inexorably being 'rationalised'. The ethical code, understood in this way, remains an omnipresent point of reference in daily life. It is that which makes certain behaviour discreditable: for example, the press will say that a non-*javânmard* (*na-javânmard*) taxi driver ran over a child (that is, he sinned by lack of respect and attention for others).[30] It is also the *javânmardi* code that assigns positive or negative value to other behaviour. Thus it is now considered a good thing to abide by laws and rules, or at least some of them. It can be seen how this idea of *javânmardi* is new and marks a break with the world of ideas of someone like Teyyeb. Respect for others and the attraction of giving and good deeds are perceived through the observance of written rules such as the highway code, the rules of sport such as football, regulations governing economic organisations and political institutions – generally, the laws of citizenship.

Of course things are not so simple, and Iranian society is going through a transition: the idea of law – religious or state law – coexists with the elusive ethic of *javânmardi*, with a certain idea of spirituality or even of mysticism (*'erfân*), and with acute attention to the requirements of the *bâten*. The world of Islamic credit, as we have described it, reflects this ambiguity well. The intangible dimension of 'acquaintance' and 'reputation', a certain informality in procedures, are made to serve 'rational' objectives such as development of the nation, as well as more 'symbolic' or 'cultural' preoccupations such as the 'honour' of families; and these social exchanges now go through organisations, interest-free loan funds or limited partnerships, however crucial the role of the 'individualities of eminence' who founded them or run them may still be. But, although it should not be seen as excluding informality in social relationships, the principle of 'rationalisation' definitely has an increasing role. In particular, the idea of the social being relates to that principle; such

29. M. Mauss, op. cit., pp. 274-5.
30. *Keyhan*, 3.3.1373 (1994).

a being is almost by definition a reasonable being, if not a calculating being, since one of the terms used to describe him, *âdam-e hesâbi*, is derived from *hesâb*, meaning calculation or logic.

At the same time, the *javânmard* of today – he who thinks of himself as one, and above all he who is considered as one – is directly involved in social activity: he is an *âdam-e ejtemâ'i*, literally a society man or a collectivity (*ejtemâ'i*) man. He can therefore no longer be considered as a marginal figure, if in fact he ever was. We should now examine how he participates, as a social being, in the redefining of private and public spaces, in the restructuring of civil society, in the reshaping of the regime's social basis centred around questions that are more national than religious *stricto sensu*. Rather than a devout character with purely other-worldly preoccupations, detached from the things of this world – in short, a Sufi – the *javânmard* wears the profile of a member of the urban middle class: certainly a believer, but definitely involved in active works in this world. His 'self-denial' will impel him to found a school, help make up a dowry for disadvantaged young girls, or finance scholarships. It will not stop him deriving material or symbolic benefits from those good deeds, for example by collecting school fees, by channelling gifts from the neighbourhood which he can always put to productive use while waiting to use them for the social objectives which he is required to pursue, or by gaining influence and distinction. As we have already seen, it would be just as vain to reduce open-handedness to mere seeking of material advantage as to deny that there is such advantage; *javânmardi* is both a style and a strategy.

In addition, it should be clearly realised that the *javânmard* quality is often not so much sought by the individuals concerned as conferred on them by the people around them or the neighbourhood. One cannot avoid thinking that this is a way of codifying and categorising behaviour which, as we have seen, sometimes borders on breaking the rules, or else of stating ideas able to ensure social cohesion. Basically the *javânmard*, although he often has a high opinion of himself and an epic idea of his actions, does not really belong to himself. He is the product of the incessant looks and gossip of society that confers that role on him, stylises him, puts him on a pedestal; he does not really exist outside the recognition, admiration and even concern which society shows for him.

But precisely by being a man involved in social action, and built up by the opinion of his fellows, the open-handed man is truly a social being. He does not only appear in the institutionalised foundations and networks close to the government or derived from it. The essence of a social being revealed in good deeds is behaviour bringing out the potential of a man of quality, even if he fits into an institutional context. The press publishes numerous reports on individuals who are not necessarily 'individualities of eminence' but who show 'rational' self-denial. In 1990 in Malayer, a city in the west of the country, 'a woman of good deeds (*bânu-ye nikukâr*) has given her own house to the Ministry of Education',[31] probably because she lived alone, had no heir and had hardly any means of subsistence. One may suppose that in return for this gesture she was to be maintained by the government, and if that indeed occurred, one can see how personal interest can go together with social commitment rather than competing with it. (In a different category, we were told during our research about a rather juicy case of a gift at Mashhad: an old woman, up against her son-in-law's covetous feelings, left her house as a *vaqf* gift in her will, while stipulating that her daughter should continue to use it during her lifetime; the family were only told of these provisions – with some disappointment – the day after the old lady's burial.)

Also in 1990, at Zanjan in Azerbaijan, a benefactor (*khayyer*) built a secondary school for 60 million rials and handed it over to the state education system without anyone knowing whether he did so out of philanthropy or to settle a debt to God or the taxman.[32] In 1995, at Shahrud in Khorassan, a 'man of good deeds' (*nikukâr*) offered 100 million rials to a hospital for purchase of respiratory equipment and there again inquisitive people wondered about his motives.[33] Some months earlier, an 'advertorial' reported 1,200 daily meals provided by another 'man of good deeds' for children in difficulty in the city of Yazd while his wife devoted herself to setting up an institute for blind people; by that journalistic method the sponsor of the article hoped to encourage other commitments to public generosity while at the same time announcing the setting up of a certain Mr. Rasouliyan's foundation, implicitly inviting readers to send contributions.[34]

In all these examples, taken from the pages of leading newspapers, we note a real social movement drawing its strength from the idea of self-denial and shown in the general practice of giving and *vaqf*. Public generosity may also be displayed by the government. During a meeting, the President of the Republic, Hashemi Rafsanjani, transferred two thousand shares in the Margarine company which were 'at his disposal' (*sic*) to five charitable and cultural institutions, including the medical foundation headed by his daughter, and it was emphasised on that occasion that the value of the gift came less from its amount than from the reminder of the 'culture of aid to the needy'.[35] But the public generosity movement extends especially far beyond the limits of the government and the leading citizens. It is the fruit of a multitude of individual initiatives, the work of Mr. *and Mrs.* Average. It records in its modes and orientation the changes in society at the same time as it contributes to the affirmation of society and possibly to the creation of a real 'civil society'.

In particular it makes use of the backing and the intermediaries available in modern urban society. For example, the written press echoes it, as we

31. *Nameh Iran*, 24.5.1369 (1990).
32. *Ettela'at*, 3.7.1369 (1990).
33. *Ettela'at*, 29.5.1374 (1995).
34. *Keyhan*, 30.11.1373 (1995).
35. *Keyhan*, 1.6.1373 (1994).

have just noted. The phenomenon is not entirely new; in the 1950s newspapers were already describing acts of public generosity on the part of leading local citizens. But those were in fact scattered initiatives whose exceptional nature was precisely what was hailed, and they had a strong charitable connotation. Today the press reflects a much wider range of activity. Open-handedness has now become 'routine'. It takes the form of a flow of funds whose personal charity aspect is being blunted, and which provides sustenance for social institutions rather than benefiting identifiable individuals in the context of a neighbourhood relationship or traditional clientage. The flow of gifts, increasingly in cash form, is coming to resemble efforts in Western societies to help medical research, humanitarian aid or Third World development; a recent trend in open-handedness involves arranging sickness insurance for families in need.

These changes in the practice of open-handedness go together with a redefining of relations between the public and private spheres, with a process of individualising roles within the family, and with the appearance of a new way of life in urban circles. Through advertisements in newspapers, giving no longer reflects only the private preoccupations of the giver, religious ones for example, but the aspirations of the community. Those aspirations certainly involve beliefs or values of a moral or Islamic type, but also, at the same time and without any contradiction, modern social needs: the need for education (it must be stressed that actions of open-handedness increasingly finance scholarships for higher studies rather than for primary schooling alone as in former times); the need for housing, in the form of houses or flats designed on contemporary lines; the need for health (hospitals are expected to have the latest equipment); cultural needs, for example in the realm of the cinema (here open-handedness can come near to sponsorship of the arts); the need for leisure activity, which the benefactor helps by providing funds especially for holiday camps for the young. In other words, the disinherited person (*mostaz'af*) whom the Revolution aimed to serve has himself greatly changed. One might be tempted to say he has become very bourgeois; he now belongs to a more precisely defined social category than before, politically favoured or at least recognised, whose social needs have become the target of public action and discussion, both by the state and by benefactors themselves.

Obviously the latter are involved in the changes in society. In particular they appear more and more often as representatives of a nuclear family whose members are autonomous individuals. It is no longer the family head who is seen as a philanthropist, but also his wife, and both may possibly act together as a couple: for example, in 1990, at Najafabad not far from Isfahan, 'Mr. and Mrs. Pezeshki' made a gift of a 1,500-square metre plot of land for an educational project.[36] Through their 'good deeds' those who practise open-handedness are increasingly involved in the political scene.

36. *Resalat*, 13.5.1369 (1990).

From the moment the *javânmard* gives up the discretion and secrecy which surrounded his generosity, when he works through the agency of an organisation which needs to be registered by the administration, he becomes a partner in dialogue with the state. The authorities summon him to meetings to concert action, they give him tax concessions, credit facilities, financial aid or subsidised products; they distribute propaganda material to him. Obviously the regime wants to seek support from the public generosity movement and make use of it for its own purposes. But it would be an oversimplification to see here nothing but a determination to impose ideological control. On the one hand the state is also responding to the demands of public policy in its most neutral sense: the people's living conditions need to be improved while the economic crisis is tackled and the country's cohesion guaranteed. From that viewpoint the use of the concept of *nikukâri* rather than *kheyrieh* is not without significance; it indicates a quiet sliding away from a revolutionary Islamic agenda to a more conventional state and national agenda to which secularists, non-Muslim minorities, and even exiles can adhere as much as the Islamists. On the other hand the public benefactors, although they are more or less obliged to declare their activities to the administrative authorities, do not necessarily feel constrained by state interference in the domain of public beneficence; they can see in it an opportunity to extend their field of activity, to increase their resources, and to add to their social responsibilities.

In practice, relations between the Republic and the movement asserting public generosity or open-handedness are just as ambivalent as those in France between the administration and the associative movement – wanting to get state support and attention, but always quick to denounce bureaucracy. The 'good deeds' agenda is autonomous in relation to the regime's, but is in constant interaction with it. This is not entirely new; the 'roughnecks' of former times played a political role alongside the Crown or the clergy while remaining distinct from them, and their intervention during the 'Tobacco Revolt' (1891-92) and the Constitutional Revolution (1905-09) is well documented; the Majles building was offered as a *vaqf* to the nation by Haj Yahya Khoi, who sat in parliament in one of the seats reserved to the clergy.[37] During parliamentary elections candidates did not fail to make use of charitable institutions to win votes.[38] What is, however, much more recent is the extension of public generosity considerations to wide sectors of the population, their increasing institutionalisation, and their association with the life style of the social being which is the mark of the city dweller.

It cannot be repeated often enough that the present-day public benefactor has the habits of a modern man; he can drive around in a Mercedes, have a villa by the Caspian Sea, marry a qualified engineer, send his children to Switzerland for education, put up a satellite dish in his home, enjoy pizzas

37. *Khandaniha*, 68, 1334 (1955).
38. *Baba Shamal*, 90, 1323 (1944).

and hamburgers; he uses a computer bought in Dubai to keep the accounts of his good works, corresponds with people by fax, makes appointments in the course of his work as a benefactor by mobile phone, and relates his 'good deeds' to the demands of national progress as well as his own religious conviction. Thus the new form of open-handedness has a largely new image of individuals' participation in society, even of citizenship, which has a relationship of mutual resemblance and attraction – or, as Norbert Elias would have said, a relationship of 'interdependence' – with a comparable but distinct process: that of the institutionalising of the Islamic Republic and state centralisation.

In this way, open-handedness, or public generosity, is helping to redefine the social base of the regime, if only because some of the main players in the Revolution were themselves big public benefactors and the popular mobilisation of 1978-79 was greatly reinforced by the social practice of giving. As we have already mentioned, religious leaders, bazaar merchants and 'roughnecks' of the fruit and vegetable market organised in solidarity with strikers, the families of political prisoners, and victims of repression during demonstrations; and it was those people who laid and secured the foundations of the Republic by reinventing the tradition of charity in a parastatal form – including all the ambivalence it contains from the viewpoint of distinguishing benefactors' personal interests and the interests of the community. In short, open-handedness is a common fund of social activities from which both actors on the power stage as well as the *vulgum pecus* can draw: rich and poor, Islamists and secularists, men and women, people of the provinces and people of the capital come together. It is in this capacity of the code of open-handedness to bridge social gaps that the basic nature of the social being is once more affirmed.

At the risk of upsetting preconceived ideas, we should admit that the Islamic Republic draws a good deal of its stability and legitimacy from this institutionalising of philanthropic 'meta-governments'. However, it would be naive to confine one's attention to this aspect. The development of open-handedness has above all made it possible for a society whose disarray should not be underestimated – due to the major changes in the 1960s and 70s, the uncertainties of the revolutionary period, the upheavals of the war and the problems of the economy – to keep within sight of familiar landmarks without ceasing to adapt to change at the same time, and even to remain in control of the process of change. Faced with the failures of the state shepherd, stuck in ideological debate and incapable of guaranteeing the sheep's property, order and security, what could the sheep do except take charge of their affairs themselves? Open-handedness has been one means among others – especially the development of the informal economy – to deal with this situation. So it can be seen that there is more to it than the simple alternatives of use as an instrument by dominant players and expression of a life style; it can also be a form of self-protection and self-organisation.

In its relative autonomy, the domain of public generosity activities is an area of debate and contradictions because a great variety of actors and interests meet there and the *javânmardi* code, as we have seen, can fit in with an equally great variety of conduct. Because of the economic crisis and the commercialisation of Iranian society this 'life style' is more and more associated with a minimum of economic capacity; it will be recalled that 'today you are a *javânmard* if you succeed in bringing home a kilo of meat'. The bazaar is, even more than before, the favoured place for getting rich. So it is not surprising that the authorities of the Islamic Republic have resumed for their own purposes the struggle of the central government to clip the wings of an economic sector that partly escapes its control – even if, in practice, it is constantly working with that sector either directly or indirectly, precisely through the 'meta-governments' of a public-generosity nature (reflecting the virtue of open-handedness) such as the Islamic Economic Organisation, the Imam's Relief Committee, the Âstân-e Qods and the big foundations. The state has not failed to denounce 'middlemen' (*dallâl, vâseteh*) before public opinion and to announce its intention to 'cut off their hands', resuming the language of the former regime. For example, the management of the Refah chain of stores, in which Mr. Karbaschi owns 51 per cent of the shares, gives as its aim 'supplying the population with consumer goods which it needs, eliminating middlemen (*vâseteh*) who are too numerous, and to give proper direction and protection to national production.'[39]

The stakes in the conflict between networks of influence and acquisition of wealth which are in competition, but which overlap partially because of the role of families, are too complex to be unravelled in this work. But it is clear that the conflict is especially about the idea of authority, the state's area of competence, and hence the boundaries of public and private spaces. What the state cannot accept is the *dallâl*'s idea of breaking free from all legal restrictions and imposing his own law on the national community, either in neighbourhoods, or in various sectors of the economy organised under the guild system. Its intention is not to suppress middlemen but to harness them in its service and to make them in some ways its own guild. There is no question of eradicating them, but rather of keeping them 'between death and sickness', to use a Persian phrase. A 'good *dallâl*' is not necessarily a 'dead *dallâl*', but one who is disciplined and accepts the rules of the game, pays his taxes to the Tehran municipality and the central government, accepts Mr. Karbaschi's urban improvement schemes, contributes to national celebrations, and has 'keenly attuned ears' to the many calls from the benefactor state always concerned to help the 'disinherited', the 'martyrs', the stricken and refugees. From that point of view there remains not much in common with the historical figure of Teyyeb, even when people invoke

39. *Keyhan*, 18.12.1373 (1995); Babak Darbeigi, 'Forushgâhâ-ye zanjirehi refâ. zarurat-e ejtemâ'i yâ abzâr-e eqtedâr-e siâsi', *Goft-o-gu*, 13, 1575 (1996), pp. 19-27.

his name. 'Teyyeb's place is empty,' lamented *Keyhan* in 1989. But the portrait drawn by the important daily of the *javânmard* able to 'work together with the state' illustrates the revolution that is expected from that sort of person, through an elementary syllogism which can be expressed thus: 'The *javânmard* are in the service of the people; the Islamic Republic comes from the people and belongs to it; therefore *javânmard* must work alongside the Republic.'

This was perhaps one of the functions of the limited partnerships in the government's eyes before. At the most difficult period of the war, the government probably used the partnerships to bypass the bazaar's monopoly of middleman trade and find new trading connections both within Iranian society and abroad, especially in Dubai, an essential place for evading the embargo. Similarly, the Nabovvat Foundation came in at the meeting-point of the interest-free loan funds and the limited partnerships and established itself in a middleman position between the public sector and the bazaar, with the almost openly admitted aim of reducing the bazaar's economic and political influence; in some ways it certainly acted like one of those *vâseteh* who needed to 'have their hands cut off', but, as a recent creation, it could have seemed more easy to control. So there should not be too much surprise that the limited partnerships, which were in theory banned and whose leaders had been brought before the courts, did not in reality completely disappear from the scene, if only because the state adopted their formula itself and financed many of its numerous infrastructure projects by share issues.[40]

Above all, the limited partnerships paved the way for companies (*sherkat*) during the two presidential terms of Hashemi Rafsanjani, causing the Iranian economy to make an irreversible change of direction between 1984 and 1990.[41] It is interesting from that point of view to compare the big scandals hitting the headlines in 1994-95 – especially the Saredat Bank scandal which involved Morteza Rafighdoust, brother of the Chairman of the Foundation for the Disinherited – with those of the previous decade. This series of scandals broke out even before the trials of the limited partnerships had been definitely concluded. They came at a precise moment, that of the pseudo-privatisations which did not really change the structure of capital or the system of production, but led to the emergence of a multiplicity of companies flanking government departments, the public sector and the foundations, in the form of subsidiaries or concessionary enterprises.

In reality, some of those companies carried on business similar to that of the limited partnerships and followed from them. They were major players

---

40. Examples are various urban improvement schemes: Navvab in Tehran, Haft bagh in Kerman, Omran-e Sistan, Tose'eh Hamadan, Tous-gotar in Khorassan and Kush-gostar in Semnan; Iranians were invited through the press to buy shares with fantastic returns, without it being made clear what were the respective private and public sector proportions of these financial packages.

41. On the *sherkat*s' activity, see _mâr-e ta'sis-e sherkathâ. Haqâyeq-e nâ govâr dar lâbelâ-ye arqâm-e bi jân*, in *Gozaresh*, 65,1375 (1996), pp. 46-9.

in the country's reconstruction and opening to the rest of the world through liberalisation of imports, in a context of continued exchange controls made necessary by the failure of the currency reform of 1994 and the burden of debt servicing. They too have been present at the meeting point of the state and the private or informal economy. Same causes, same effects: the main accusation against their executives is of eating up or wasting the 'treasure belonging to the people' (*beytol-mâl*), especially through their foreign currency operations. They obtained their foreign currency at the favourable official rate but failed to keep proper accounts of transactions carried out at the free market rate; this allowed them to make fantastic profits without anyone knowing who was benefiting. The people accused answered that they had really wanted only to serve the nation and the beneficiaries of their open-handed activities, but that they were victims of fraud. Far from having embezzled money, they made loans to people in need, even if they were family members, and the 5 per cent commissions which they charged were not at all illicit in their view; in any case, they could not have broken the law because there was in fact no legal framework fixing sales prices of goods.

These scandals, accusations and defences are surrounded by confusion which had already been seen in the limited partnerships episode. There has been confusion between the private and public spheres, which is at the basis of the so-called privatisation process in the so-called public sector. But there is confusion, also, between the world of personal connections (*râbeteh*), whose logical manifestation is pulling strings or favouritism or even clientage, and the world of regulations (*zâbeteh*), which is supposed to find its expression in the state and the law. We have here one of the major issues at stake in the recent presidential election, to which we shall be returning. But already we can see two assumptions challenged. Although open-handedness relies on personalised relations between giver and recipient, it does not necessarily go against the world of regulations; it is rather a place of negotiation between it and the world of personal connections, since it has been a quite important vehicle for business orientation, for the spread of cash transactions, in short, for rationalisation. On the other hand it would be naive to see in economic opening-up or liberalisation a move promoting law by definition, since companies first showed favour to what the Chinese call *guanxi* – personal or family contacts present below the surface in the 'Republic of Initiates'.

Those two public-generosity networks – the interest-free loan funds and the limited partnerships – had the effect of promoting the greater autonomy of Iranian society, or at any rate *within* Iranian society. To schematise: the interest-free loan funds ensured increased autonomy of savings in relation to the state. They were inseparable from development of the informal economy on the one hand, and on the other, the political domination of the Right, which was able to take control of parliament in 1992. The limited partnerships, on their side, have acquired autonomy in relation to the

4

SOCIAL BEINGS, POLITICAL BEINGS: THE STORY OF AN ELECTION

On 8 March and 19 April 1996 Iran elected its fifth parliament since the 1979 Revolution. In the Islamic Republic, elections are more important than is too often supposed because the Assembly (*Majles*) is not without power under the 1979 Constitution.[1] The experience of the last few years has shown in any case that the Assembly had the ability to cause trouble for the President's plans, and that its opposition was probably the main obstacle to the economic reforms made necessary by the worsening financial situation. Opening the country up to foreign investment, a *sine qua non* for the success of structural adjustment, requires the approval of the *Majles*. But the Assembly has remained the stronghold of economic nationalism since 1990 and rejects modernisation of oil legislation or of the arbitration rules for commercial disputes. In addition, deputies can vote members of the government out of office and have not hesitated to use this right to dismiss some of Mr. Rafsanjani's colleagues in government, notably his Minister of the Economy, Mohsen Nourbakhsh, in 1994, and his Minister of Culture, Mohammad Khatami, in 1992.

Above all, as the editorial writer in the daily *Resalat* – the organ of the outgoing parliamentary majority – admitted, the 'outcome of the vote in March-April 1996 will largely influence the presidential election scheduled for 1997.'[2] Mr. Rafsanjani could not seek re-election, and it was public knowledge that the Speaker of parliament, Mr. Nategh Nuri, who had also been one of the main leaders of the conservative Right in the majority since 1992, was planning to succeed him. Hence the importance, in the view of observers, of the results that the conservatives would achieve. Clear success for them would place Ali-Akbar Nategh Nuri in an excellent position, even though his credit had been somewhat eroded since July 1995 because of the resignation of Ayatollah Mahdavi Kani from the chairmanship of the Society of Fighting Clergy and the growing divisions among the conservative majority on certain crucial questions such as respect for private property, creation of political parties and *velâyat-e faqih* (the guardianship of the Islamic jurist).

---

1. One third of the articles of the Constitution deal with Parliament; the Leader of the Revolution is the only authority with power to dissolve the Assembly. See Dorri-Najafabadi, 'Nezârat va majles-e shorâ-ye eslâmi', in *Faslnâmeh shorâ-ye eslami*, p. 65.
2. *Resalat*, 5.11.1374 (1996).

The Election Campaign

In this situation it is not surprising that the parliamentary elections were preceded by a real campaign from mid-1995. Innumerable meetings, round tables and other seminars, organised at the university or in mosques by various associations (especially student associations), and by the press and on television, sought to examine the record of the fourth parliament and define the main issues to be faced by the next Assembly. Polemics were often lively, numerous senior officials were transferred in the ministries, and tension reached a height when the independent philosopher Abdolkarim Soroush, who has the sympathy of the Islamic Left, was violently molested in October 1995 by the Ansar-e Hezbollah group, close to Ayatollah Janati, in the cause of defending the gains of the Revolution and for having refused to debate with the audience.

All this agitation showed from the autumn onwards that nothing was decided. In the following months, the debate on the method of choosing candidates and the possibility of forming political organisations or even parties – a real bogey for the Islamic Republic since the Revolution – accordingly increased in intensity. Confusion was at its height when it was learned, on the one hand, that it was not necessary to be a declared party to take part in the elections; and on the other, that the National Liberation Movement had no right to put forward candidates, but they could try their luck as independents, without claiming to represent their organisation.[3] On its side the Islamic Left, which had been thrown out of parliament in 1992, drew the conclusion that the Constitution Guardianship Council was definitely exercising stricter control of candidatures than before, and that its selection would be equivalent to a real pre-election in advance of the people's choice. As for the conservative Right, it went ahead boldly to take advantage of those constitutional provisions to impose its hegemony, at the risk of arousing discontent that could turn against it later.

The month of Ramadan, which coincided with the registration of candidates, was in fact the start of the election campaign proper, although this was not opened officially until 29 February, a week before polling day, with publication in the newspapers of the list of candidates selected by the Guardianship Council and the Ministry of the Interior. The candidates made use of daily fast-breaking meetings for their campaigning. In fact Ramadan is the principal occasion when families in the most extended sense of the term meet together and when people exchange visits. This social contact, in which all sections of society join, takes place in a mood of religious sentiment which prevents anyone from suspecting the intentions of those who unfold a table cloth, cover it with varied dishes and invite everyone present to help themselves. Shame on anyone who has unworthy thoughts!

The indispensable Mayor of Tehran, Gholamhossein Karbaschi, made

---

3. *Keyhan*, 18.5.1374 (1995); *Akhbar*, 3.10.1374 (1995).

his own contribution to the election campaign which had still to call itself by that name. Faithful to his determination to curb the power of the bazaar and the role of commercial middlemen, he cut the prices of *zulbiyâ bâmiyeh* (the principal sweetmeat for that holy month, which is eaten just at the moment of breaking the fast) on the municipal markets whose number he was constantly increasing.[4] But above all, he signed jointly with 15 other leading figures a declaration of loyalty to the President, Hashemi Rafsanjani. The signatories[5] – notably ministers, advisers, and the governor of the Central Bank – who were to be called from then on the 'Servants of Reconstruction' (or 'of the People'), advocated an assembly composed of 'experts' and 'scholars'. They praised the role that Hashemi Rafsanjani had played in the development of a parliamentary tradition since the Revolution. They declared their intention of backing a programme which Rafsanjani embodied as 'great commander of reconstruction' and which was summed up in three slogans; 'the honour of Islam', 'perseverance in reconstruction', and 'the fertilising of Iran'.[6]

According to statements by the President himself,[7] the catalyst that led to publication of the open letter of the sixteen was the refusal of the Society of Fighting Clergy to have their protégés put on the list of candidates in Tehran. But the 'Servants'' initiative rapidly went beyond that episode. It completely transformed the electoral scene and the balance of political forces. First of all, it provided the various sections of opinion with the opportunity to advertise themselves. Then it aroused innumerable declarations of views, more or less well thought out. On the parliamentary Right there was a storm of protest, with some deputies going so far as to implicate the President,[8] while others sought a happy medium, an area of compromise. The 'Servants' replied that their initiative was in no way illegal and that anyway they had no intention of standing as candidates themselves, which their respective offices barred them from doing. In his deliberately ambiguous style, half political and half religious, the Leader of the Revolution, Ali Khamenei,

---

4. *Akhbar*, 8.11.1374 (1996).
5. The three successive declarations of the 'Servants' were signed by 16 people, including ten ministers - Messrs. Najafi (National Education), Mohammad Khan (Economy), Torkan (Transport), Forouzeh (Reconstruction Crusade), Nematzadeh (Industry), Zangeneh (Energy), Shoushtari (Justice), Kalantari (Agriculture) and Shafei (Cooperation); four advisers to the President - Messrs. Mohajerani (Legal Affairs), Amrollahi (Atomic Energy Organisation), Hashemi (Executive) and Hashemi-Taba (Physical Education Organisation) - and the Governor of the Central Bank, Mr. Adeli, and the Mayor of Tehran, Mr. Karbaschi. But as the Constitution Guardianship Council had recalled that the electoral law prohibited ministers from supporting candidates, election posters were then put up presenting a list of candidates backed by 'A Group of Servants' or 'A Group of Reconstructors'. The voters themselves did not bother themselves with paraphrases, and spoke quite simply of the 'Servants' or the 'Reconstructors', identifying them perfectly well.
6. *Akhbar*, 28.10.1374 (1996).
7. *Salam*, 7.11.1374 (1996).
8. ibid.

implicitly backed them on the first point;[9] to that extent he played down rumours of a conflict between him and Hashemi Rafsanjani. Finally, in its desire to prove too much, the Association of Fighting Clergy widened its divisions, already obvious since the previous autumn. The names of the 150 deputies who had criticised the 'Servants' for attacking the legitimacy of parliament were never published, despite pressing requests from a section of the press.[10] Worse still, several deputies expressed anger at having been considered as signatories of that petition quite contrary to their wishes, or without having been able to learn about the manifesto of the sixteen in full.[11]

Thus the Right, which had thought its victory was assured – if only because the Society of Fighting Clergy had decided not to enter the contest – suddenly found itself in an awkward situation. Sure of its position, it was joining the calls for mobilisation of the voters, for the sake of democratic proprieties, and in its own words it was working to 'stoke the fire of the elections', where it expected to be the sole winner. By stoking the fire, while not being able to put forward someone who was presidential material, it aroused the feeling that it wanted to rush ahead among a section of opinion for which Mr. Hashemi Rafsanjani was not necessarily finished. But in that game it was overtaken by the President's 16 'Servants' who put their champion's card on the table.

Never, perhaps, had the political arena in Iran in the reconstruction period been so open. In the end 3,228 people out of the 5,359 who had fulfilled the formalities for candidature were accepted as candidates in the contests for 270 seats. In addition, for the first time, competition among the various groups to which these candidates claimed allegiance was openly displayed. Those reasons explain why the turnout was noticeably greater in the first round of these elections than previously. According to official figures it was 74 per cent (24.8 million voters), compared with 65 per cent (18 million voters) in 1992.[12] It should be noted however that abstention was much greater (at 38 per cent) in Tehran. These figures need to be qualified a little. There is no electoral register, strictly speaking, in Iran. To vote it is sufficient to be of Iranian nationality, to be 15 years old,[13] and to present one's identity document for stamping; one can then perform one's civic duty in the constituency of one's choice. At any rate the atmosphere of the campaign, especially in the provinces, made this increase in turnout credible, and the first round was a real contest despite the restrictions brought in by the process of selection of candidates under the aegis of the Guardianship Council.

This part of the campaign, in addition, produced here and there real phenomena of popular mobilisation. That happened especially in Tehran

---

9. *Akhbar*, 8.11.1374 (1996).
10. *Salam*, 12.11.1374 (1996); *Akhbar*, 7.11.1374 (1996).
11. *Akhbar*, 7.11.1374 (1996).
12. *Iran*, 26.12.1374 (1996).
13. That law was adopted on 26.1.1363 (1984).

with the candidacy of Faezeh Hashemi, the President's 33-year-old daughter, who by her sporting activities and personal charisma symbolised a particularly dynamic but not very political idea of women's condition, and who made her impact on the electoral scene by supporting the 'Servants'. Her result was awaited with great interest. She was elected in the first round, winning second place on the Tehran list after Mr. Nategh Nuri. Malicious tongues even said that the latter's lead was made possibly only by a trick – because the phrase 'known as Nuri' was used in his election literature, half of the voting slips which only had the name 'Nuri' written on them were allocated to him, as nobody knew whether these were meant for him or his very strong rival Abdollah Nuri. On the other hand Faezeh Hashemi, who had wanted to stand under the name of Rafsanjani, was not allowed to do so, despite intervention by the President himself.

The case of Tehran was not unique. In several cities, exceptional personalities, outstanding because of their youth, their looks, their professionalism or efficiency, their academic qualifications, their energy and their independence emerged in the first round: for example Mrs. Iran Ahu-riya in Tabriz, Mrs. Nayyereh Akhavan in Isfahan, Mrs. Bibi Qodsiyeh Alavi and Mr. Farhad Jafari in Mashhad, Mrs. Elaheh Rastgu in Malayer, Mrs. Jamileh Kadivar in Shiraz. Most of those candidates came up against strong political or local resistance, which did not always stop them getting elected (as with Mrs. Akhavan in Isfahan and Mrs. Elaheh Rastgu in Malayer, although Mrs. Rastgu's election was annulled), but which could lead them to withdraw (as in the case of Farhad Jafari in Mashhad, who was forced to give up when the vote count seemed likely to put him in a very favourable position in the run-off). In smaller centres passions were no less strong, even if the candidates had less prestige; at Torbat-e Jam, in Khorassan, all taxis were hired for the campaign, tea flowed in torrents, restaurateurs and confectioners did not know where to turn, and no less than nine candidates sought the voters' support, with the help of musicians; the main street, covered with carpets and decorated with pots of flowers, had a quite unusually lively appearance.

From the First Round to the Second

In the first round 140 deputies were elected, after winning the required one-third of votes cast. This voting must now be interpreted. A section of the foreign press at once spoke of a victory for the majority in the outgoing parliament. The reality was more complex. In most provincial constituencies explicitly political divisions were shown to be less important than other issues, social or local ones, to which we shall be returning. It was not possible in that situation to know, in March, whether the newly elected people would join the ranks of the conservatives; realignments of factions are frequent, and some candidates had taken prudence so far as to claim support from several lists at once, following the example of Mr. Nategh Nuri himself. In addition the latter's score (35.9 per cent) was not particularly glorious if one considers the means at his disposal and compares him with his predecessor, Mr. Rafsanjani (more than 80 per cent of votes in 1988). Conversely, the Left's results were not negligible, in view of the small number of candidates that it was allowed to put up, the bad media coverage which was a handicap for it, and the refusal of the Fighting Clergy to take part in a contest which they considered unfair.

As for the 'Servants', they did not really win their bet, if it was for them a matter of obtaining a parliamentary majority; their leading candidates were well placed in the second round, but they had only stood in the big cities, and over the country as a whole the conservative Right's hegemony seemed more or less unchanged, if only because it alone was properly organised nationally. However, it was more likely that the 'Servants' had been trying above all to score a point, to put up opposition to the power of Mr. Nategh Nuri, to provoke a change in the political landscape and leave the coming presidential election open. That objective seemed to be well and truly attained on the evening of 8 March.

In any case, the three main tendencies in the race expressed satisfaction with their respective performances. After the Noruz holiday the battle resumed and became fiercer.

First of all, elections were annulled in about ten constituencies, including those for nine seats in Isfahan province where Mrs. Nayyereh Akhavan – wife of an outgoing deputy, Dr. Kamran, whose candidacy had not been approved by the Guardianship Council – had been elected, coming ahead of all her rivals and putting champions of the Right out of the contest, but also at Miyandoab in Azerbaijan province in the west and Malayer in Hamadan province.

Then the political climate became noticeably harsher in several places. In Shiraz Mrs. Jamileh Kadivar, wife of one of the Vice-Presidents of the Republic – Ataollah Mohajerani, who was one of the 16 'Servants' – and herself a renowned intellectual, had to campaign in difficult conditions.[14] In Isfahan and the surrounding towns, the Friday prayers Imam, Ayatollah Taheri, who could not be classed as a left-winger, protested against the cancellation of the first round which he called an outrage and denounced 'lawless' incidents such as attacks by a group of 'troublemakers' against scientific centres, a religious school and a mosque;[15] while the Prefect of the province, Ehsan Jahangiri, noting the frequent overturning of election results in the province since the Revolution, regretted the latest snub all the more because the turnout had increased noticeably (to 63 per cent compared with 44 per cent in 1988 and 35 per cent in 1992) and was near the 1980 level of 68 per cent.[16]

14. See interview with him in the daily *Salam*, 15.2.1375 (1996).
15. *Salam*, 1.1.1375 (1996).
16. *Akhbar*, 18.1.1375 (1996); *Salam*, 24.2.1375 (1996).

Finally, polemics broke out at the national level, with the conservative Right using a speech by the Leader of the Revolution on 23 March, at Mashhad,[17] to attack the 'Servants' supposed 'liberalism' and weakness towards the United States, at the height of the emotion aroused by the resumption of war in Lebanon and the massacre at Qana. Four candidates thought it necessary to distance themselves from them;[18] General Rezai, Commander of the Revolutionary Guards, called on people to 'bar the way to the liberals, that is those who challenge the principles of the Front and the War, of spirituality, of the clergy and of *velâyat-e faqih*, and to vote for *hezbollahi*'.[19] According to some rumours Gholamhossein Karbaschi and Faezeh Hashemi were even physically attacked.

The second round did not end the uncertainties arising from the first. The turnout was considerably lower. However, such declines had been seen in previous elections. What mattered essentially was the political direction that was supposed to emerge from the voting. It was in fact ambiguous, although each camp again claimed victory. It appeared that 90 to 100 deputies could reasonably be ranked with the Right, 70 to 80 among the 'Reconstructors' and about 40 with the Left, which had definitely made a comeback in parliament. Apart from the five seats reserved for religious minorities other than the Baha'is (two Armenians, one Jew, one Zoroastrian, one Assyro-Chaldean) and assigned in the first round, the remaining deputies (about thirty in number) were unclassifiable from a political viewpoint, while they represented permanently one eighth of the Assembly. And this was where the too rapid forecasts and too sweeping analyses ran into problems. In the Iranian factions system alignments by this or that person are temporary; they do not at all exclude compromises or reversals. Thus majorities are subject to change. It was obvious that a number of the deputies would swim with the current. The re-election of Mr. Nategh Nuri to the chair on 2 June, by 132 votes against 105 cast for Mr. Abdollah Nuri, gave an early first indication of this.[20] But it should be noted that Hassan Rohani, reputed to be close to the 'Reconstructors', was almost unanimously elected Deputy Speaker, and 145 deputies responded to an invitation from the 'Reconstructors' on 23 May.[21] So it was advisable not to look only at the figures, but to make a more subtle analysis.

In the first place, the Right's relative victory in the 1996 parliamentary elections aggravated its internal contradictions. In fact the victory was won, with some difficulty, by only one wing of that tendency. It will be recalled

17. *Keyhan*, 5.1.1375 (1996).
18. *Keyhan*, 28 and 29.1.1375 (1996).
19. *Keyhan*, 29.1.1375 (1996).
20. More precisely, Parliament only elected a provisional bureau on 2 June. That vote was confirmed on 5 June, and Mr. Nategh Nuri then received 14 more votes; this illustrates the fluidity of the factional alignments and deputies' propensity for backing the winner. *Keyhan*, 17.3.1375 (1996).
21. *Salam*, 5.3.1375 (1996).

that Ayatollah Mahdavi Kani had resigned from the chairmanship of the Society of Fighting Clergy in July 1995, and let it be known that the health reasons mentioned by some leading figures in that movement were not the only explanation for his action. According to certain commentators whose statements were not denied, he disapproved of the transformation of the Society of Fighting Clergy into a political organisation or even a party,[22] and more generally of the politicisation of the clergy, which he saw as the 'father of the people'.[23] His religious authority is considerable, and in the 1980s his name had been mentioned frequently when the filling of this or that top level post in the Islamic Republic had been under discussion. This meant that his resignation damaged the unity of the Right and hence the leadership of Mr. Nategh Nuri, even though Fighting Clergy election posters had shown his photo next to those of the Imam, the Leader and the President.

In addition some leading figures in the Fighting Clergy had decided not to stand in the parliamentary elections; probably they were placing themselves in the Islamic Republic's reserves, perhaps to save themselves for the top job to be awarded the following year or, more modestly, for ministerial posts. This was the case with Mr. Abdollah Jasbi, chairman of the powerful network of Free Universities – established in 130 cities, with 10,000 teaching staff and 530,000 students[24] – and Mr. Ahmad Tavakkoli, one of the founders of the newspaper *Resalat*; those two men had won respectively 9.1 per cent and 23.8 per cent of the votes in the 1993 presidential elections. Others again did not get elected, starting with the most eminent representatives of the Jam'iyat-e Motalefeh, of which the leading dignitaries of the bazaar are members – such as Mr. Ali-Naghi Khamoushi, President of the Chamber of Commerce; Mr. Asadollah Badamchian, Adviser to the President of the Supreme Court; and Mr. Habibollah Asgaroladi, former Minister of Trade in Mir-Hossein Moussavi's first government and today one of the highest office holders in the Imam's Relief Committee. So it is clear that while Mr. Nategh Nuri was re-elected to the parliamentary chair, important traditional sectors traditionally supporting the Right, such as the Free Universities, the Chamber of Commerce and the network of interest-free loan funds, were deprived of parliamentary representation.

Secondly, the Right, in contrast to the previous parliament, had to define itself in relation not to a defeated minority, but to at least three tendencies whose boundaries were in addition very fluid, and which were in a position to claim a share of election victory. These were the 'Servants of Reconstruction'; the Left, represented by the Alliance of the Imam's Cause; and the nebulous collection of independents who had been elected because of personal factors without openly adhering to one of the major national

22. *Ettela'at*, 19.4.1374 (1995).
23. *Akhbar*, 30.11.1374 (1996).
24. *Akhbar*, 29.2.1375 (1996).

political tendencies, either because they did not wish to do so, or because they had not been accepted by the groupings' leaders. So it could be presumed that the parliamentary majority was not defined according to strict ideological considerations.

Local Issues in an Election

Whatever may be the explicit political meaning of elections in the Islamic Republic, there is another way of interpreting them: they can enable us to get some inner core data from the depths of Iranian political society by revealing some of its fundamental dynamics which, it must be stressed, do not necessarily follow the institutional agenda. This brings out marked continuities which are not permanent phemonena, but in fact bring in innovations, and whose rhythm is specific and does not correspond to that of the political system whose development has been dominated by the 1979 Revolution, the proclamation of the Islamic Republic, and the Republic's various phases and electoral and institutional landmarks. In other words, looking at the 1996 elections we get another look at the question of the relationship between social and political change.

From this point of view, the parliamentary elections, especially in the provinces, involved numerous social issues whose urgency contributed greatly to the vitality of the campaign.

In many respects, the Islamic Republic has resumed the old regime's efforts at centralising and rationalising the state, with other methods, but also other resources. These efforts involve increased unification and even some homogenisation of Iranian society, conveyed through various agencies: for example, development of rail and road links, the spread of university education over the country, the interest-free loan funds network, the spread of a Persian and Islamic way of life in consumption, dress and education, the sometimes authoritarian uniformisation of the urban landscape, and the institutionalising of Friday prayers. However, this analysis must be supplemented by a different observation: centralisation goes together with increasing 'localisation' of political and economic life, which is not viewed favourably by all the factions on the scene because of the disorder to which it gives rise.[25] The assertion of local power is both autonomous in relation to the centralising logic of the Islamic Republic and involved in close interaction with central institutions. This vigour of local dynamics is favoured by a real development of the rural and regional economy (which the gravity of the financial situation should not conceal): the action of public and semi-public organisations – especially the Crusade for Reconstruction and the Imam's Relief Committee – has contributed to

25. A. Azam-Beygui, 'Negahi digar be 'amalkard-e namatlub-e tarha-ye 'omrani va masuliyat-e dolat va majles', in *Ettela'at-e siyasi-eqtesadi*, 97-98, 1374 (1995), pp. 111-17; *Salam*, 15.12.1374 (1996).

this, and so has the informal sector. Two major conclusions can be drawn: the stability of the Islamic Republic depends on the scale of these dealings with the provinces, and its capacity for change on the social transformations they make possible; in addition, the unity of such a multi-ethnic and multi-cultural country as Iran does not seem seriously threatened by centrifugal tendencies.

In any case, the re-localisation of Iranian political life is very obvious, and the principal leaders of the Republic are less and less hesitant to link themselves to their regions of origin, following the example of Hashemi Rafsanjani, whose interest in the prosperity of his native province of Kerman is known to all.

The elections were a good indicator of this process, and also formed part of it. In practice the selection of candidates in 1996 was to a great extent delegated by the Constitution Guardianship Council and the Ministry of the Interior to 'local councils' (*shorâhâ-ye mahalli*) consisting of 30 'people of trust' (*mo'tamed*) chosen by the administrative authorities for their good reputation among their fellow citizens, and from the ranks of major property owners and traders, clerics, and former civil servants. The criterion of age, a guarantee of wisdom, seems to have been decisive in the recognition of such a reputation; the criterion of wealth too, but one can perfectly well be a *mo'tamed* without being rich. In practice the local councils entrusted nine *mo'tamed*, from their own ranks or not, with the approval or rejection of people who had registered as candidates. Among these nine *mo'tamed* there were supposed to be one or two clerics. Inclusion of women in these councils was explicitly provided for by the official forms, but in reality their involvement in this stage of the election process seems to have been particularly negligible. It goes without saying that the central or regional authorities had the last word, to be used possibly to strike out names or, on the contrary, to impose a candidate because of his service record. But the outstanding fact remains that candidate selection was, on a massive scale, a local affair.

So competition was organised above all on the basis of local solidarity and local issues. It also promoted certain political qualities, firstly that of honour (*âberu*), which on its own sums up all that is expected of a good man who can hold his head up high. From the selection of candidates onwards struggles for influence raged. They intensified as the decisive day approached, although the rivals maintained a certain restraint; while a rival's posters could be torn down and his moral character attacked before the authorities, on occasion the rivals had relaxed moments together, for example at the printing works during the printing of posters. Election materials were made available for common use (as in Mashhad) and above all there were efforts to avoid physical violence. However, in the first round, clashes appear to have occurred in Azerbaijan; Farhad Jafari in Mashhad seems to have withdrawn only after being seriously manhandled, probably because his candidacy threatened well entrenched interests; and these tensions seem to have become general in many constituencies as the second round approached.

In these conflicts there were alignments following six sorts of solidarity: religious (among Shias and among Sunnis, but also among religious schools or leaders), ethnic, family or *qawm*, neighbourhood in the widest sense (*mahalleh*), professional (according to guilds or occupations), and political (following trends derived from the country's history). Certainly none of these divisions was decisive on its own, and most of them varied from one situation to another. Thus the electoral game remained very open and fairly unpredictable, although local episodes in the game could on occasion be dominated by one or another form of solidarity. In addition, the contending parties in these local conflicts resorted to mobilising resources from outside their constituencies, for example by bringing in leading figures in national political life to back up local candidates, or, more prosaically, by bringing in coachloads of voters to take advantage of the provision allowing someone to vote in any part of the country with his identity document alone.[26]

The Strategy of Companies (Sherkat)

The liveliness of the electoral process required candidates to invest considerable sums in their campaigning. This opened the way for the entry of enterprises or companies (*sherkat*) into the political game. They have continued to grow since the defeat of the command-economy Left and the liberalisation of the economy, as we saw in the last chapter. This change in the economic scene is itself inseparable from the various logics of solidarity that we have mentioned, and recalls the phrase, 'the Republic of Initiates'.[27] This has gone so far that financing of political life by business has become, in Iran as in France, a major subject of polemics, in the unfavourable context created by the Saderat Bank and Tobacco Corporation scandals, in which senior dignitaries of the regime and local authorities were very directly involved. In Tehran, for example, the daily *Resalat* made a barely disguised accusation that companies working for the municipal authority were contributing to the 'Servants" campaign.[28] When asked about the origin of her campaign funds Faezeh Hashemi confined herself to answering: 'The same as those of the Society of Fighting Clergy' – meaning gifts from individuals or companies; this was a way of both confirming *Resalat*'s suspicions and advising it not to open the Pandora's Box of accusations. It seems that tensions of the same sort were noted at Mashhad.

26. It should be explained, however, that a voter cannot change constituencies between one round and the next.
27. J.-F. Bayart, 'Entre "dirigistes" et "libéraux": la République islamique', in F. Adelkhah, J.-F. Bayart and O. Roy, *Thermidor en Iran*, Brussels, Complexe, 1993, pp. 15-53.
28. *Resalat*, 23.12.1374 (1996).

But the role of business in the electoral game has not been limited to its financing. It has also encouraged change in the style of politics by promoting the qualities of competence and efficiency (*takhassos, kârâ'i*), which were just the qualities that a whole series of reformers claimed to have, starting with the 'Servants of Reconstruction', as did a good many independents who were variously called 'liberals', 'technocrats' and people 'who think differently' (*degar-andish*). It is no longer sufficient to speak to win over voters, it is necessary to act and act successfully. In this respect the conservatives' victory was a Pyrrhic one in so far as the centre of gravity of Iranian society and the economy is tending to move towards an increased professionalism which the people, rightly or wrongly, are inclined to identify with the conservatives' opponents. It is revealing that 9 per cent of the candidates were clerics and 5 per cent people who had not completed secondary education, but 7 per cent were doctors, 12 per cent had Master's degrees and 39 per cent first degrees.[29]

However, there were obstacles to change which must be taken into account in the continuing authority of the clerical political nomenklatura (*hozeh*) and the influence of the regime's clientage networks, such as the families of martyrs. The campaign for the second round saw precisely a return in force of the '*Hezbollahi*' tendency, in the form of condemnation of 'liberals' owing allegiance to the Americans and a return to forceful language which might have been thought to belong to the past. The quality of political debate was affected by this development, with protests, recriminations and accusations gradually replacing exchanges of arguments in the newspapers; the numerous warnings by the Leader or the President were unable to halt this trend. Whereas the pre-election period had been dominated by confrontation of ideas on the need to create political parties, the management of the economy, the Left-Right division and social justice, the post-election phase turned to more trivial questions: how much had such a candidate spent? Where had the money come from?

Notably, the Ansâr-e hezbollâh militants, representing the feelings of ex-servicemen and families of martyrs – who have problems in readapting to society, are suspicious towards all those who have not known the sacrifices at the front, and readily get angry at the materialist compromising of the present time – affirmed their determination to preserve the gains of the Revolution. They moved into action, turning on women cyclists in Chitgar Park (a thinly disguised attack on Faezeh Hashemi); interrupting the showing of the film *Tohfeh hend* (Gift from India) at the Qods cinema and removing its sign; manhandling Abdolkarim Soroush again, attacking inadequately veiled women, demanding the adoption of a law making wearing of the *chador* compulsory; and possibly even attacking a theological college at Isfahan.

To some extent, this movement was a return to the tradition of the 'roughnecks' and other 'swaggerers' who had distinguished themselves

29. *Ettela'at*, 12.12.1374 (1996).

throughout the history of rioting in Iran. The Ansâr militants act out of revolutionary conviction or the feelings of the war volunteers, *bassiji* – which does not at all exclude professional agitators lending a hand. Until now the 'liberals' and the Islamic Left have been the main targets of this violence, which seems to have spared the Right. But it would be wrong to conclude that the Right is wholly manipulating it, even if one or other of its factions may share the militants' ideological standpoint, for example joining the Qom *hozeh* to condemn bad use of sport. In reality the Ansâr movement, sincere though it is, is in a small minority in the country, if only because of its claim to the right to interfere in private lives, unacceptable to much of the Right. Its activism is for the moment confined to Tehran and some provincial centres. It illustrates all the difficulty involved in the necessary synthesis between the ideals of the Revolution and the war and the necessities of reconstruction and modernisation; it contributes to some extent to expression of all the contradictory dissatisfactions, but without offering a viable political way ahead.

Politics in its Own Right, No Longer Sacred

The progress of the election campaign was also a vital indicator of Iranian political society's loss of its sacred aspect, due to its increasing professionalism and even commercialisation. The election followed precise rules – however vague and questionable they might be by Western democratic criteria – and was subjected to constant scrutiny by the press and the legal authorities. For example, uncontrolled putting up of posters was more or less kept within limits by various administrative bans, accompanied by arrests, fines or clean-up orders,[30] and perhaps most of all by social pressure from the people who did not want to see road-signs or public buildings covered or the city made untidy. In addition, the Constitution Guardianship Council, anxious to limit election expenditure and to put candidates on something of an equal footing, issued a certain number of orders which reinforced the primacy of central law over runaway local enthusiasm – notably by banning colour photographs of the candidates, insisting on a choice of one negative for each, and setting limits on the format of posters.

But this rationalising and bureaucratising process did not stop at this sort of regulation of election passions. There was also an endless debate, in the press and in conversation, on the costs of the campaign. Financial costs were incurred by free distribution of *chelo-kabâb*, the multiplication of posters, renting of offices and hiring of cars, the abundance of leaflets, convoys of voters from other areas filling up entire coaches – perhaps even pure and simple corruption in the form of vote-buying? All this lent credence to the

---

30. For example in Tehran, where 800 posters were removed by order of the Prosecutor's office on the second day of the election campaign. *Resalat*, 13.12.1374 (1996).

idea that the elections, if they required so much expenditure of energy and money, should bring in big rewards. Thus there prevailed not only a very utilitarian idea of political commitment – at the opposite extreme to the revolutionary Messianic fervour and mobilisation of 1978, or the ostentatious simplicity of someone like Ayatollah Taleghani who refused to sit in an armchair at the Assembly of Experts and squatted on the ground during televised official sessions – but also a fairly disillusioned attitude towards the political class. If the candidates were so devoted to the cause of the people, should they not have devoted those fabulous sums to building schools and hospitals or distributing exercise books for children? From before the first round a certain number of them in fact withdrew from the contest, after obtaining the endorsement of the Guardianship Council, saying that they would after all devote the money meant for their campaigning to building schools: was that not a way of proving their good reputation and their eligibility, fixing a date for the next parliamentary elections in the year 2000?

At the same time, this commercialisation of the electoral space illustrates the professionalising of political life in the Islamic Republic – professionalising of a revolutionary or post-revolutionary elite, the essence of a phase corresponding to Thermidor 1794 in the French Revolution. Iranians are in fact very aware of this change in the political arena; the age of passion (*shour*), they say, has been followed by the age of reason (*sho'ur*) or, some say, even the age of 'personal interests' (*manâfe'-e shakhsi*).

It is obvious that as politics has lost its sacred aspect, this has completed the separation of the political sphere from the religious – a trend that had already been revealed in a paradoxical way by the conditions in which the Leader of the Revolution acquired the status of *marja'iyat* in 1994 and Mahdavi Kani resigned from the chairmanship of the Society of Fighting Clergy in 1995. It is revealing that the new Assembly includes only about 50 clerics (compared with 65 out of 259 deputies in the fourth parliament and 98 out of 216 in the first). Here we need to examine whether the time has not come for a revival of a religious and philosophical approach that had been expressed at one time in the *hojjatiyeh* Organisation – created in 1953 and wound up at the Imam's request in 1983 – but goes well beyond that movement alone and represents a real school of thought underlying a number of associations and institutions. Initially intended to combat 'the Baha'i heresy', turning to scientific knowledge and reason for that purpose, this approach resembles a movement for religious reform and modernisation, although it is rather quietist and politically conservative.[31] In the turbulence of the Revolution, the first years of the Republic and the

---

31. 'Eya Baghi, *Dar shenâkht-e hezb-e qâ'edin-e zamân, mosum be anjoman-e hojjatiyeh*, Tehran, Nashr-e dânesh eslâmi, 1362 (1983); Nashriyeh râh-e mojâhed, *Anjoman-e hojjatiyeh, nasli ma'yus az harekat va enqelâb*, Tehran, Enteshârât-e râh-e mojâhed, 1368 (1989).

ordeal of war, it was the target of violent attacks from the *hezbollâhi* who alleged that it had collaborated with the old regime, was relying on the appearance of the Twelfth Imam rather than on *velâyat-e faqih*, placed knowledge above militancy, and was too concerned with material and technological progress and therefore with the things of this world, at a time when the prevailing slogan was the necessary identification of faith with politics.

With hindsight one can understand better that the differences between this tendency and militant voluntarism were probably dramatised by the prevailing situation. The imperatives of the struggle against the Shah and then the preservation of the Republic against opposition terrorist activities and Iraqi aggression led some to dissociate themselves from the *hojjatiyeh* Organisation which had been one of the main circles of socialisation (*dowreh*) until the Revolution. According to Sami Zubeida, Abbas Vali and Camille Verleuw, the authorities' relatively mild treatment of that movement, after it had been asked to dissolve itself in 1983, could be explained by the fact that a considerable number of the leading figures in the Revolution were among its sympathisers.[32] Some of them are in fact still seen as such, without any doubt being cast on their revolutionary commitment on that account. However, the conflict was in fact more complex. Mobilisation for the war led to new forms of social commitment: at the front, of course, but also in the city neighbourhoods and villages too, since the recruitment of *bassij* was generally carried out by groups of friends or neighbours and was accompanied by many collective actions in support of the volunteers from families, schools and mosques.[33] In this situation where passions were aroused, the rationalist considerations and intellectual methods of an organisation like the *hojjatiyeh* were frankly not in tune with the current mood.

There was also the whole process of intellectual questioning in the 1980s, in Iran and also in university circles abroad (for example in France), which saw the realities of the Islamic Republic through the prism of the immediate and tragic issues of the political struggle. Since 1989 the years of reconstruction have considerably altered the terms of the debate. So much so that one may wonder if there has not been a major though still implicit political regrouping related to the electoral calendar, leading to the rapprochement or reconciliation of opposing historical and religious trends within the *hozeh*, the elite of society or the revolutionary political class.

---

32. A. Vali, S. Zubaidda, 'Factionalism and political discourse in the Islamic Republic of Iran: the case of the Hujjatiyeh society', *Economy and Society*, 14/2, 1985, pp. 139-73; C. Verleuw, 'L'Association hojjatiyye mahdaviyye', in B. Badie and R. Santucci (eds.), *Contestations en pays islamiques*, vol. II, Paris, CHEAM, 1984-87, pp. 81-117.
33. N. Riahi-Jozani, 'Enfant soldat: corps dissous, corps morcelé', in E. Volant, J. Lévy and D. Jeffry (eds.), *Les risques et la mort*, Montreal, Méridien, 1996, pp. 41-63; F. Khosrokhavar, *L'islamisme et la mort. Le martyre révolutionnaire en Iran,* Paris, L'Harmattan, 1995.

From that point of view what matters lies not so much in the interplay of inevitably changing factional alliances as in the growing legitimation of one issue: that of 'separation', for example between ethics and politics and between private and public. The 1996 parliamentary election campaign was a special moment in this general process of differentiation, especially because the pattern of electioneering favoured candidatures targeted according to category (the targets being women, the young, the clergy, students, traders, retired people, Turks, people of Yazd, Sunnis, the handicapped, etc.); also by the very act of voting, because candidacies followed the logic of increasing individualising of roles and people within the family, and the choice of voting slips by family members turned out to be highly autonomous and varied.

Although the number of women elected – 13, compared with nine in 1992 and only four in 1980 – was in the end less than one would have expected from the large number of women candidates (179, compared with 81 in 1992) and the first round results, the special part played by women in the election deserves to be emphasised. First of all, as we have seen, it was often women candidates who dominated events and occupied the front of the stage: not only Faezeh Hashemi in Tehran but also Jamileh Kadivar in Shiraz, Elaheh Rastgu in Malayer, Nayyereh Akhavan-Bitaraf in Isfahan, and Ahou Riya in Tabriz. These women often obtained scores higher than those of male candidates, the high point occurring in Mashhad where Mrs. Alavi was elected but her husband Mr. Fattahi, who was also standing, was defeated.[34] In addition, this participation by women went well beyond the token moves usual until then, typified by the royal family. Wives and daughters of leading figures of the Islamic Republic, before the eyes of all, took up responsibilities and were more visible on the political stage than the sons. The direction of their commitment was individual: Faezeh Hashemi and Jamileh Kadivar chose the side of the Servants, Nayyereh Akhavan-Bitaraf sided with the Left, Maryam Behrouzi with the Society of Fighting Clergy, Nahid Shid with the independents.

In Tehran there were no less than 11 women among the the 60 candidates still standing in the second round; the Islamic Republic Women's Assembly, led by Imam Khomeyni's daughter Zahra Mostafavi, sponsored a list of 30 candidates including eight women of all political tendencies. Similar phenomena were to be observed in the other big cities, but also, with due allowance made for variations, deep in the heart of the country. At Torbat-e Jam in Khorassan, for example, the candidates – all men – were actively backed by female 'propaganda fronts' (*setâd-e tabliqâti*), consisting of their wives, sisters, female cousins and various women activists who held meetings in the neighbourhoods and mosques, or even wrote large numbers of anonymous letters to discredit opponents. Lastly, the female electorate

---

34. According to *Salam*, 10.1.1375 (1996) the women candidates in Tehran won on average 384,000 votes, the men 364,000 (compared with 282,000 and 301,000 respectively in 1992).

was very active at the grassroots. Women voters could of course do their duty in any polling stations, but, for the very first time, the 'Executive Commissions' made a point of opening special stations for them, probably to make it easier for a certain category of women to take part.[35] Within families, men did not at all have a monopoly on political discussions, and the progress of the women candidates most in the public eye, starting of course with Faezeh Hashemi, inspired plenty of comment, rather like that inspired by the heroines of fashionable television films; from that viewpoint mobilisation of voters was carried out less through ideological speeches than through a whole process of daily conversation[36] arising from the various events during the campaign.

The hidden core which we have brought to light in analysis of the electoral process definitely reveals a society engaged in full-scale internal debate. This was not so much a resumption of the fundamental debates which dominated the 1970s or the early period of the Islamic Republic as a much more modest process of reflection and exchange of views concerning various aspects of man's relationship with his environment. Constant social commentaries on the elections, however anecdotal they might seem, in fact guaranteed real interaction between the upper and lower levels of the Republic. For example, the theme of honour (*âberu*) was a recurring one both in the constituencies – candidates disqualified by the Constitution Guardianship Council complained that their 'honour' was being besmirched – and at the highest level of the State, where the same Council explained that its refusal to approve a candidate did not cast doubt on his integrity. Similarly, the Leader of the Revolution echoed rumours about the sums of money that certain interests were said to have handed over to candidates, saying that a deputy must not be a 'debtor' (*vâm-dâr*). Thus there emerged a 'moral economy' of the elections, which did not fail to modify that of the Republic, and which was based on diversifying rules from one area of society to another or from the private to the public sphere. For example, something that is acceptable between two private individuals, or in restricted social circles – accepting money to do this or that thing – becomes questionable in the political sphere as soon as it affects equality among the voters; not everyone has the means to get a candidate's attention to defend his personal or corporate interests, and not everyone has the good luck to choose the right candidate, the one who eventually wins! Similarly the distribution of *chelo-kabâb*, respected on the part of a man of open-handedness who organises public meals on the feast of Âshurâ, takes on a more suspect meaning in the middle of an election campaign. As for the most conservative candidates, they surround themselves with women

---

35. Only since 1992, thanks to the intervention of the Association of Fighting Clergy, have women been authorised to represent candidates at polling stations. *Salam*, 20.2.1371 (1992).
36. We have borrowed this term from Victor Perez-Diaz who used it in connection with the democratic transition in Spain.

dressed in the traditional *châdor*, which denoted the need not to lose a single vote, rather than religious principles.

The content of the moral economy of the elections is very 'legal-rational'. It does not go back to first principles of community ethics, religious or other, but deals with the action of a social individual subject to rules. Candidates went so far as to present voters with detailed biographies in the form of a 'curriculum vitae' (*zendegi-nâmeh*) giving a candidate's family situation, level of education, past or present jobs and above all personal commitments and service record as a revolutionary or martyr (mentioning imprisonment or war service, victims of war in his entourage, etc.). This initiative spread sufficiently far for some to decide to play the card of individualism in response; in Mashhad, Farhad Jafari had posters produced showing an original and daring picture of him without a beard, explaining his profession and his occupations in three words – writer, journalist, student – and giving potential voters this self-effacement as food for thought: 'My past? It's not worth spending any time on it' (that did not prevent him – quite the contrary – from being in all schoolgirls' work folders and, apparently, winning a considerable number of votes). Generally, the election campaign illustrated this trend towards a society where the grand speeches of the revolutionary epic are giving way to more fragmentary commentaries – those which develop less on a national scale than in the narrower circles of the family, the sports team, the guild, the cultural foundation, the university, the school, religious meetings in the mosque, and which weigh up the pros and cons, criticise, question and mock.

It remains to examine whether the electoral procedure is proving open enough for this change to become institutionalised. The electoral 'market' – this expression is in fact used in Persian, *bâzâr-e entekhâbât* – is sufficiently diversified ('hot', people say in Iran) for voters to be able to bring a number of social distinctions into play for the best pursuit of what they see as their interests. They have a very utilitarian and rational idea of those interests; the deputy is now expected to plead the cause of the village, the town, the landlords, landless peasants, transport operators, teachers, students – specific interest groups – in the *Majles* or before the local administrative authorities. The qualities which make a good deputy in the eyes of public opinion reflect this state of mind very well. He must be close to the people, know how to listen to them and receive their grievances (*bedard-e mardom bereseh*), show simplicity – in short, 'sit down and get up with the people' (*bâ mardom neshast-o barkhâst dâshteh bâsheh*); but he must also be capable of getting his views accepted in the corridors of bureaucracy or within parliament, he must be a man of weight and influence (voters often use a metaphor recalling the skill of a tailor cutting his cloth: *boresh dâshteh bâsheh*). Nowadays this ability assumes that one has had a good education, if possible higher education, and is an expert in the noble sense of the word (*motekhasses*) and not just a man of conviction (*mote'ahhed*) – 'Of course parliament needs experts, but choose those who are the most committed',[37] the Leader of the Revolution urged during the campaign; and one needs to make a good impression on television.

In reality, this utilitarian profile of a deputy obviously fits in with the more classical or traditional ideal of a man of importance. Hossein Ghazi-Zadeh, deputy for Fariman/Sarakhs, scored a definite success by ostentatiously paying back to parliament unused travel expenses for a foreign mission, in a gesture worthy of a true *javânmard* but also of a genuine revolutionary, ready to serve the people without extracting advantage for himself. Similarly Farhad Jafari – whose clean-shaven look, so popular among secondary schoolgirls, was enough to place him in the category of people who 'think differently' – told the weekly *Khavaran*, which was surprised that he had not boasted during the campaign about his record of service at the war front, 'I do not think one should claim glory for having served the people, or think they are in one's debt';[38] thus he showed that it is possible to act simultaneously as a *javânmard*, a revolutionary and a 'liberal', to use the term employed by the Right.

The utilitarian view of political action is more and more asserted at the local level, at the expense of national Messianic ideas which have prevailed for a long time. The general language used by the 'reconstructors' and 'independents' during the elections subtly suggested this equivalence between pragmatism and local action. According to them, if the good deputy is the 'man of the district' or of the 'place' (*ahl-e mahal*) as general sentiment favours, he is also ' the man of expertise' (*ahl-takhassos*) – the same idea of belonging (*ahl*) is expressed in both cases. There is no contradiction between this local belonging and the national or international dimension. It is because he is a 'child of the district' (*bacheh mahal*) and shares in the life of his voters that the deputy can serve their interests. However, those interests are now inseparable from a wider context: assertion of local or national interests goes together with the will for integration with the centre or with the world.

The utilitarian view of politics is reflected at the top level of the state in the code of values which Ali Akbar Rafsanjani highlighted from 1989 to 1997; the President explicitly called his government a 'working' (*kâr*) cabinet, causing consternation among the command-economy Left. The distance travelled in a few years can be seen: the theme of 'work' is now widely used over the whole political spectrum, even though some differences of outlook remain between the Right, which places 'social justice' ahead of economic development although it may mean leaving the bazaar to be its guarantor; the Servants, who give priority to economic development and especially industrial investment, which alone can ensure

---

37. *Keyhan*, 29.1.1375 (1996). To Mr. Hashemi Rafsanjani those two qualities complement each other: see *Akhbar*, 7.12.1374 (1996).
38. *Khavaran*, 145-6, 1375/1996.

social justice; and the Left, which sees salvation only in development of the nation's political expression and potential. Despite appearances, the emotional and divisive impact of these debates has been considerably softened; the long arguments over the two five-year plans proposed by Hashemi Rafsanjani were a sort of soothing bath for feelings. From that viewpoint there was not so much a fundamental difference between the Leader of the Revolution and the President of the Republic as complementarity between two distinct roles: the President embodied the necessities of governmental action, 'reconstruction', 'progress' (*pishraft*) and 'fertilisation' (*âbâdâni*), the last expression being the very one preferred by the Mayor of Tehran in his municipal policy, and also used in the Servants' posters, or by the voters when it comes to praising the record of the deputy in their town.

However, the issues of 'work' and 'fertilisation', although no longer sufficient to decide between the major political tendencies, are not a factor for consensus themselves; they naturally cannot serve all the interests involved, and inevitably provoke conflict among them. These contradictions recur at the highest state level, where the economic policies of various players or factions can prove contradictory, as was shown by the outbreak of a large number of financial scandals, for example in the banking sector, local government and various branches of industry.

The 'fertilisation' of Khorassan, in the literal sense, involves many difficult decisions concerning allocation of water and arable land and the economic use to which those two scarce resources are to be put. Should subsistence farming be given priority over cash crops? Is it reasonable to continue to grow sugar cane, lucerne or market garden produce when they require large quantities of water? Would it not be better to favour industrialisation as some experts think?[39] The deputies have to address these questions which concern their constituencies very directly. For example, one candidate is said to have won support in Torbat-e Jam from landowners who wanted to see a ban on the use of about a hundred wells lifted, and were disappointed in the failure of the outgoing deputy to obtain this measure. What is interesting is that this candidate was supported by the Âstân-e Qods, which had itself had those wells closed on the grounds that the water table was too low. Similarly the deputy for Torbat-e Heydariyeh, Sahmi Hesari, a clergyman who had inspired a refinery project in the hope that it would be implemented in his town, was disagreeably surprised to see the refinery built

39. Sa'dollah Velayati, 'Nokâti chand pirâmun-e manâbe' va masâ'el-e âb-e ostân-e khorâsân [Some comments on water resources and problems in Khorassan]', *Faslnâmeh tahghighat-e joghrifayai*, 4, 1366 (1997), pp. 80-103. On the political economy of Khorassan, cf. also B. Hourcade, 'Vagf et modernité en Iran. Les agro-business de l'Âstân-e qods de Mashhad', in Y. Richard, *Entre l'Iran et l'Occident. Adaptation et assimilation des idées et techniques occidentales en Iran*, Paris, Éditions de la Maison des Sciences de l'Homme, 1989, pp. 117-47; N. Hakami, 'Pélerinage de l'Emam Reza', doctoral thesis, Paris, EHESS, 1977.

at Nishabur for strategic and industry-related reasons, even though he had threatened to burn himself alive in the parliamentary chamber; his defeat in the 1992 elections relieved him of the obligation to go to such an extreme. Exacerbation of these conflicts over water, land, industrial schemes and the creation of new administrative units cannot be ruled out in the years to come. To some extent, elections mediate and institutionalise these tensions. But they are also able to dramatise them, causing frustration or upsets.

There is one particular division that the electoral system expresses badly. In practice, the Sunnis, to whom the Constitution does not give the status of a minority, have great difficulty in obtaining senior government jobs, and the demarcation of constituencies makes it difficult to elect one of their people to parliament. The reservations on the part of the political class, and even a good number of intellectuals, on this subject are due in part to the worries aroused by the war in Afghanistan, immigration of workers and refugees, the supposed very high birth rate among the Sunnis, the power of the Baluchi drug networks, and the activities, at least financial, of Saudi Arabia in the region. The ideological talk of 'unity' among Muslims by the Islamic Republic does not alter the case. Today the Sunni elites seem to be besieging the liberal professions so as to ensure their upward social progress and the advancement of their community. But the state of the Sunni-dominated districts and villages in Khorassan shows an alarming disparity. Moreover, Sunni families, especially immigrant ones, are reluctant to send their children to Shia schools, and the rate of illiteracy and school dropout is particularly high.[40]

Even if one leaves aside the problems of social and cultural integration posed by the Afghans, the question of political representation of the Sunnis has some urgency. Cities such as Sarakhs, Taibad and Khaf, where they are in the majority, have not been able to elect one of their people to parliament because they are swallowed up in majority-Shia constituencies, and it seems to be a lost cause in advance for a Sunni to seek election in that region. At Khaf none of them stood in 1996, in contrast to the 1992 elections where four of them tried their luck and one was only narrowly beaten, the final winner being a Shia cleric, Habibollah Habibi. At Taibad their only candidate – Abdolghassem Mowdoudi, a sociologist – did not get beyond the pre-selection stage. It follows that the Sunnis are even more without a voice in places where they are in a minority, as in Torbat-e Jam, and in any case they are very commonly absent from the various bodies running the electoral process. To all this must be added the divisions among the Sunni leaders themselves, the *molavi* – dissensions which do not help them get access to the election market. Although those events have not been fully explained, the Mashhad riots of 1992, the destruction of the Sunni mosque

40. M.-H. Papoli Yazdi, 'Asarât-e siyâsi-ye hozour-e panahandegân-e afghâni dar khorâsân' The political effects of the presence of Afghan refugees in Khorassan, *Faslnameh Tahqiqât-e joqrâfiyâ*, 15, 1368/1989, pp. 5-35.

at Feyz, and the explosion of a bomb at the Imam Reza shrine in 1994 suggest that the persistent marginalisation of the special interests of a considerable fraction of the population, on the pretext of religious or cultural difference, will not be without risk.

However, there is a much more general problem raised by this particular case: the problem of the institutionalising of political mediation, which is likely to continue to dominate the scene in the coming years, in view of the heterogeneity of Iranian society and the rapid changes which it is undergoing. The concept of minority is insufficient and even unsuitable to convey it. On the one hand, there are also difficulties over the representation of social categories – for example youth, or the recently urbanised suburbs (the riots in the Kouy-e Tollâb district in Mashhad in 1992 and in the mushrooming town of Islamshahr near Tehran in 1995 were reminders). On the other hand, groups such as the Sunnis of Khorassan, but also the Baluchis, the Lors, the Arabs and *a fortiori* the Azeris, besides not being homogeneous themselves, have relations with the central government that are not confined to separatist feeling leading to autonomist claims – differing there, it is true, from the Kurds.

Elections and Political Reformulation

Being as ambiguous as they were, the 1996 parliamentary elections revealed the great debate, or rather, the numerous debates shaking the Islamic Republic twenty years after its birth. Its legitimating principle remains composite, based on both 'the guardianship of the Islamic jurist' (*velâyat-e faqih*) and the sovereignty of the people (articles 5 and 6 of the Constitution). By definition, elections are at the heart of this theoretical contradiction, but they are also one of the main ways of overcoming it and one of the special moments of that process of overcoming it within the institutions of the Islamic Republic, as daily activity goes on. In any case, the problem is not posed in terms of an alternative; while nobody directly or publicly attacks the idea of *velâyat-e faqih* (in the autumn of 1997 Ayatollah Montazeri attacked the Leader's *personal* competence), nobody is now reopening the debate on elections by universal suffrage, which Imam Khomeyni said was 'the sole criterion of assessment'. The Islamic Republic seems to have decided to live according to these two agendas and to reconcile them. But this process is not without polemic and tension.

There is first of all something very classic, the difficulty of arbitrating between the national interest and special interests, especially local interests for which the deputies make themselves the defence counsel (*vakil*). Secondly, there is discussion on whether the title of *velâyat-e faqih* which the Leader of the Revolution bears describes an official function or is of divine origin – whether it derives from *vekâlat* (the principle of delegation) or *velâyat* (the principle of transcendance). The Islamic Left respects the position but gives it a constitutionalist interpretation, according to which the

Leader, before the law, is equivalent to a simple citizen; it strongly contests the '*velâyat*ist' interpretations by the Assembly of Experts. The Right, in the majority, recognises the Leader as having a transcendental position which gives him in particular the power to dissolve parliament. The 'Servants' let their daily *Hamshahri* publish a series of articles by Ayatollah Javadi Amoli commenting from a purely theological point of view (not a political one as *Resalat* claimed to believe) on the book by Mehdi Haeri Yazdi, *Hekmat va Hokumat* (Wisdom and Government), banned in Iran and favouring a '*vekâlat*ist' interpretation of *velâyat-e faqih*. In this way, too, they seem to have come closer on this subject to the ideas of the Left, although they give priority to public action rather than ideological disputes.

But it should be noted also that the Right itself is not unanimous on the subject, as was shown by the circumstances of Ali Khamenei's elevation to the *marja'iyat* in 1994. The clerics are not the last to indulge in reflection, and this contributes to the division among the conservatives who claim to follow them.[41] The religious scene is enlivened by numerous theological colleges which often give general education also, and which today have become clearly differentiated institutions, headed by distinct boards and relying on the support of varied, even divergent economic interests. This network of establishments publishes a fairly considerable number of magazines whose content – religious, certainly, but also philosphical, historical, social, cultural and political – examines the future of the *hozeh*, Shia Islam and the Islamic Republic.

The Republic is too often imagined as a theocratic regime upheld by the dictatorship of the clergy. The reality is less simple. Even excluding the fact that a not negligible proportion of the clergy has steered clear of all political activity, today there is a reformulation of their social role. Defence of their special corporate identity no longer seems a crucial issue, since an increasing number of the men of religion participate fully not only in the exercise of power, but much more widely in the life of society – as doctors, journalists, deputies, mayors, military personnel, even television producers.[42] It was in this way that the clergy were a prominent player throughout the elections, taking stances on the qualification of candidates, the organisation of the campaign and the important affairs of the country, and declaring that the act of voting was a legal, social and political 'duty' (*taklif*). It was in this sense also that Faezeh Hashemi told journalists, who asked her what lay behind clerical opposition to her initiatives and

41. See a series of articles published by Hojjatoleslam Mohsen Kadivar, 'Nazariyehâ-ye dolat dar feqh-e shi'eh' [Ideas of the State in Shia *fiqh*], in the weekly *Bahman*, 1-5, 1374 (1996), and in the magazine *Rahbord*, 4, 1373 (1994), pp. 1-41.
42. It is interesting to note that, out of 91 deputies in the fourth parliament who had received clerical education (including those reaching the top level of *ejtehad*, that of the Sources of Emulation), only 65 declared themselves to be clerics (*mo'amem*) and wore clerical garments. See Edâreh koll-e omur-e farhangi majles shorâ-ye eslâmi, *Mo'arref-i-ye namâyandegân-e majles-e châhârom*, 1371 (1992).

questioned her about the influence of the clergy in the elections, that their 'abâ was 'like [her] veil'; in other words, the problem did not come only from the clerics as clerics, and the cowl no longer made the monk! This secularisation of the clergy and its inclusion in society are inseparable from other movements of realignment, such as the rapprochement between lay intellectuals wearing 'hats' (mokallâ) and the turbanned intellectuals (mo'ammem), for example in the magazines Kiyan, Farzaneh, Zanan, Payam-e zan and Iran-e farda.

It definitely seems that the scholarly or ideological dispute over velâyat-e faqih is connected with tangible social processes. One of those – this is our third point – involves the formation of political groups which fall short of parties strictly speaking, but are already setting out terms for the possible emergence of parties. That eventuality is now something openly discussed by almost everyone on the political scene. It seems necessary for the rationalisation of the interplay of factions; only real parties seem able to ensure a minimum amount of transparency for political life, to discipline members of parliament and to arbitrate between local interests and the national interest. Of course the Left and the 'Servants' seem more enthusiastic at this looming prospect, while the Right does not conceal a certain anxiety. But, as Mohammad Javad Larijani nicely put it, the Right gives the impression of a bad pupil who puts on a spurt on the eve of an examination,[43] despite the worries of someone like Mahdavi Kani about politicisation of the clergy. Here, too, the conservatives are adopting a theme that was originally put forward by their rivals.

However, left-wing and right-wing parties, if they are to be formed, will start off from two fairly distinct organisational traditions. The Right meets more in 'societies' (jâme'eh), the Left in 'associations' (anjoman); thus people speak respectively of the Society of Fighting Clergy and the Association of Fighting Clerics. The significance of these ideas is sufficiently obvious in Iran for a Society of Islamic Associations of Guilds and the Bazaar (on the Right) to be formed out of concern to mark distance from the Islamic Associations of Guilds (on the Left). The introduction of a multi-party system would thus confer approval on an organisational tradition, of associations on one side and societies on the other, which goes back essentially to the 1950s and was historically the starting point for social thought in modern Islam. However, it is not certain that the form of a party will be able to channel effectively the very fragmented and diffuse expression of the various political movements; as we have seen, both Left and Right have backing in a multitude of professional, educational, religious and business institutions, more or less autonomous. One may wonder whether these are not putting together an authentic 'civil society', and they cannot easily be reduced to unitary political representation because of the weight of local, personal and professional interests.

43. Resalat, 6.10.1374 (1996).

In the paradoxical way they turned out, the parliamentary elections of 1996 revealed the legalising and rationalising trends in Iranian society and many other things besides. If there has to be rationalisation and bureaucratisation, they will not be in one direction. Lastly, ambiguity is shown in the electoral fate of the 'Servants'; they lost in one sense as a political group, but not necessarily as a political renewal movement; their ideas, in many respects, came to prevail as the legitimate issues for discussion. This was shown a year later by the outcome of the presidential elections of 23 May 1997.

This political earthquake was explained by many factors. In the first place, Mohammad Khatami's campaign was extraordinarily professional. It benefited from the combined skills of the Servants of Reconstruction and the militants of the Left Alliance, two tendencies which were originally behind his candidature and have solid experience in communication. Mohammad Khatami's candidacy and the dynamism of his campaign very quickly changed the situation which had been thought to be a straightforward one in which Ali-Akbar Nategh Nuri was frontrunner, after the possibility of Ali-Akbar Hashemi Rafsanjani standing for a third time – which was prohibited by the Constitution – had been definitely abandoned in the autumn of 1996, and after the former Prime Minister Mir-Hossein Moussavi had decided not to stand, and the Society of Lecturers in Theology at Qom had come out in support of the speaker of parliament.

Steadily, the new herald of the Reconstructors and the Left expanded his audience and brought an increasing number of forces on to his side. Some members of the Society of Lecturers in Theology at Qom let it be known that the motion passed in support of Ali-Akbar Nategh Nuri in November 1996 had been voted in a different context and with some haste. Similarly the Leader of the Revolution denied, a few days before the vote, that he had any preference for one of the four candidates standing. As for the *motalefeh* movement and the Society of Fighting Clergy, they had declared for the speaker of parliament in the absence of some of their leading figures, such as Ali-Akbar Hashemi Rafsanjani. It was public knowledge that Rafsanjani wanted Mohammad Khatami to win. In this situation Ali-Akbar Nategh Nuri's candidature became like that of Edouard Balladur – an early seeming frontrunner who ended up losing – in the French presidential elections of 1995. This possibility had been foreseen since the beginning of 1996, as Nategh Nuri had declared his candidature so early, and it should have been shown as more likely by detailed analysis of the parliamentary elections of 1996;[44] on 7 February 1997 by-elections in several constituencies confirmed that voting trend, especially in Isfahan.

Secondly, Mohammed Khatami's candidacy turned out to crystallise in the political arena some profound changes in Iranian society, not that society

44. F. Adelkhah, 'Ébullition préélectorale en Iran', *La Croix*, 10 January 1996.

should be seen in a simplistic fashion as opposed to the 'government' or the 'regime'. Mohammad Khatami's full strength came precisely from the fact that he combined the characteristics of a man of the inner circles of power, close to Ali-Akbar Hashemi Rafsanjani, and those of an outsider; the respectable Islamic standing of a Hojatoleslam and the prestige of a university don; the top-class credentials of a former revolutionary militant who had worked closely with Ayatollah Beheshti and the open mind of a polyglot influenced by experience of the West. He presented himself as the man of reform rather than the man of a clean break, and that in no way dampened the hopes placed in his name. The voter turnout was so massive that the authorities had to delay closing of polling stations by four hours; it was 88 per cent, compared with hardly more than 50 per cent in 1993. In that way also the 1996 parliamentary elections had set the tone, and during the presidential election campaign the active mobilisation of 'propaganda fronts' that had dominated the scene the previous year was seen again.

The results are a good illustration of some of the trends in Iranian society for which Mohammad Khatami has made himself the spokesman. First, he had the massive support of young people and women, as most observers noted. But his impressive score in Tehran and the thorough defeat of Ali-Akbar Nategh Nuri also showed that the bazaar no longer coincided with the conservative Right. It had been considerably transformed from a sociological viewpoint, and is now differentiated and is escaping at least partly from control by the traditional networks and guilds. This change goes together with the increasing power of businessmen and companies (*sherkat*) which we have mentioned. Similarly, the clergy, which had been assumed to identify itself with the Right and Ali-Akbar Nategh Nuri, took much more varied positions; not only did Ayatollahs such as Montazeri, Ardebili and Sanei come out on the side of Mohammad Khatami, the city of Qom gave him 59.4 per cent of its votes and Mashhad 70 per cent. Lastly, Khatami's recognition of special regional interests ensured him enthusiastic support from the Turkish, Arab, Kurdish and Lor votes, at a time when relations between the provinces and the capital were being renegotiated and a less centralised way of running the Republic seemed to be emerging after a period of strong centralisation, which had been partly a necessity due to the war with Iraq.

This reshaping of the political landscape, made obvious by the parliamentary elections of 1996, the by-elections of January-February 1997 and the presidential elections of 23 May, is incomprehensible unless account is taken of the growth of a public space in the last few decades, a public space to whose growth the religious field has made a big contribution.

5

A NEW PUBLIC SPACE FOR ISLAM?

When Islam in Iran is discussed, it is often in strictly political terms. Under the Pahlavis, it is argued, there reigned an authoritarian modernisation process restricting the influence of religion fairly brutally to the private sphere, with the aim of building a centralised secular state; this regime, it is further said, was violently rejected by society and replaced, in the 1979 Revolution, by an Islamic Republic exerting in some way God's vengeance against an impious enterprise, sinful in its excessive modernity. This view is not entirely false. But the clear-cut picture given in this interpretation of events is not wholly convincing, and its main elements have been reconsidered by historians.[1] It is now known that the monarchy had solid support among the clergy and formed a real alliance with at least a part of the hierarchy. Similarly, the view of the revolutionary mobilisation of 1978-79 as exclusively Islamic must be qualified, and it has been shown that the Republic, possibly without being conscious of it, continued some of the dynamics of the old regime, for example the processes of centralisation and bureaucratic rationalisation.[2] Similar debates also continue about the Constitutional Revolution of 1905-9.[3] In addition, analysing the Revolution in terms of a crisis of modernisation or secularisation does not tell us why things happened in 1978-79 and not in 1963, when Imam Khomeyni was exiled, or in 1971 during the festivities at Persepolis where the Shah was seen ostentatiously drinking wine, or in 1975 when he tried to increase tax pressure on the bazaar – or, on the other hand, several years later.

But our intention here is to alter the terms of the debate. Political change in Iran does not just mean more or less Islam in institutions or in society.

1. See especially S.A. Arjomand, *The Turban for the Crown. The Islamic Revolution in Iran*, New York, Oxford University Press, 1988; R. Mottahedeh, *The Mantle of the Prophet: Religion and Politics in Iran*, New York, Simon and Schuster, 1985; N.R. Keddie, *Religion and Politics in Iran. Shi'ism from Quietism to Revolution*, New Haven, CT, Yale University Press, 1983; H.E. Chehabi, *Iranian Politics and Religious Modernism. Liberation Movement of Iran under the Shah and Khomeyni*, Ithaca, NY, Cornell University Press, 1990.
2. F. Adelkhah, J.-F. Bayart and O. Roy, *Thermidor en Iran*, Brussels, Complexe, 1993.
3. V. Martin, *Islam and Modernism: The Iranian Revolution of 1906*, London, I.B. Tauris, 1989; J. Afary, *The Iranian Constitutional Revolution, 1906-1911. Grassroots Democracy, Social Democracy, and the Origins of Feminism*, New York, Columbia University Press, 1996.

One also needs to know whether Islam has been an invariable factor throughout the century. Of course it has not been so at all. The religious arena itself has been through formidable changes and is an area of social change, especially because it partially occupies the public space – political space and also media space.

We can start off by illustrating the distance travelled between the Iran of the mid-1970s and that of the 1996 census. The former was a country of 33.7 million people of whom 47 per cent lived in towns of over 100,000 inhabitants. By 1996 the country had 60 million inhabitants, 61 per cent of them town dwellers. Over the same period the number of people receiving schooling rose from 59 per cent in 1976 to 85 per cent for men and from 28 per cent to 74 per cent for women.[4] Greater Tehran, which had 4.5 million inhabitants in 1976, is today a megalopolis of about 10 million people. This shows the extent of the changes brought about both by universal modernisation and by great events (the Revolution, the war with Iraq, exceptionally rapid population growth, the uncertainties of the oil-based economy, etc.). The religious sphere could not fail to be affected by these changes.

Some examples drawn from daily life are sufficient to illustrate this. Thirty years ago, in a middle class family living in the capital and practising their religion in just an everyday way, it was customary to apply special precautions in handling the Koran or Koranic verses, to show proper respect for their sacredness. The Book was a rare 'presence'. It was shelved high up, wrapped in a piece of cloth, to avoid its being soiled by contact with unclean hands or dust, and to keep it out of children's reach. People arranged their movements around the room in relation to the holy Book; you did not turn your back to it, you avoided any rude or – even worse – any immoral attitude, you did not stretch your legs out in the direction of the Book, even to sleep. It was considered unfitting to get up when the Koran was open for reading.

At every important moment of life people had recourse to the Koran; a verse (*va en yakâd*) was pinned on to a new-born baby's clothing, during the marriage ceremony people absorbed themselves in reading the Koran at one point and the young bride had her photograph taken with the Book in her hand; you passed under the Koran three times and under a glass of sugar-water before going on a journey; you consulted it through a religious authority before taking any important decision; it was used to ward off bad luck, in case of illness for example, and naturally there were recitals from it for the dead. Daily life itself was placed under its protection; the pediments of houses were often decorated with ceramic or wrought iron verses. The sacredness of the Koran was so well understood, and implied so many obligations, that people took care not to have many copies of it in their

4.   M. Ladier, 'La Transition se confirme en Iran', *Population et Société*, 328, October 1997, pp. 1-3.

possession. One civil servant under the Pahlavi administration could prefer to get rid of a particularly precious copy, in calligraphy on gazelle skin, by 'giving' it to water, on the understanding that it must be pure running water. This was the normal procedure for destroying all religious writings, especially spoiled or incomplete fragments of the Koran. A pious person could even systematically cut out the Koranic verses appearing in newspapers, to preserve them from any disrespectful treatment and make them disappear in accordance with the rules, even if it meant crossing the city to find a well or a stream of guaranteed purity.

Many of these customs are still common. Some of them have even become more marked, and have acquired the status of 'invented traditions'.[5] Thus the *va en yakâd* pendant or brooch pinned on to the baby's clothes is now a personalised gold jewel. As for the bride's Koran placed at the head of the dowry, it is now at the heart of the ceremony; its binding can be of high quality, and the young bride is absorbed in the reading of it more solemnly than before. The moment has to be immortalised on video as recorded by professionals – a new occupation which women have learned on the job, to respond both to the new expectations of families in tune with modern life and to the Islamic norms valued by the Republic. Then there is the long photo session where the bride is snapped in numerous poses, the Word of God (*kalâm ollâh*) in her joined hands and her ecstatic face looking up to heaven. In many respects, new-style family sociability, the consumer urge and modern techniques give substance and ritual form to older practices, including the most religious ones.

But the most obvious changes relate to the actual distribution of the Koran. It is now printed in large quantities. Numerous editions have appeared and there are differences among them; whereas previously there was some homogeneity in calligraphy, binding, format and Persian translation, a great diversity has taken over. With the help of a real effort of exegesis, translations have succeeded each other, and are less literal than before. The believer has a choice of versions which may correspond to differing uses, ranging from the pocket Koran protected by a leather or plastic case with a zip fastener, to the high-value copy meant to adorn the home and impress everyone around. The Islamic Republic prides itself on putting the final touches to the world's biggest edition of the Koran, while micro-Korans are sold, with cases again, to serve as keyholders, the writing being so small as to be illegible. It would probably be going too far to speak of a process of 'commercialisation' of the Koran. Nobody, for example, will ever speak of 'buying' a Koran, nor will anyone enquire directly about its price; the ritual formula is rather to ask 'how much is the gift of the Koran?' (*hedye-ye qorân chandeh*), and in bookshops the labels say, 'Gift of the Koran: 5,000 rials'.

---

5. E. Hobsbawm and T. Ranger (eds.), *The Invention of Tradition*, Cambridge University Press, 1983.

However, the wide distribution of the Word of God has considerably altered people's relationship with it. It is transmitted through the written press. Some newspapers have chosen a Koranic verse as motto, others punctuate current socio-political affairs with sacred quotations, and most devote articles to theological debates punctuated by Suras of the Koran. It has become impossible to take as many precautions as before in everyday handling of the holy Scriptures. None the less a section of the clergy and believers is angry about the way sacred things have become an everyday part of life, especially because newspapers, whose paper is often subsidised by the state, supply particularly cheap wrappings for butchers and greengrocers, and end up in dustbins. This wide distribution of the Koran has dissociated it from the feeling of mourning to which it was often linked. This has gone so far that the '*besmellâh*-mania' of the leaders of the regime, who do not start a speech without invoking the name of God the Almighty and Merciful, has become a subject of derision in everyday jokes. When a reporter asks a peasant what he places around the roots of his fruit trees, the peasant answers, 'In the name of God the Merciful, sh*t!'

It goes without saying that many practices and customs predominant thirty years ago are still current. But the combined effects of, on the one hand, changes inherent in a 'mass society' in the areas of consumption and communication, and on the other, the Republic's special impulse towards Islamisation have irreversibly altered the idea of sacredness and people's relationship with it. Beside the fact that the Book now inspires socio-ideological debates in the daily and periodical press (no longer just legal, theological and philosophical disputes confined to clerical circles), it is the object of practices hitherto unknown on the part of the believer-consumer. The latter can now hear the Sura of his choice chanted by dialling 114 on his telephone (the number recalling the 114 Suras of the Koran), and it seems that this service is on the way to becoming available on the on-screen telephone information terminal, although that has only been distributed very sparsely and its marketing seems actually to be linked with the opening of the 114 Koran dialling service. In the same area of innovation, the television recommends replacement of the tunes played over the phone for waiting callers by recorded Koranic verses. This has in fact been implemented (as of the spring of 1995) on the Ministry of Justice phone lines. However, these new forms of Islamic socialisation do not really correspond to a return to revolutionary militancy. This period is comparable to Thermidor 1794, and these innovations coincide with new consumer practices considered important by *Homo Iranicus* (although he is also *Islamicus*). Thus, at the same time, telephone callers to the Special Elections Office at the Presidency, headed by Mohsen Hashemi, were greeted by the tune of a famous song by Graeme Allwright: '*Petite bouteille, sacrée bouteille!*'

On a more serious note, the believer concerned to perfect his knowledge of the Book can obtain at least three disks of what should really be called

'Koranic games' – *Toubâ, Rezvân, Tâhâ* – which can help him to familiarise himself, in an interactive fashion, with the verses of the Koran, religious knowledge and the lives of the saints, in Persian, English or French. There is no reason to suppose that the 'Koranic games' will supplant electronic games of the 'Atari' type which are all the rage among the young generations. But they show at any rate that Islam has entered the era of mass media and new information technology. The foundation of the Republic itself gave added speed and a special colour to these religious changes through innovations in the politico-theological domain, for example, by imposing the doctrine of *velâyat-e faqih* which was not at all 'traditional' in the sense in which Imam Khomeyni meant it, and in the legislative domain's in civil law matters.

It should be added that in any case Islam is not homogeneous from a social point of view. To understand this point better we shall start with the impressive development of neighbourhood religious sociability customs since the 1979 Revolution: for example, celebration of the main feasts of Shia Islam, especialy the Âshurâ ceremonies (*ta'zieh*); pious gatherings of men (*hey'at*) and women (*jaleseh*); attendance at the mosque; and less regular meetings linked with major events in life (essentially with mourning) and with the expression of wishes and thanksgiving for their being granted (the tablecloth ceremony, *sofreh*, that is, the gift of a dish).

Analysis of these customs makes it possible, first of all, for us to discern three major categories of religious sentiment: one which can be called popular, in the sense that it is practised not by unimportant people exclusively, but rather by just anyone, and is a constant and regular occasion for ritualised mobilisation; a second that is undeniably learned, in the sense that it is based above all on the Book, theological works and written traditions (*Hadis*), practiced especially but not exclusively among the clergy; and a third that is ideological, more or less explicitly linked with the Islamic Republic's political aims deriving from the Revolution, or with the idea of political Islam.

It can be seen straightaway that this classification is somewhat arbitrary and that these three categories of religious sentiment are constantly penetrating each other in neighbourhood socialising practices. For example, the 'lady' (*khânum*) who holds the role of religious authority in a religious women's meeting (*jaleseh*), and who is also called 'speaker' (*sokhanrân*) or 'announcer' (*guyandeh*, the word used for radio and television newscasters), may have received training at a theological college, and claims privileged relations with clerical circles. But, at the same time, she adopts at least some elements of the regime's ideological discourse, if only because it is predominant in most theological colleges. In addition, she is inevitably held accountable to the expectations of an audience who is more attached to continuity in practice despite the increasing rationalisation of its ideas, and is not at all insensitive to an *imaginaire* which some place in the realm of superstition.

In addition, these meetings called 'religious' and considered as such by the sociologist or anthropologist studying religious activity are not necessarily just that. People talk of many other things besides God there. They are, very classically, an occasion for exchanging precious information relating to daily life – about housing or marriage matters, for example – and for displaying one's social distinction by one's appearance, one's financial contribution or the dishes laid out on one's tablecloth; they are even occasions for trading in consumer goods brought from one of the country's Free Zones, from Dubai or from a place of pilgrimage, or in home-made works of craftsmanship produced under the compulsion of the economic crisis. Not only are the different levels of religiosity constantly mingled, but they are also inseparable from extra-religious and often everyday practices; it is perfectly possible, and entirely legitimate, for people at the same meeting to pray, to make vows, and to fix the time for the next body-building session.

Secondly, the regime, following one of the intellectual traditions of the *hozeh*,[6] has for obvious reasons emphasised the social dimension of religious life rather than private and mystical expressions of the faith. Confronted with the exigencies of revolutionary mobilisation and the country's isolation, threatened by Iraqi aggression, it based its revolutionary message on the principles of religious legitimacy so as to take over the public space, especially through mass demonstrations. The official Friday prayer ceremonies[7] are the best example of this process; they include a first sermon on strictly religious lines and a second that is explicitly political or social in tone, the latter being the one which foreign news agencies do not fail to quote. It is even common today for the first sermon to be preceded by an address, possibly quite technical, by a minister or a technocrat who explains the main outlines of his actions in the area of 'reconstruction'. Today the preoccupations of daily life override other considerations and people take less part than before in that sort of rallying. But the expectations to which it responded in the early days of the Revolution – the assertion of unity of the family and social cohesion through a ritual of mobilisation – now find a response in other forms of sociability, including the very neighbourhood religious gatherings just described. So there are phenomena of mobilisation and transformation on the borders between the religious and political, and movements within the urban space; in this context, much more fluid than is often supposed, religious sociability remains an area for innovation as much as permanence.

6. See especially the work of the great Islamic scholar Allameh Tabatabai, one of the first clerics to deal with such subjects as *Social Relationships in Islam* (n.d,n.p.) and *Islam and the Real Requirements of Every Age* (Tehran, Mohammadi, 1348/1969).

7. Started first in Tehran in July 1979 on the initiative of Ayatollah Mahmoud Taleghani, the official Friday prayers have preserved a symbolic period of political and religious rallying in the Islamic Republic: Y. Richard, 'Clercs et intellectuels dans la République islamique d'Iran', in G. Kepel and Y. Richard (eds.), *Intellectuels et militants de l'Islam contemporain*, Paris, Seuil, 1990, pp. 29-71.

It follows, thirdly, that politico-religious issues in the Islamic Republic are not played out solely on the national scale according to the totalitarian or authoritarian style of religious and ideological control alone. More precisely, religious sociability is differentiated in all sorts of ways: between urban and rural life, between men and women, and in Tehran between the affluent north and the densely populated south. As the Revolution has become routine, this diversified aspect of religion has been more emphasised, along with its unitary direction: *jaleseh*, and women's associations and newspapers, tend to emphasise special characteristics according to religious criteria (in relation to theological matters, for example) or political ones (relating to the main factional trends in the regime, for instance) or else social ones (the standard of education of believers, for example, and their age and social status). But there are at the same time unifying effects, coming in some way 'from below'. State control is not the only homogenising factor in Iranian society. Forms of religious practice are developing that converge towards a mingling of outward expressions, habits, ritual acts, and symbolic practices regarding clothing, food and other aspects of life.

For example, the feast of sacrifice, a traditional practice *par excellence*, is now more and more in the public space, notably through the media, and is a major event in the country's social life, if only because of the way it causes the price of sheep to rocket. It gives rise to a big public debate, now a recurring one, on what is to be done with the sacrificial meat: should it be distributed to the needy or to the neighbourhood, or go into the family freezer? It is the occasion for a host of actions which are commonplace, but shared by everyone: buying the sheep, enduring its bleating, meeting as a family, cutting the animal's throat in front of the house by the gutter, giving or receiving one's share of the meat, etc. Above all, the feast of sacrifice is the subject of plentiful discourse, a true social narrative in favour of the needy, coming from the media and from neighbourhood social interaction.

It is important to stress that in reality, the effects of differentiation and the effects of unification peculiar to religious practices merge together; in particular, one cannot distinguish the 'high' and 'low' sides of society's cultural homogenisation. The 'feast of charity and good deeds' on the eve of spring, and the feast of 'affection' at the beginning of the school year, were started by the Imam's Relief Committee to help destitute people and disinherited children respectively. They well illustrate the political authorities' concern to see open-handedness and religious giving institutionalised. But they are no less popular for that, and families are crazy about them; on the day schools reopen for the new year, the stands collecting alms are never empty.

These observations show that the politico-religious issues of the Islamic Republic not only confound too rigid categorisations between the popular, learned and political forms of religious activity, but also arise at the meeting point of the national and the local, of control and participation. Indeed they can only be understood in terms of the creation of a public space, even of a civil society. From that point of view, it is important to grasp the specific aspects of neighbourhood religious sociability, as expressed in the *jaleseh*, *hey'at* and *ta'zieh*, or to a lesser extent in mosque attendance. The *jaleseh* are summoned by women of the neighbourhood, often taking turns, and are generally attended by people of the district. It is not taken for granted that one can pass through the open door into a meeting if one has not been notified in one way or another; the information is passed around in a relatively limited circle. The *jaleseh* more often than not give their blessing to previously established networks of relationships, but they are also places where people get acquainted; a women moving into a district will come to fit in especially by going to *jaleseh*. The feminine character of these meetings strengthens their local roots, and it is revealing that the people attending them usually go to the meetings on foot. The *hey'at* operate in a comparable way, with the difference being that the believers attending them have, or have had, work activities that go beyond the bounds of the neighbourhood, notably in the guild networks; so they often arrive at the meetings by bus or car. Even so, the sociability principle of the *hey'at* remains the same, and is based on the idea of a certain intimacy or at least comradeship among their members; there, too, one does not frequent just any circle of people, and information is passed around in restricted circles.

While *jaleseh* and *hey'at* bring habitual participants together at given intervals – weekly, fortnightly or monthly – the mosque represents a more neutral space, also a public place, but one where anyone, even a passer-by, can enter without being invited and is at least in theory the equal of anyone else, and where the role of host is played by God himself. In short, you go to the mosque on your own initiative, while you generally go to a *jaleseh* or a *hey'at* when you are invited, possibly by a public notice. In addition, the Imam of the mosque does not (yet?) have the same role in society as does the parish priest, to perform ritual; there is no baptism in Islam, and neither circumcision nor marriage takes place at the mosque; only mourning ceremonies are now held within it, often out of convenience or even as a mark of distinction, but even so the funeral itself is not held there. But the mosque still forms part of the neighbourhood space (at least in districts where it is the central point). On the one hand it is the connecting link between the religious life of those districts and clerical circles, especially the 'sources of emulation' (*marâje'e taqlid*);[8] on the other hand, every day it welcomes at least some categories of inhabitants or workers from surrounding areas, such as old people or traders looking for a place to pray

8.   This title, formalised in the nineteenth century, is given to the theologians best qualified to serve as a reference and model for the faithful, especially because of their proficiency in Islamic law (*fiqh*). At different periods the community of Shia faithful has recognised as a guide of consciences one or several 'sources of emulation', who generally live in the holy cities in Iraq - Karbala and Najaf - or at Qom in Iran, but also in the major Iranian urban centres.

as well as a place to rest – not counting the real public service it offers, less and less systematically it is true, in providing running water and toilets.

In contrast, participation in the organised Friday prayers cannot, or can no longer be seen as a form of neighbourhood religious sociability. In the first period of the Revolution they were well organised at that neighbourhood level; local public benefactors did not fail to put *salavâti* (free) buses at the disposal of the faithful; in addition, organised fleets of cars helped to take people of the districts to the University of Tehran. Today, as many fewer believers are observing the ritual, as noted, this connection has been loosened and attendance at the Friday prayer ceremonies is more and more an individual act that does not involve neighbourhood sociability much. In addition, one may note that mosques do not seem to have assumed a special position for that purpose. Friday is definitely not the Lord's Day in the Islamic Republic, at least not in places of worship; people prefer to be with the family, so much so that it is not uncommon on that day for religious buildings to be quite simply closed until nightfall.

The changes and differentiation in Islam suggest that the religious sphere should be understood in three aspects: its increasingly institutionalised character, which goes with a continued process of state centralisation but also marks its boundary; rationalisation, which goes with increasing emphasis on the individuality of the believer; and its 'economic orientation', which modifies ritual and ceremonial practices.

Institutionalising the Religious Sphere

If one accepts the hypothesis that the foundation of the Islamic Republic amplified the movement towards the centralising and institutionalising of Shia Islam in Iran, it is important not to confine the analysis to the hierarchy alone. Bureaucratising of Islam is a larger phenomenon which is found at all levels of society. In a certain way, the Islam of the Republic contributes to social legitimation of state centralisation and is becoming an expression of that process itself, as we sought to demonstrate in the first chapter of this work. But above all, it contributes to the spread of the bureaucratic model in the fabric of society.

To give one example among others, religious education is more and more organised on school or university lines. It is provided in buildings that are differentiated from sacred buildings, unlike the *hozeh* and *madreseh* of earlier times, and are laid out according to Western-type arrangements (classrooms, lecture and reading rooms, tables, chairs, laboratories, etc.); it lays down precise criteria for admission, for example criteria of age, marital status, military service and level of education, and often a contractual commitment; it involves regular assessment by examination; it can be given full time, part-time or by correspondence[9] according to the pupils'

9. See for example the admissions notebook of Hoseh'elmieh Shahid Sahabadi, 1369-70 (1990-1).

preferences and means; it deals at the same time with Islamic matters, themselves more and more specialised, and extra-Islamic disciplines (foreign languages, sport, etc.). Religious education, in addition, maintains ever closer links with national education, especially through equivalence of qualifications. And it sets out to provide career possibilities outside strictly religious ones, notably in the civil service and the regime's foundations. It is also open to girls who can now follow a curriculum similar to the boys', higher levels included. A category of women taught by this system has thus achieved social recognition which is itself a factor for change in the religious sphere, and which can be expected to go on expanding, in view of their dynamism and initiatives.

In addition, the 'legitimate' (in the Islamic sense, *shar'i*) circulation of money has been very much institutionalised over the past twenty years. Collection of religious taxes continues to be bureaucratised. If one looks back to the work of Naraghi, at the beginning of the nineteenth century, one can see that this process was indispensible in regulation and centralisation in the religious sphere in a context of recurring dissidence, even before becoming an issue in relations between the clergy and the power of the state.

In theory, a Muslim is liable to two major taxes on his wealth: *khoms*,[10] which everyone must pay at the rate of one-fifth of his overall income after deduction of daily expenditure, and *zakat*, which only applies to certain sorts of income. Half of the *khoms*, called 'the Imam's share' (*sahm-e emâm* or *vojuhât*), is generally collected by the network of mosques and centralised by the 'sources of emulation' (*marâje'e taqlid*), the leading dignitaries in the religious hierarchy. It is meant to pay for the material support of the clergy. For the rest, the believer can hand over the amount due to a clergyman or a devout person of his choice, or manage it himself for charitable purposes. This ideal arrangement is effective only in relation to the actual organisation of the clergy, and this has continually changed from one historical period to another.[11] It is known, for example, that the hierarchical organisation of the clergy, especially the institution of the 'sources of emulation', is a consequence of the predominance of the *Osuli* theological school over the *Akhbari* school, and goes back only to the nineteenth century. In addition, the consecration of the holy city of Qom as one of the principal places of Shia religious power only occurred just after the Second World War, in particular following the occupation of Karbala and Najaf by the British. It illustrates the emergence of a new concept of the clergy, its role, its teachings and its prerogatives in relation to the traditional model represented by the Najaf authorities.

Under the successive leaderships of Ayatollah Haeri (died 1935) and Ayatollah Borujerdi (died 1961), Iranian Shiism continued to follow a

---

10. H.A. Naraghi, *Hodud-e velâyat-e Hâkem-e eslâm*, Tehran, Ministry of Culture and Islamic Guidance, 1365 (1986).
11. Y. Richard, *L'islam chiite, croyance et idéologie*, Paris, Fayard, 1991.

modernising and bureaucratic institutionalising process. But Borujerdi's death altered the religious scene again; none of the 'sources of emulation' could immediately claim primacy, and theological authority was divided among a number of eminent figures such as Golpayegâni, Khomeyni, Shariatmadari, Khoi and Qomi. After 1979 most of the 'sources of emulation' distanced themselves from the Islamic Republic, some of them even entering into conflict with the regime. At the same time, the middle ranks of the clergy, who saw their influence increasing with the founding of the new regime, formalised their status. It was at this time that the titles of *hojjatoleslam* ('proof of Islam'), *ayatollah* ('sign of God') and *ayatollah ozmâ* ('supreme sign of God') were popularised to designate, if only in an arbitrary way, a duly constituted hierarchy, which had never been the rule in religious life; they became elements of social distinction both among the clergy and among the faithful.

At all events the increasing bureaucratic differentiation in the religious domain, the deaths of the major sources of emulation, the regime's need to retain its monopoly of Islamic legitimacy, its 'open-handedness mania' and '*shorâ*-mania', its trend towards managing innumerable charitable activities and mosques through foundations and associations – all these changes have brought in a new phase in the rationalising of religious taxation. The gifts of the faithful needed to be developed and at the same time to be centralised in the interests of the authorities. Thus the state gradually tried to take over control of the clergy's financial resources. A central *khoms* fund, Sandoq-e Akhmas, was set up, to channel the contributions of the faithful. Similarly a central alms fund, Sandoq-e Kheyrât va Sadaqât, seeks to provide a new channel, through collection boxes on the public highway and in government offices, for charitable donations formerly made to help works by the mosques or handed to devout people of the neighbourhood to use. However, the bureaucratising of 'legitimate' circulation of money goes beyond the bounds of state control. The network of interest-free loan funds, which as we have seen is giving popular savings or even popular speculation something of a 'banking orientation', is the fruit of individual or social initiatives that have escaped from the central authorities' power while often enjoying state support.

With these changes, the religious domain has undergone continual differentiation, both institutionally and structurally, into a multitude of specialised organisations whose remits are more or less precisely defined and – a bureaucratic inevitability! – often overlap. At the national level, the Ministry of Culture and Islamic Guidance, the Ministry of Education, the Islamic Propaganda Organisation and the Qom Islamic Propaganda can coexist to ensure the Islamic direction of society. In a more fragmented fashion, the Mosques Management Centre, the Society of Preachers, the Friday Prayers Front, the Friday Prayers Imams Council, the Prayer Revival Front, the Koran Apprenticeship Centre, the Front for Ordering Good and

Banishing Evil, and other Central Councils for religious gatherings compete with each other in publications, seminars, collections, motions, congratulations and condolences, which have at least the merit of testifying to their existence and justifying the funds they receive. Obviously this overflowing of institutions is directly connected with the factional struggle which is the driving force of the regime, although it is not possible to establish a congruence between the chart of religious organisations and that of political tendencies; by definition, the alliances and loyalties are fluid and changeable.

This extreme fluidity shows us that bureaucratising of the religious domain can be both a factor for state centralisation and a brake on that process. On the one hand, every one of those institutions is flanked by a representative of the Leader of the Revolution: it relays the regime's ideology, it establishes control over the clergy who were originally rather reticent towards the government, it contributes to covering Iranian society with 'a network of complicated, minute and uniform petty rules' (as Tocqueville put it). On the other hand, each of them adds to the disorder in a very fragmented political landscape, helps to paralyse central government action, favours some waste in the allocation of resources, and can even become a focus of autonomous power – archetypal examples being the Âstân-e Qods at Mashhad, the Organisation of the Sacred Threshold which runs the Imam Reza shrine, the Shahzadeh Abdolazim shrine at Rey and the Imam Khomeyni mausoleum in the south of Tehran.

This double movement of bureaucratisation and structural differentiation in the religious field plays a part in the – still very uncertain – development of civil society, just as much as it shows the power of an authoritarian regime's ideology. Of course the regime has sought to impose its Islamic code and its prerogatives with its well known methods. But it is far from being able to control the dynamics of a country in the midst of demographic growth, reconstruction, and a change of identity, stimulated by trade liberalisation and changes in the regional environment. The complex relationship between state and society is largely mediated through Islam, that is, through Islamic institutions, practices, intellectuals, financial resources, etc. For example, one aspect of the proliferation of Islamic organisations is the flourishing of publishing companies, magazines, encyclopaedias and audiovisual centres which deal with religious questions, not usually at the instigation of the clergy but rather in response to lay intellectuals, and which are opening a public space for rationalising, reflection and debate.[12] This change needs to be placed in the context of the wider spread of literacy, urbanisation, and above all the rise of a middle class which the Shah's regime created through oil income while keeping it politically impotent, but which eventually ensured its hegemony through the Revolution in spite of the economic crisis.

12. Daftar tabliqât-e eslâmi-ye howzeh-yeh 'elmiyeh qom, *Râhnamâ-ye farhangi-tahqiqâti-ye shahrestân-e qom*, Qom, published by the author, 1372 (1993).

The terms of the debate surrounding the elevation of Ali Khamenei, the Leader of the Revolution, to the rank of 'source of emulation' in the autumn of 1994-95, after the death of Ayatollah Araki, are a good illustration of the emergence of such a public space through institutionalising of religious society. It was unprecedented in the history of Shia Islam for an appointment of that sort to be accompanied by such a media campaign, both within Iran and abroad. Traditionally it had been an internal affair of clerical circles; the public was interested only in the death of a 'source of emulation'; then the believer, left on his own by fate, learned in entirely informal ways, through the intermediary agency of mosques and religious meetings that he attended, of the names of people who might succeed the dead man. It was up to him to choose in his mind his preferred new 'source of emulation', according to his own religious principles but also, perhaps especially, the preferences of his professional, ethnic or political circles. It was very different in 1994. The press took up the question for several weeks, and Ayatollah Jannati went so far as to exclaim strongly, during Friday prayers, 'the choice of the *aslah* [the most suitable – see below] belongs to the people'![13] The process was not however entirely public; discussions among the clergy remained confidential, and when Ayatollah Behjat recited the prayer for the dead over the tomb of Ayatollah Araki – traditionally an explicit sign of eminence and suitability to succeed the deceased as a *marja'* – the media said nothing or almost nothing about it, even though his elevation had probably been desired by the deceased dignitary. In addition, a large portion of opinion lost interest in the matter because, in fact, the *marja'iyat* is conferred according to criteria that concern only a limited number of clerics.

But the debate echoed by the media indicated a fundamental swing in the organisation of society. The episode was very far from increasing the power of the Leader of the Revolution over the political system by his elevation in the religious hierarchy, or the absorption of the sacred domain by the political, as some thought at the time; rather, it revealed the increasing dissociation of the state from the religious sphere. A number of Iranians could even have been surprised by the announcement of Ali Khamenei's promotion to the rank of *marja'*, having thought this was more or less automatic since he had succeeded Imam Khomeyni as Leader of the Revolution. The retrospective realisation that one could be the one without being the other was in fact the start of a parting of the ways between the political and religious spheres, even though one of the justifications given for legitimising Ali Khamenei's elevation was precisely the need to avoid a separation between the two.

Paradoxically, the criteria put forward by the different sides in the public debate contributed to the differentiation precisely because they went beyond strictly religious considerations and emphasised the supposed political abilities of the candidates. Thus it was said that 'preserving Islam must

13. *Keyhan*, 12.9.1373 (1994).

override preserving its commandments'; 'Islam is not just the *fiqh*'; and 'two thirds of the *fiqh* deal with political and social matters.' In other words, the debate recognised at the same time the autonomy of the political in relation to the religious and that of the religious in relation to the political, a double differentiation to which Imam Khomeyni was attached, whatever anyone has said. In addition, one issue at stake in the elevation of the Leader as a 'source of emulation' was related to the balance of power within the Republic. The aim was certainly to mark the permanence of the religious dimension both as a principle of legitimacy and as a diplomatic source of strength, but it was also to define the Leader's area of competence in relation to that of the President: one to embody the principle of religious legitimacy, the other to take charge of 'reconstruction' and conduct of public affairs, with relations of necessary complementarity between the two, rather than rivalry. The eloquent silence of Hashemi Rafsanjani, his advisers and his ministers throughout these debates was revealing about this division of roles. Briefly, while there had never been so much talk of giving a sacred dimension to politics in Iran, never had there been, either, such efforts to distinguish the two spheres of religion and politics.

The ambiguity of the statement by Ayatollah Rasti Kashani, a member of the Council of Guidance, about the designation of Ayatollah Khamenei as *marja'* well illustrated this phenomenon of autonomy for the two spheres: 'For all questions relating to state order, it is right to follow the opinion of the *velâyat-e faqih* [of the Leader of the Revolution]. For every individual question, two situations are possible. Either there is no basic disagreement between the *marâje'*, and the individual is then free to follow the source of emulation of his choice. Or there is such a disagreement, and then one must submit to the opinion of the *aslah*. If the *aslah* has not been chosen, the believer adopts the opinion of his choice according to conscience, and obviously the Leader is then the first source of emulation to whom one should turn.'[14] It would be premature to assume that this movement towards autonomy for the political sphere is certain to go all the way, or that this is a proto-democratic trend; it is equally possible to see in such developments either the emergence of issues of a liberal type, or the determination of the clergy to keep a monopoly over management of individual lives in the face of a government with claims to hegemony. At the very least the debate remains open for many years to come.

The way in which Ali Khamenei attained the status of *marja'* is far from having given him absolute supremacy over one or the other of the two spheres, or consecrating him as *aslah*. A distinction needs to be made between the function of *marja'* and the qualities of *aslah* (the most suitable) and *a'lam* (the wisest) attributed to the most eminent person among the *marâje'*. Recognition of these titles is as informal and as little institutionalised as that of the *marja'* status, and similarly comes from the

14. *Keyhan*, 19.9.1373 (1994).

common knowledge of the believers and clergy. Even so, the difference among these attributes is important. While the *aslah* does not have a legitimacy allowing him to question the positions of the other *marâje'*, he has a larger number of disciples around him and a greater following as a 'source of emulation'. It is to him that people quite naturally turn in cases of disagreement among the *marâje'* on some given question or another. This diffused primacy, characteristic of Iranian society's ways of organisation, allowed Imam Khomeyni to act as a referee and handle certain disputed matters arising from the novelty of the post-revolutionary situation. For the moment, Ali Khamenei has acquired only the position of *marja'*, and if the Iranian press is to be believed, nobody seems to have talked of his designation as *aslah*. It is possible that the Leader of the Revolution may in the end rise to that position, but it is not absolutely certain.

Ali Khamenei was not the only one to be elevated to the rank of *marja'*. His name appeared alongside those of six other clerics who were at the same moment considered by the Society of Lecturers at the Islamic School at Qom to be fit to hold that position. While seven names thus filled the headlines of the Iranian press, one did not need to be a leading clergyman to see that they did not have unanimous backing among the various religious authorities. For example, the Society of Fighting Clergy only recognised the fitness of three of them, and made it known in an entirely independent way before the Society of Lecturers at the Qom Theological College published its own list.[15] In fact, among the seven names, only that of Ali Khamenei apparently aroused general approval. The six others elevated to the status of *marja'* had as their common denominator the fact of having rejected all political commitment since 1979; their appointment thus confirmed the breaking of ties between the two spheres. It could even be said that the issue of the structures of Iran's political and religious societies went together with a geopolitical dimension which reinforced the effects of differentiation: the Iranian regime aimed to take over the leadership of the community of Shia believers all over the world. The two holy cities of Karbala and Najaf in Iraq seemed to support the candidacy of Ayatollah Sistani, like Ayatollah Fadlallah in Lebanon. It was in connection with this foreign policy objective that Ali Khamenei finally accepted the dignity of *marja'* in relation to the Shia Muslim community abroad, after having given the appearance, like a good *javânmard*, of considering his nomination premature – a subtle way, not without some mysticism which he is known to have, to acknowledge the irreducible sacredness of the religious sphere, but also an elegant way of not rushing ahead too much, so as to mollify opponents irritated by his irresistible rise since Imam Khomeyni's death.

In any case, today people rarely speak of the Leader of the Revolution as *marja'*, although he is obviously very present on the political scene. His

15. It is to be noted that the religious sphere on this occasion used the list system for voting: *Keyhan*, 10.9 and 12.9.1373 (1994).

thesis (*resâleh*) seems less widely circulated than those of – for example – Ayatollah Montazeri and Ayatollah Sanei, and in January 1997 it was a certain Ayatollah Nuri-Hamadani who laid down the conditions in which travellers were bound to respect, or could be dispensed from, the Ramadan fast, an important subject at this time of globalisation and international dealings! Significantly, the personality who seems to be exerting undeniable ascendancy over the religious scene is the very one who was deprived of the succession to Imam Khomeyni in March 1989, who lives under virtual house arrest in Qom, whose declarations often cause scandal and earn him the wrath of the security services, but whose teachings are followed on a massive scale: Ayatollah Mohammad-Ali Montazeri. One of the leaders of the populist Left, Dr. Ghaffari, could say at a Round Table on the theme 'Religion and Freedom' at the University of Tehran, in the autumn of 1996, that he followed Ayatollah Montazeri as a 'source of emulation' while feeling glad that he had been excluded from power; and he was supported in this by Ayatollah Hojjati Kermani, close to the conservative Right tendency or rather, perhaps, to the Foreign Ministry. More generally, a Muslim naturally remains master of the choice of his 'source of emulation'; that choice may not take account of his political or social views, and he may also continue to prefer a deceased dignitary, such as Imam Khomeyni.

Rationalising and Individualising Processes in Islam

Bureaucratisation of the religious domain, in so far as it is a dimension of rationalisation (to follow Max Weber), goes together with an individualising process. Religious socialisation combines these various aspects. Girls are initiated into prayer at the age of nine (while boys are only bound to religious duties after the age of 15). Since the early 1990s, television has been broadcasing the ceremonies marking this initiation, the 'feast of duty' (or 'feast of devotion'), which, it must be emphasised, is of a sort completely unknown hitherto in Iranian society. The girls, in white veils, recite for the first time, all together and in public, the prayer that they have been learning during the school years; they are fêted, and crowns of flowers are given to each of them, together with gifts and a Koran. This ritual, which has parallels with First Communion in the Catholic Church, is a mark of social recognition and the value accorded to the child, who is celebrated as a true individual; it gives blessing to the autonomy of the believer in relation to the family, autonomy that has been instilled by teaching. This new form of religious socialisation shows that the bureaucratising of Islam both limits the area of intervention by the family, leads to a certain degree of homogeneity in rituals celebrated and broadcast by television, and in that context favours individualising from the youngest age.

Today Islam is a matter of reason as well as faith. This was already clear before in the writings of people like Motahhari. But since the Revolution, the wide spread of the regime's ideological discourse, especially through the

Friday prayer ceremonies, and the conquest of the media by religion have reinforced this rationalisation of the Islamic message. For example, Ali Khamenei, at the first Friday prayer ceremony in Ramadan in January 1997, suggested that the prayer of contrition had two dimensions: it had a spiritual aspect, but it was also socially useful, in that it helped restore balance and dignity for the sinner.[16] Believers themselves, in an increasingly systematic way, use logical arguments, which claim to be scientifically based, to justify their practices. Thus polygamy is considered harmful in the light of the teachings of Western psychology; a woman who is a victim of polygamy has every chance of being a bad mother and not being able to perform her role in society well. If only because times are hard and pennies have to be counted, the Martyrs' Foundation and the Foundation for the Disinherited back up this line of thinking by recognising the rights of one wife only in awarding their social benefits.

This rationalisation of religion, and its relation to the process of individualisation among believers, are greatly helped by the development of the media in public space which we mentioned earlier. For example, religious meetings are readily called with the aid of neon signs, or small posters produced by computer, or banners laid over the public highway, or small-ads and display advertisements in the daily press. The radio also carries advertisements of them. The names of participants who are to provide the religious stimulation for the meeting are clearly mentioned, and where necessary it is explained that there will be *porsesh-o pâsokh*, questions and answers. In other words, religious meetings are now an individualised space where reaction is expected, whereas before one went above all to listen. Thus they are the object of choice on the part of the believer, who will prefer one speaker to another or one sort of sociability to another.

It must be explained that this change concerns also the *jaleseh*, subjected to the same rules of publicity and rivalry. Without repeating our earlier analyses,[17] we can recall that the religious field – not necessarily the running of the Republic's legal and religious affairs – has given women numerous opportunities for access to the urban public space in an entirely legitimate social, even political way. At present, many of them manage Islamic institutions or associations, especially in the charity field, and they play a full part in the structural differentiation of the religious field mentioned earlier. This does not mean that women's emancipation passes necessarily through Islam in Iran; after all, some women prefer to open body building halls (it is true that running them is in perfect conformity with the Islamic morality favoured by the regime, and is legitimised by segregation of the sexes). But in a given historical society, religion can be a decisive area for individualisation. It might be interesting in this respect to compare Iran with

16. *Keyhan*, 29.11.1375 (1997).
17. F. Adelkhah, *La Révolution sous le voile. Femmes islamiques d'Iran*, Paris, Karthala, 1991.

Victorian England; it has been said that women's charitable works paved the way for the birth of the militant feminism of the Suffragettes, in a context of urbanisation, industrialisation and the development of the mass popular press.[18] The institutionalising of the 'feast of duty' has given rise to a lively debate, especially in the pages of the quarterly magazine *Farzaneh*, inspired by 'Islamic feminists'[19] who find no trace of such age discrimination between girls and boys in the Koran and fear the psychological and educational consequences, the Ramadan fast being hardly favourable to preparation for examinations.[20]

Similarly, people's relationship with death has been profoundly altered in the last few decades, and again it can be seen that the media have had much to do with it. During the war with Iraq, the memory of martyrs fallen on the field of honour was glorified in the press and on television; their life stories were published, their next of kin interviewed. In this context funeral ceremonies were modified. To the extent that they were often taken over by state or parastatal institutions, they tended to become bureaucratised; they borrowed from the dramatic organisation of Âshurâ processions; they began to give rise to advertising, through death notices with black borders; there was feasting surrounding them; they were organised around representation of the deceased person, whose portrait was painted on large cloths coated with plastic, while his photograph was reproduced on the death notices and placed on the tomb at the same time as some of his personal objects or letters. By this new ritualisation, the dead person is no longer absent from the living as he was before; he remains among them as a hero.[21]

Most of these innovations continued after the war. This is partly because the cult of the martyrs has continued to be celebrated and has become a not insignificant source of advantages, even of social privileges, even though the bitter feeling about useless deaths is now predominant. It also continues because funeral ceremonies as a whole are based on the model established in the 1980s: the portrait of the dead person can be carved on the tombstone and the custom of a procession has revived; in addition, the final resting place is abundantly covered with flowers or trees and regularly visited, and deaths are announced publicly through posters, personal announcements or notices in the newspapers.

One noteworthy fact is that women are not the last to 'benefit' by this change. Even in the 1970s it was not usual to call them publicly by their first names, and when they died, any condolences that may have been expressed – for it was not such a usual custom then – were addressed to the family

18. L.A. Tilly, 'Industrialisation and Gender Inequality', in M. Adas (ed.), *Islamic and European Expansion. The Forging of a Global Order*, Philadelphia, Temple University Press, 1993, p. 253.
19. A. Kian, 'Des femmes iraniennes contre le clergé. Islamistes et laïques pour la première fois unies', *Le Monde diplomatique*, November 1996, p. 8.
20. *Farzaneh*, 5, 1373-74/1995.
21. F. Khosrokhavar, *L'islamisme et la mort*, Paris, L'Harmattan, 1995.

without the dead woman's name being specified. Imam Khomeyni's behaviour was a departure from the norm because the names of his two daughters and his wife were known. His wife in fact gave an interview after his death, readily recalling some epiodes in their private life, such as his proposal of marriage and the criteria for her consent.[22] Similarly, his son Ahmad spoke in his will, published in the press, of his wife *'Fati azizam'* ('my dear Fati'), preferring to use this intimate abbreviation rather than the full first name Fatemeh.[23] On the other hand, Ali Khamenei's family remains in the background, and even someone like Hashemi Rafsanjani, who readily travels with his wife and whose daughters have shown themselves very active on the public stage, prefers to speak of 'Our family' to describe his other half: 'our family threw itself on me [to protect me]', he said after the first attempt on his life shortly after the Revolution. But such behaviour, which may seem more suitable in some circles, is increasingly out of place. In everyday life, politics included, women's first names are known and used. A *fortiori*, wives and daughters sign condolences with others or alone, in the Western manner, giving their respective forenames in the same way as men; they no longer hide behind the formula 'the X family shares the grief of the Y family.' Messages of condolence are sent to them, when it is not they themselves who take the initiative in announcing the death of a husband or another near relation.

In the obituary columns or on the graves, the portraits of dead women can be reproduced just like those of deceased men; whether one likes it or not, this public portrayal of the death of women was only made possible by the wearing of the veil, which altered the bounds both of decency and of what is permitted in the religious sense. Hashemi Rafsanjani himself, who as we have seen was so traditional in his attitude towards his wife, allowed photographs of his mother to be published after she died in late 1995, and the funeral took place beneath a giant poster of the old lady, while television cameras broadcasted the President's emotion.al reaction It was a remarkable scene, in that the publicity given to the private grief of the public man contributed to the creation of the national space; for the first time there was an official funeral of a woman, really quite an ordinary one, with whom everyone could identify. It was only a few months earlier that the press had spoken of a visit by Hashemi Rafsanjani to his mother at her village in Kerman province; the public had then learned of the modest conditions in which she lived, and the President had derived great popularity from the simplicity of this episode.

Thus death plays a part – rather late, it is true – in the individualising of the deceased person; but also, we should not doubt, in that of living people. For example, the funeral oration, at the moment of lowering into the tomb, expresses both the virtues of the dead person and the suffering of the

22. *Ettela'at*, 12.3.1373 (1994).
23. *Keyhan*, 9.1.1373 (1994).

survivors who are named one by one, often by their first names, with stress
laid as required on the shocked state of the wife or the husband, and the jobs
or titles of near relations recalled – a discreet mark of respect for the quality
of the dead person or the status of the family. It is thus not surprising that
death costs more and more and is becoming a permanent preoccupation. The
concern is to raise in good time the necessary amount to pay for a funeral
fitting one's status, and especially to acquire a plot, whose price is continually
going up. Through speculation in cemeteries, preparation by a restaurant or a
caterer of the funeral meal, the sums charged for funeral services, the
publication of notices in the newspapers and the printing of announcements
of the event, death is now part of that 'commercialised' world to which the
middle classes belong and more and more Iranians want to belong.

Death is a space for individualisation and social distinction and also, by
that means, for rationalisation and bureaucratisation. The dynamic Mayor of
Tehran lost no time in taking charge of the destiny of Behesht-e Zahra, the
'Paradise of Zahra' (Zahra was a daughter of the Prophet), a 400-hectare
cemetery in the south of Tehran, next to the Imam Khomeyni mausoleum,
the place where the Imam went on his return from exile and where many
martyrs of the Revolution and the war lie. The cemetery mortuary plans to
centralise all the deceased of the capital for registration, even if it means
providing families with the means to transfer them to the provinces if they
so wish. The stress is on public health (the dead person is carried in an
ambulance and hospitals are most often against returning the body to the
home for the funeral wake, the body is washed by professionals and the
family is kept back behind a glass partition); on precision (the cemetery
office is able with computer aid to give information rapidly on the location
of tombs, and statistics on cause of death are published); and on speed, the
administration taking pride in not needing more than twenty minutes to carry
out registration formalities, to sell a plot outright or lease it for thirty years,
to supply funeral services at a price – such as the hiring of a speechmaker
(*maddâh*) plus public address system or a reception hall, or the provision of
flowers, mourning clothes or a tombstone, or printing of posters and
publication of a notice in the daily press.[24] The municipality's rage for
rationalising and for public health has gone as far as considering mechanised
washing of corpses, a plan that has until now come up against theological
obstacles and could only be authorised by a *fatwa*. But already a visit to
Behesht-e Zahra tells a good deal, with its appearance as an ideal city, its
straight avenues, its flower beds, its fountains, its numbered squares, its lines
of tombs already dug in accordance with Muslim tradition and waiting for
bodies, and often tragi-comic scenes.

Rationalisation often means innovation. Two-storey tombs have been
possible since 1983, shrouds are sewn in ways contrary to traditional rules,

24. Mo'âvenat-e khadamât-e shahri, 'Tarhâ-ye khadamâti, projehâ-ye 'omrani va zist-mohiti-
ye sâzemân-e beheshet-e zahrâ', *Ketâb-e sâl-e hamshahri*, 2, 1373/1994, pp. 858-61.

believers are encouraged to donate their organs by filling up and signing a consent form in their lifetime, distances between tombs have been reduced to allow 1,200 instead of 1,000 to enter into a square plot – most of these changes being given legitimacy by an array of *fatwa*s, revealing the aim of ridding the faith of practices with no religious, rational or scientific basis.

But rationalisation often means inequality. The space in Behesht-e Zahra is very differentiated socially between the more tree-filled square plots and the leased graves which are generally much less well maintained; family vaults are, as in Europe, a sign of wealth, while some parts reserved to martyrs and artists symbolise political or cultural distinction.[25] This partly explains why the bureaucratising and individualising process regarding death is not without conflicts. For example, the administration of Behesht-e Zahra, always in favour of contracting out its activities to private enterprise – for the sake of efficiency and profitability, in line with the state's economic liberalisation policy – has only been able to privatise washing of the dead, which caused it many problems because of the storm which that scheme aroused in the press.

Last but not least, the development and improvement of cemeteries has become an area of intense conflict in town planning, extending the field of property conflicts which divide Iran's modern cities all the way to the grave. For example, at Isfahan the University, concerned to acquire a former Christian cemetery for its extension scheme, encountered resistance not only from the important Armenian community, which assures everyone that Shah Abbas gave it the land in perpetuity and wants to build houses there, but also from a municipal department always eager to widen its field of intervention by creating a new amusement park. The quarrel was (temporarily?) suspended when a researcher suggested classifying the historical site as a symbol of the city's specific past and its acceptance of foreigners.[26]

In Tehran the Emâmzâdeh Abdollah cemetery, on the road to Rey, is the object of comparable conflicts. A ban on selling new plots there, issued before the Revolution, led to real speculation and large-scale fraud relating to ownership deeds for the tombs, as that necropolis was highly rated among well-to-do families because of its location and charm. To stop that racket monopolised by some middlemen – the famous *dallâl* so despised by the Mayor – the municipality eventually prohibited all new burials there. The rumour then spread that it was planning, there too, to turn the cemetery into a park, to the great anxiety of owners of plots. The Mayor's office defended its good intentions, assuring everyone that it only wanted to improve the site and put an end to speculation. But, once again, its forceful methods led to

25. In 1995 a grave could be let for 10,000 tou-ans or bought for a sum ranging from 30,000 to 200,000 toumans. A family vault cost around 3 million toumans (a touman, equal to ten rials, is equivalent to about one eighth of a British penny).
26. The cemetery contains the graves of the first Westerners, some of them famous, who went to work for the Safavids.

dispute: 800 owners of tombs certified that, contrary to the administration's statements, they had never given their consent for the tombs to be demolished, and demanded that they should henceforth be involved in the improvement plan for Emâmzâdeh Abdollah. Thus, management of death became an opportunity for displaying civic expectations of participation.[27] Similarly speculation around the last resting places of Behesht-e Zahra led the authorities to issue strict regulations on their possession and use; only holders of the deeds or their family members could be buried there, any further alienation now being banned, so as to dissuade middlemen who were buying up whole square plots to sell the tombs there at a high price – in a sense, according to the customary phrase, to 'cut off their hands'.

What can now be clearly seen is that the process of individualising, bureaucratising and rationalising the most universal act of all, the act of dying – an act that is almost universally experienced in religious terms in Iran – is a factor contributing to the creation of a public space. We have already noted numerous indications of this. But the point deserves to be explained once more. We must emphasise first the investment – emotional, as well as social and economic – which almost all Iranians place in death. Every Thursday afternoon, the time set aside for commemoration of the dead, and every Friday, the day of rest, families flock to the tombs of their kin, the ritual being prepared at home or in the neighbourhood, especially through preparation or purchase of dishes and fruit which are distributed to the neighbourhood and passers-by for the repose of the souls of the dead. This form of religious sociability fits clearly into the public space. One consequence is the serious traffic jams on the motorway from Tehran to Qom. To this must be added the specific commemorations of the third, seventh and fortieth days and the first anniversary of death, as well as the various festivals, including Noruz; each of these occasions is an excuse for distribution of food and receiving guests, some of the halls at Behesht-e Zahra being able to accommodate up to 5,000 guests.

This funeral sociability is not at all unrelated to other dimensions of life, just as *jaleseh* are not exclusively religious meetings. Young people exchange glances there and potential mothers-in-law weave match-making schemes; as for the singers (*maddâh*) who chant the virtues of the deceased, and whose talent is measured by the flow of tears that they draw from the audience, it is they also who liven up weddings, they may even strike a deal for that by the side of a tomb. These various practices, by their intensity, give rise to an ever greater concentration of pronouncements by the authorities. Thus the Behesht-e Zahra administration is planning to distribute freely or at low prices publications describing precisely and rationally the various stages of committal to the ground, in the hope, so it says, of comforting the families, reconciling them as far as is possible with the idea of death, and disarming any possible conflicts with people they have to deal with in the

27. *Akhbar*, 15.1.1375 (1996).

future. It even wants to encourage publication of academic works. The act of dying, more and more, involves writing, going beyond registration and statistics to scientific knowledge. It is also coming to depend on images, since an increasing number of ceremonies are photographed and filmed on video, like marriages and 'feasts of duty'.

This creation of public space through practices relating to death also involves the world of companies (*sherkat*), which, as we have seen, are taking charge of funeral ceremonies on an increasing scale in accordance with the general trend in society, but which also sponsor the funerals of employees, martyrs and the dispossessed in a spirit of open-handedness. Lastly, public management of death brings together in an obvious fashion two basic processes of creation of a public space: the establishment of municipal parks and sporting events. The Behesht-e Zahra administration has in its cemetery the biggest green open space in the capital, and commemorations of the death of Imam Khomeyni include athletics, cycling, and even football contests.

Enough has been said to show that a dying man is more and more frequently an *âdam-e ejtemâ'i*, a social being. It is also revealing that messages of condolence published in the press are more and more signed by business concerns, as membership of the world of *sherkat*, not only of that of the guilds, is now the real sign of social recognition. In the same way open-handedness in the funeral domain is more and more often the expression of rationalised giving: rather than offering a meal to the next of kin at ceremonies commemorating a death, people prefer – and this is conveyed through the press – to pay a sum of money to a charitable institution, a mosque or a family in need to help it arrange a dowry or obtain treatment for a child.

Towards Money Orientation in the Religious Field

In a certain way, then, this public Islamic space produced by religious practice takes the form of a 'bourgeois civil society' merging on a large scale with the processes of commercialisation, privatisation and building of a middle class whose way of life is tending to acquire hegemony on the national scale. This interaction affects the whole body of a believer's daily religious practice. The mosque lists fees for its services, from funerals and commemorations to the rite on return from pilgrimage or the rite for breaking of the fast during Ramadan, in accordance with the preferences of the faithful, who are brought more and more to define themselves as customers: for how long do they want to participation by the Imam? What is the Imam's rank and prestige? Do they want tea, cakes, fruit, a meal? Is a reading from the Koran being ordered? For how many hours has the room been hired? Is it planned to invite people of both sexes, which would mean using two rooms? A mosque in the Piruzi district, in the west of Tehran, gave the following bill for a funeral service in June 1996: it listed in the right column the services for which there was a charge (250,000 rials for the preacher, *vâ'ez*; 20,000 for the reciter of the Koran, *qâri*; 7,000 for the waiter serving tea; 7,000 again for distribution of prayer books; 5,000 for the attendant looking after shoes; 60,000 as a 'gift' for the mosque; a total of 124,000 rials); in the left column there was an exhaustive list of services offered free: the space (*sic*), carpets, the prayer books themselves, the ritual cloth called *shâl* which symbolises the presence of the deceased, electricity, water, heating or fan and air conditioning, the samovar, tea glasses and their saucers, the teapot, the tray, water glasses, ashtrays, rose water censers, public address system.

As a logical expression of this process, traditional *hoseynieh* and *zeynabieh*[28] are proliferating, and changing in a certain way into 'multi-purpose halls': they are hired out for mourning ceremonies or returning pilgrim ceremonies, but also for guild or *bassij* meetings and cultural activities; they can even be available to candidates at elections and their supporters, or be used as hostels for delegations coming from other cities, all the more so as they often have an ethnic-regional (*qawmi-mahalli*) connotation and have something of the function of clubs for 'sons of the soil'. It goes without saying that the public benefactors who own the *hoseynieh* and *zeynabieh* alone or in partnership call for contributions from people using them. Those centres of sociability are involved in some respects in a 'privatisation', in the economic sense, of the religious field – people speak, for example, of the Leader of the Revolution's *hoseynieh* – and this development has not failed to arouse the concern of some clerics, following the example of Ayatollah Mahdavi Kani who has criticised the proliferation of such centres inasmuch as they risk 'emptying the mosques'.[29]

The religious sphere is more and more money-oriented. In a case of manslaughter the 'blood price' laid down in *fiqh* can be commuted for staggering sums of money; in 1992 the amount rose from 700,000 to 7 million toumans, payable to the family of the deceased through the agency of the court, and it seems to be to some extent indexed on inflation, at the same time as being fixed at the national level – while there has also been public debate on the very concept of *dieh*. Similarly, the Leader of the Revolution estimated in 1995 that the *fetriyeh*, a religious tax corresponding to three kilos of wheat and now paid by the faithful at mosques at the end of Ramadan, would go up to 120 toumans, that being an intermediate price between the free market price and the state-subsidised flour price. He has issued a *fatwa* to authorise the Welfare Organisation, a charitable body of the old regime which has just been rehabilitated, to collect gifts equivalent to the purchase of a sheep during the Feast of Sacrifice, so as to contribute to the

28. Places of worship dedicated, respectively, to Imam Hussein and Hazrat-e Zaynab, the children of Imam Ali.
29. *Resalat*, 12.3.1373 (1994).

financing of social work to help the deprived. As for the operators in the religious domain – such as the Koran reciters (*qâri*), male and female choirs (*tavâshih*), and the authors of a new literary genre called 'mosque literature' (*adabiyât-e masjed*) and consisting of stories and poems – they are frequently invited to take part in contests, called in plain language 'competitions' (*mosâbeqeh*, the word used for sporting contests), which systematically involve prizes, sometimes in gold pieces (but not cash).

The money orientation of religious practice assumes that it is being progressively subjected to what Max Weber called 'capital accounting', on the part of the political and religious leaders and also of the ordinary believer. Iranians have seen the Leader of the Revolution issuing a *fatwa*, on the basis of expert scientific advice, to allow consumption of a certain sort of fish which has been shown under the microscope to have scales, explaining that this particular species lives particularly in the waters of the Persian Gulf and the Gulf of Oman:[30] a firm encouragement to the national fishing industry and a protectionist measure in a good devotional disguise!

As for social differentiation among the tombs in the cemeteries, it follows a classic process of attribution of value. The rise and fall in prices of plots is influenced by strictly cultural or political criteria, such as the proximity of tombs of martyrs or saints, as well as apparently more objective criteria such as convenience of access and the 'fertility' of the square cemetery plot, a guarantee of tidiness and absence of dust and mud; pure and simple speculation also comes in. It is according to these elements that families choose their graves, from the moment that dead people are no longer buried in the order in which they arrive, but rather in accordance with an economic and business transaction: the calculated purchase of a plot from the administration of the cemetery.

To give a final example: a Muslim who in a dream saw his deceased father held up at a border and showing his empty suitcase was advised by the Imam whom he consulted to have prayers recited for a year for the tidy sum of 60,000 toumans, to allow the dead man to enter Paradise. He made a twofold economic response to this advice. On the one hand, he went to a reciter who charged him less for his prayers than the person recommended by the Imam; on the other hand, he took care not to tell his dreams to men of religion any more when his father appeared in them!

This story, which is true, has the advantage of reminding us that the process of creation of a religious public space, widely broadcast by the modern media, is nothing like a linear transformation. It is incomprehensible unless it is related continually to concrete practices by people acting in given situations, and the contexts in which it is revealed. In particular, however much the idea of a public space may be indissociable from the national idea, it is nonetheless embodied first of all in neighbourhood practices.

---

30. *Keyhan*, 25.11 and 27.11.1373 (1995).

One last look at religious sociability will confirm this. Without resuming the description of the *jaleseh,* two aspects of them deserve special attention. First, these meetings channel considerable amounts of money: the 'ladies' collect alms and religious taxes which women frequenting their groups spontaneously give them. They can also appeal, quite legitimately, to the generosity of the faithful, whether for making up the dowry for a needy girl, for helping a family struck by illness, or for contributing to the building of a mosque. These giving practices are an integral part of the *jaleseh;* it is impossible to imagine one without the other. There are precautions surrounding the circulation of alms; they are slipped into plastic bags which clearly specify their destination, the believer being thus assured that her religious intention will be carried out while the woman taking the collection is placed beyond suspicion. This aspect of such meetings is very directly related to the subjectivity of the faith – to the personal feelings and history of individuals and families – and at the same time to the growing money orientation of society, especially as, it will be recalled, *jaleseh* are also an occasion for more prosaic dealings, of a commercial sort.

Women's sociability, thus understood, has a paradoxical relationship with followers of ideological and learned religious sentiment. On the one hand it is a response to some of their admonitions about charity, and in that way satisfies some of the economic needs of the regime and the clergy, especially by collecting religious taxes that are more and more centralised by the government. But, on the other hand, the *jaleseh* thus manage considerable sums in a relatively autonomous fashion, and as a result gain increasing independence and to this extent relativise the bureaucratising of open-handedness which the regime is seeking. In that way, Islamic pluralism, which had been classically guaranteed by the diversity of the 'sources of emulation', is now perpetuated or even sometimes strengthened by resolute differentiation of the public space.

Secondly, at the *jaleseh* there is recital and interpretation of dreams, the most individual and most direct way to the supernatural, the invisible world and the divine. The faithful can thus foresee and, through almsgiving, avert a danger; they acquire some power of divination. Even though women's dreams are reputed never to be more than reality turned back to front (*khâb-e zan chapeh*), they willingly recount their dreams, interpret and assess the most simple ones themselves, or ask for learned interpretation by the religious authority presiding over the meeting; on her side the speaker at the meeting may choose a theme connected with dreams as the focus of her sermon. Another way in which the world of imagination appears in the *jaleseh* is the description of Paradise and Hell. Dreams are a permanent exposition of religious practice. In addition they are not alien to scholarly religion: interpretation of dreams is a recognised skill of the clergy, in the same way as astrology, even though theological schools are divided over the validity of teaching those subjects and they are not taught, for example, at Qom and Mashhad. The religious ideologues of the Islamic Republic, for their part, have not neglected this domain of dreams and the other world: did not Imam Khomeyni appear on the face of the moon during the Revolution? Did not the families of martyrs receive premonitory signs of the death of their flesh and blood in their sleep a few days before the fatal day? Is it not also by dreams that the son fallen in battle communicates with the living? Does Iranian cinema, especially 'war films' (*cinemâ-ye jang*), not place the moment of awakening of the hero's national, Islamic and revolutionary consciousness during his sleep? And does not the way in which President Rafsanjani escaped so many attempts on his life derive from the special logic of the invisible world revealed, among other things, by dreams?

The aspect of religion relating to dreams and the other world gives rise to constant exchanges of ideas between scholarly or ideological religion and the popular variety. From that viewpoint the bureaucratising and rationalising process is not necessarily opposed to what is often seen as superstition; an official of the regime once showed people a genuine photograph of the Prophet Mohammed found in Imam Khomeyni's bedroom after his death, without batting an eyelid. But, at the same time, dream-related practices are likely to crystallise conflicts between the political or religious authorities and the population of the urban districts. After dreaming and recounting their dreams, women and men find themselves being credited with special healing powers, and a crowd of people queues up at their houses to obtain healing or comfort, entrusting them with their alms. Others may see in their sleep the site of the lost tomb of a saint or hear unpleasant truths confided to them about the behaviour of certain religious dignitaries of the regime. Extraordinary events arouse real public movements which naturally worry both the political and the clerical authorities. One famous healer of Tehran, who operated during religious meetings and who specialised in treatment of cancer among other things, had to go underground, while in the industrial city of Foulâd-e Mobârakeh, 50 km from Isfahan, Revolutionary Guards intervened to halt the activities of a saint who aroused too much popular emotion. The thin dividing line between the scholarly, popular and political spheres is even more obvious in that the forces of order are sometimes called in by the divided and perplexed people of a neighbourhood themselves.

So it can be seen that dream-related practices are a meeting point between the people and the religious and political authorities, as much as they are a subject of disagreement among them and an avenue for movement towards greater autonomy for civil society: occasional repressive operations do not exclude pursuit of a more continuous debate to which books, magazines and sermons contribute generously. Seen in this way, dreams also favour the cultural unification and integration of society. It is for example revealing that, in Tehran and near Orumiyeh, some figures versed in dream lore have overcome ethnic and religious divisions; Muslims are interested in Armenians' visions and dreams, and vice versa; one such expert received a visit from his deceased father-in-law, surrounded by a group of senior religious dignitaries of all faiths paying tribute to his qualities as a pious man and his purity. Dream lore is a truly social fact; it presents modern Iran with its current leaders – not those of the era of Medina – and with its roads, its aeroplanes, its factories and its new places of pilgrimage such as the Imam's tomb in the south of Tehran, but also with its contradictions and diversity. Through dream-related, activity Iranians, above all, weave the fabric of their own future and not the future of the state;[31] the *hejâb*, whose contribution to the country's socio-cultural homogenisation is well known, was often worn earlier by Muslim women after a dream in which Fatemeh herself dressed them.

If one takes account of these religious phenomena it is clear that contemporary Iran is much less disillusioned and controlled than is sometimes supposed and than the extent of the processes of rationalisation, bureaucratisation and commercialisation might suggest. It seems like a very 'post-modern' society where the relations between the scholarly, political and popular fields, potentially but not necessarily relations of conflict, are managed at the individual level with an imaginary element readily added.

However, we have to stress once more the role of religious practice in the creation of a public space which is thus a religious space. The paradox is only apparent because it is known since Tocqueville that the idea of a public space has to do with the *imaginaire*, it being understood that the latter has unbreakable ties with the material world.[32] The public space accordingly belongs to the order of belief, which can – why not? – be religious belief. In Iran there have been new examples of several religious processes which are shown by historians to have contributed to the growth of the city. According to Peter Brown, the Christian bishops of western Europe, in the fifth century, 'founded cities in the cemetery'; '(they) came to orchestrate the cult of the saints in such a way as to base their own power within the old Roman cities on these new "*towns outside the town*". The bishop's residence and his main basilica still lay within the city walls. Yet it was through a studiously articulated relationship with great shrines that lay at some distance from the city – Saint Peter's, on the Vatican hill outside Rome, Saint Martin's, a little beyond the walls of Tours – that the bishops of the former cities of the Roman Empire rose to prominence in early mediaeval Europe.'[33] There is an obvious analogy with the Marqad-e Emêm/Behesht-e Zahra complex, run respectively by the Khomeyni family for the Imam's mausoleum and by the

---

31. As also in the case of Ismaël Kadare's *The Palace of Dreams* (London, Harvill, 1991).
32. J.-F. Bayart, *L'illusion identitaire*, Paris, Fayard, 1996, p. 142.
33. P. Brown, *The Cult of the Saints: Its Rise and Function in Latin Christianity*, London, SCM Press, 1981, p. 8; author's emphasis.

Tehran municipality for the cemetery. Since the Imam went there as soon as his plane landed bringing him back from France, Behesht-e Zahra has been one of the leading places where the legitimacy of the Republic is rooted, and the mausoleum is an obligatory part of the itinerary for official guests. Every Friday morning the ritual of reading of *do'âye nodbeh* takes place there, while families pay their respects to their dead at Behesht-e Zahra, and *salavâti* buses transport the faithful there. The leaders of the regime do not fail to make speeches there at regular intervals, while it is recalled, for example, that it was there that another attempt on Ali-Akbar Hashemi Rafsanjani's life took place in 1994. In short, the shrine and the cemetery dominate the centre of power symbolically from the outskirts of the city.

At first sight, the other major shrines in Iran do not conform to this pattern, as they are built in the very heart of the cities, or at any rate are there today. That is notably the case for the Imam Reza mausoleum in Mashhad, the Hazrat-e Ma'sumeh mausoleum in Qom and the Shahzadeh Abdolazim mausoleum in Rey. But in these situations there is also a relationship of exteriority between the shrine and the centre of political power, and between it and the mass of believers who frequent it; that relationship goes with the strength of its symbolic radiance. Qom is situated 120 km south of Tehran, but its influence over the institutions of the Republic is no less strong for that – especially through the teaching authority of the Society of Theology Lecturers who, as we have seen, intervened in the process of selection of candidates for the elections and, *a fortiori*, for the 'sources of emulation'. The holy city is like the duplicate, or alternatively like the godmother, of the capital: everyone turns to it in expectation of its agreement. Similarly the Âstân-e Qods in Mashhad, although autonomous, represents a fundamental mainspring in the national political game. The Leader of the Revolution is very close to it and regularly 'sweeps' its shrine clear of offerings left by pilgrims. In the nineteenth and twentieth centuries, at least until the 1970s, Shia Islam was already the constituted national religion of Iran through the preeminence of Karbala and Najaf, and it was from Najaf that Imam Khomeyni conducted his preaching against the Shah's monarchy.

It is clear that the shrines, understood in this way, launder the accumulation of wealth and patronage, as Peter Brown put it; the economic function of the holy places, with their numerous bazaars, is obvious. But that function should not be separated from the accumulation of political influence or visibility which it makes possible, or which goes with it. Control of a shrine is not only a matter of good administration. It becomes a trump card to play in the political struggle, even an entry ticket to the political scene. It is very largely because of the Imam's mausoleum that Ahmad Khomeyni continued to play a role after his father's death and that today his son Hassan, previously relegated to the background, is making himself known more and more on the public stage, benefiting, it is true, from his personal presence just as much. Similarly Hojjatoleslam Mohammad

Rey Shahri, the senior official in charge of Iranian Muslims' pilgrimage to
Mecca, is building his political career on the foundation of the Shahzadeh
Abdolazim shrine, where he was appointed administrator by the Leader of
the Revolution in 1990.

The 1997 presidential election illustrated very well the position of the
holy places in the laying out of the public space. The aura of each of the major
candidates was mixed up with the prestige of a particular shrine: Ali-Akbar
Nategh Nuri with Âstân-e Qods, Mohammad Khatami with the Marghad
shrine, and, of course, Mohammad Rey Shahri with the shrine of Shahzadeh
Abdolazim. In the same realm of ideas, religious ceremonies, readily relayed
by television, are becoming key moments of political expression. As we have
seen, candidates for the parliamentary elections had earlier used the *eftar*
during Ramadan in 1996 to get their messages relayed and carry on discreet
campaigning even before the campaign was officially started.

It is understandable then that the state is concerned to keep a systematic
record of the places of veneration of saints, to renovate them, improve their
appearance, and try to keep them under its control by entrusting clerics with
their administration. On its side the local population can itself aspire to this
recognition 'from the top' of its shrines, which are a source of finance or
accumulation of wealth, even though conflicts inevitably arise between its
drive for autonomy and the intervention of the clerical bureaucracy. As in
Latin Christianity there is a true 'expansion' in veneration of saints, and it is
the work of the citizens themselves. There is a vast movement, all over the
country, towards the institutionalising of shrines, and this cannot be
explained simply by the strategies of politicians, the aims of the state or even
the plans of leading local citizens. It is the mass of the faithful that is
involved and that, in a more or less confused way, negotiates over the
outlines and orientation of this religious dimension of public space. Thus
they may, as 'men of good deeds', revive the memory of a saint unjustly
consigned to oblivion, or they may prefer, as for example during the war
with Iraq, the peaceful Imam Hassan to the intransigence of Imam Hussein
who is glorified by the ideologues of the regime; or they may create an
entirely new saint from among living or dead people in their close entourage,
as a result of a dream or on the basis of an extraordinary chain of
circumstances. This process of conferring sacredness 'from below' in
practice makes it impossible for the political authorities to impose complete
centralisation of the religious sphere, apart from the fact that those
authorities are not unanimous in their religious ideas. There is rather
interaction between different religious agents, and a public space emerges
precisely from that. This, at least, is the hypothesis that can be reasonably
argued.

So it is useful to widen the circle of the entrepreneurs who are at the
origin of this social mobilisation in support of the saints: '...far from
describing a grudging or politic concession to the mindless force of habits

formed among the "common herd", we have met a group of *impresarios*, taking initiatives, making choices, and, in so doing, coining a public language that would last through western Europe deep into the Middle Ages',[34] Peter Brown wrote about Latin Christianity. In Iran, the saints' *impresarios* are also recruited among the 'men of good deeds' who are always ready to lay out a tablecloth in honour of the saint dear to them. The creation of this religious public space recalls in this respect the issues surrounding pilgrimage as expounded by Victor Turner and later by Benedict Anderson, writing about the national 'imagined community'.[35] This is especially so as pilgrimages to the tombs of saints, which bring together millions of the faithful every year, are not just religious in character; they are also an occasion for family visits, tourism, indulging in the pleasures of consumption, and even for business ventures. People readily speak of 'pilgrimage and amusement'[36] (*ziyârat-o siyâhat*) or 'pilgrimage and trade' (*ziyârat-o tejârat*).

In other words, the process of creation of a religious public space is mixed up with the process of creating a 'bourgeois' civil society, a consumer society and a political society. It is difficult for the analyst to separate the institutionalising of a differentiated religious field, in which rationalising of practice and its inclusion in the imaginary world contribute to the individualisation of the believer, from the rise of *sherkat*, the commercialisation of daily life, and the extension of political or more particularly electoral participation. The social specificity of the religious field is relative.

For example, pilgrimages to the tombs of saints provide women with the opportunity to be 'social beings', especially in middle class circles; they now travel to Mashhad, Damascus or Mecca with female relatives or among female friends (*dust*), or else on journeys organised among people of the same religious circle, the same school, the same government department or other workplace. They see an occasion for expressing devotion to their saint or the Prophet, but also for staying at a hotel, eating at a restaurant, seeing the sights and doing shopping; for being, like men, the absent ones that the family wait for and welcome eagerly on their return; for having adventures to share by describing their journeys. To refer to Peter Brown again, the Islamic Republic has designated in the religious sphere 'a new class of givers',[37] that of women, whose charitable or public generosity activity is tireless and extends, when the occasion arises, into the political arena; many women have made donations to help the fighters at the front or, during the visit by Yasser Arafat in 1979, to help the Palestinian cause, as was

34. P. Brown, op. cit., pp. 48-9.
35. B. Anderson, *Imagined Communities: Reflections on the Origin and Spread of Nationalism*, London, Verso, 1991, chapter 3.
36. In many respects, the development of tourism in Iran owes a good deal to the organisation, by various institutions, of so-called pilgrimage-tourism (*siyâhati-ziyârati*) tours.
37. P. Brown, op. cit., p. 46.

immortalised by a cruel cartoon showing the PLO leader rushing with a triumphant smile to thank his audience of women and coming back with a bundle filled with gold jewels. The massive presence of women at the shrines – shrines that are now places not only for devotion alone but also for bureaucratic innovation, economic rationalisation and political participation – illustrates their integration into the life of the citizen.

Similarly, disputes among clerics do not arise only from theological, factional or political disagreements. They often concern conflicts over material interests, or more basically about different ideas on government, society, the nation, the faith of believers, daily religious practice, the family, business or the state. It has often been said that Iranian religious life was dominated by the dispute between Akhbari and Osuli in the nineteenth century and by the victory of the latter over the former. Thus, it is said, the Islamic Republic displays continuity with the supremacy of the Osuli whose principal 'source of emulation', Morteza Ansari, was the spiritual mentor of Imam Khomeyni. In fact things are more complicated and do not lend themselves to a clear dichotomy separating two defined schools or sets of beliefs. It is probable that the bureaucratising of the religious sphere owes less to the victory of the Osuli than to the dynamics of their conflict with the Akhbari. Above all, one must not see the debate as definitively concluded. In many respects it has continued steadily throughout the twentieth century, and it is the same debate that is heard again, in a changed form, in contemporary discussions or conflicts in the religious domain.

The institutionalising and bureaucratising of that domain are expressed notably through growing specialisation of religious knowledge. A person with that knowledge is becoming increasingly an 'expert' (the term is used explicitly: *motekhasses*), and while he is acknowledged as an *'âlem* to have a general competence in *fiqh*, he is valued above all in relation to the field of specialisation in which he has particular authority. The idea of an *'âlem-e motejazzi* (specialist scholar), commonly expressed, is very revealing of this change. For example, only the part of Ayatollah Sistani's *resaleh* dealing with questions relating to youth is widely distributed, and he is seen above all as a *motekhasses* on that question, his general authority in matters of *fiqh* being more diffused. The expert *faqih* will end up by making hardly any pronouncements except on highly specific problems such as the 'blood price' following road accidents, just as the practice of medicine has tended to become differentiated according to specialisation; the metaphor is used by clerics themselves.

It follows automatically that this change in religious authority has consequences in the political arena and for the more or less rational idea of *velâyat-e faqih*. In a certain way it perhaps favours (or expresses) not so much the secularisation of sacred knowledge – as is often said – as precisely the specialisation and compartmentalising of that knowledge, without any loss of its special nature or its status. In other words, we see another example here of a more general process of dissociation between the divine and the worldly, or between the management of the sacred and religious (*din*) on one side and that of the state (*dolat*) and the social field (*donyâ*) on the other. Imam Khomeyni admitted this change in practice himself, when he entrusted the *velâyat-e faqih* with the task of preparing for the coming (*zohur*) of the Twelfth Imam, without however attributing to him the ability to embody the ideal government.

We have seen that the division of roles between the President and the Leader of the Revolution, and especially the conditions in which the latter was elevated to the rank of 'source of emulation', approved and extended such a diversification of political society between 1989 and 1997. The same was true of the last presidential election campaign. For example, the deeply religious word *aslah* (the superlative of *sâleh*, 'worthy' or 'able', which came to be used to describe the most eminent 'source of emulation') was widely used to describe the various candidates. In the eyes of his followers it was clear that Ayatollah Rey Shahri was the *aslah* candidate. But the other candidates were also presented as such, having regard to the more or less precise provisions of Article 115 of the Constitution, made more explicit by the Guardianship Council. The quality of *aslah* is now the object of precise definition which limits its meaning and relevance. It is no longer related to a principle of transcendance, but recalls criteria according to which one is more or less suited for the honour. This suitability is assessed by a college consisting of six clerics appointed by the Leader and six legal experts proposed to parliament by the judicial authority and elected by the deputies.

As a result, the idea of *aslah* in the political sphere is becoming institutionalised and joining the ranks of legal principles. Similarly, it has tended to extend itself, to join in the movement towards individualisation, even to become more democratic; 238 people, including nine women, have deemed in their own opinion, or following the opinion of those around them, that they were potentially worthy of being recognised as *aslah* by the Constitution Guardianship Council, and displayed this conviction in the public arena – starting to campaign, giving press interviews, and questioning the very foundations of the Constitution. For example, Mrs. Azam Taleghani, daughter of one of the most eminent figures in the Revolution – Ayatollah Taleghani – intended, by declaring herself a candidate, to resolve the uncertainty over the possibility or otherwise of a woman becoming President of the Republic. She only received a partial answer: she was indeed ruled out, along with the other eight women candidates, but no mention of their gender was made by the Council to back up its decision.

From the point of view of political society's development, these episodes are important in themselves, and it would be too easy to laugh at the undoubtedly undemocratic character of the elections due to the decisive roles played by the Leader of the Revolution and the Constitution Guardianship Council. Other issues are at stake in the jousting – in fact very much under control – between candidates and factions: they are issues of the orientation of society, the place occupied by various categories of the population in society, and the principles of legitimacy of the government, as Mohammad Khatami's victory proved.

At first glance, it could also be concluded that religious expressions and activities have 'colonised' the electoral domain. But it is perhaps more interesting to ask questions about the other side of the coin: will the rationalising of the idea of *aslah* in the political arena remain without effects in the religious sphere? Will the 'sources of emulation' themselves not be assessed according to specific criteria and in the future be recognised as *aslah* in respect of this or that quality? For the present it is best to halt at the idea that the Republic is recording the start of a process of creating a public space and institutionalising that 'public use of reason',[38] a process in which religious institutions and practice are massively involved. The mark of a social being is indeed to use his reason in the public arena. To that extent the process of which we are speaking started before the Revolution. But the theorists and precursors of the Revolution, people like Morteza Motahhari, Bagher Sadr or even Allameh Tabatabai, brought the social aspect out of its secularist or secularised ghetto and gave it an unquestionable Islamic legitimacy, even if that meant painting over the surrounding Positivism with Islamic green. Social behaviour did the rest.

38. J. Habermas, *L'espace public*, Paris, Payot, 1993.

6

LOOKING AFTER NUMBER ONE:
A COMPETITIVE SOCIETY

We noted in the previous chapters that pigeon fanciers entered their birds into competitions, that commemorations of the death of Imam Khomeyni now included sporting events, and that operators in the religious arena – Koran reciters, choirs, authors of the 'mosque literature' genre – competed with each other in contests, quite plainly called competitions and systematically including prizes. The public space is in fact imbued with this idea of competition.

For example, the daily *Keyhan*, always lamenting and nostalgic, expresses its 'holy' (*sic*) concern at the increase in 'cultural competition and the culture of competition' between cultural and educational centres, which are often motivated by a '100 per cent lucrative preoccupation': 'the alarm bell has been rung!' The journalist lamented, 'Rare are those who do not regularly respond to notices about such and such a competition, with prizes in cash or in the form of household electrical goods. Some of these cultural centres do not hesitate to make people pay fees for entry to their competitions without anyone knowing exactly where the money thus collected goes. In addition they resort to real advertising tricks, giving a dazzling picture of gifts of great value as first prizes, even going up to people's homes, while at the same time planning items with no real utility, even frankly defective, for the runners-up.' In *Keyhan*'s view the height of scandal is reached when a mosque takes such initiatives and announces it in leaflets distributed at Friday prayers, as in one northern city which it does not name. As for the prizes promised, from a house to a trip to Cyprus or a Walkman, they hardly fit in with the culture and expectations of the faithful at the Friday prayers, if our censorious journalist is to be believed. In short, he suggests, it is truly a 'cultural bazaar' that is opening up, alongside the other bazaars already in existence.[1]

But what distresses some, can make others happy. Proof of that is seen in the star pupils who every year harass their parents into taking them to the Play City, the huge amusement park of the Foundation for the Disinherited; they intend to use their tickets for the big wheel or the ghost train which the Mayor of Tehran provides free of charge for children at the top of the class.

1. *Keyhan*, 1.11.1373 (1995).

Similarly, a future home owner, who has actually already put down a comfortable advance payment, does not conceal his joy at drawing in a raffle enough to pay the balance of the cost of his house in the Ekbatan suburb, and his family celebrates what seems like good luck rather than the fruits of saving. In this pursuit of luck and merit, devout people are not left behind: when asked by the religious authority at a *jaleseh* about the age at which Khadijeh married the Prophet, the participants only livened up when promised the work of Al-Kafi in four volumes as a prize, although that meant the most ridiculous answers being suggested in cheerful disorder to increase one's chances, making it a game of chance.

A Sports-Mad Republic

However, in Iran as elsewhere, it is probably through the increasingly important position of sport in social life that this phenomenon can best be grasped.

Honour where honour is due – the leading role belongs to football, as was shown by the scenes of joy that accompanied the qualifying of the national team for the France '98 World Cup in November 1997. The famous scene from the film by Abbas Kiarostami, *Life Goes On,* which shows the inhabitants of a village destroyed by the 1990 earthquake concerting efforts to put up a television aerial hastily so as to receive the Scotland-Australia match, has symbolic importance and is mentioned by Bromberger; the exploits of Michel Platini were no secret for the young people whom he played with in the Gilan.[2] In fact national television readily re-broadcasts matches, generally with a slight delay to avoid any breach of the Republic's Islamic code; the districts of the big cities organise football tournaments, especially during evenings in Ramadan; small boys like kicking a ball around and find in the wrappings of their sweets and chewing gum the pictures of their favourite players.

However, this fashion for football has been accompanied by the success of a whole series of other sports, such as volleyball, basketball, swimming, riding, cycling, table tennis and of course gymnastics, body-building, running and walking, sometimes even on Friday mornings on the mountains that surround most of the big cities, starting with Tehran. Sport is now the object of public concern. The specialised sports press abounds in the kiosks and has become one of the most profitable publishing lines. As one would expect, Gholamhossein Karbaschi has taken numerous initiatives in this area, sponsoring marathons along the asphalt of his city at regular intervals, for example. There are more and more investments in the form of stadiums and sports complexes, while most of the parks, as will be recalled, are also provided with playing fields, ping-pong tables and volleyball nets. The

2. C. Bromberger, *Le match de football, Ethnologie d'une passion partisane à Marseille, Naples et Turin*, Paris, Editions de la Maison des Sciences de l'Homme, 1995.

litical arena itself is affected by this craze. Faezeh Hashemi, as we have seen, derived some of her popularity from her position as vice-chair of the Olympic Committee and chair of the Islamic States Women's Sporting Solidarity Congress. Similarly, the Minister of Agriculture and the Minister of Industry and Mines have succeeded each other at the head of the Olympic Committee, the Minister of the Reconstruction Crusade is the Chairman of the Polo Federation, the Minister of Transport is Chairman of the Wrestling Federation, and Ali-Akbar Nategh Nuri's brother heads the Boxing Federation. As for the deputies, more and more of them have responsibilities in the sporting domain, and about fifty of them have even set up a 'sports faction' (*fráksion-e varzesh*) whose spokesman, Dr. Ghafurifard, is a member of the Assembly's Bureau.[3] The clergy is also involved in the movement, if only through the intermediary of the *imam jom'eh* who have *de facto* administrative authority rank and represent the Republic at competitions in the same way as prefects. A man like Ahmad Khomeyni actively supported the National Horsemanship Association in Iran, which promotes the export of thoroughbreds – highly prized in the Gulf states – in particular, and he organised two congresses on horse breeding, held in the conference halls of the Imam's shrine. More generally, mosques have since 1991 tended to provide a setting for, or have even organised sporting competitions, and in this way have organised the youth through the agency of the *bassij*, in a way rather reminiscent of parish sponsorship in the Catholic Church.

In some ways, the importance of physical activities in Iranian society is not entirely new. Imam Ali, the subject of devotion for all Shia Muslim believers, himself excelled in vigour and good looks. He remains the model *par excellence* for all sportspeople, and it is his name that they shout during a contest; he was for example the inspiration that Mostefa Hashemi Taba, placed in charge of Physical Education by President Rafsanjani, claimed to follow.[4] In former times the 'houses of strength' (*zur-khâneh*), where people practised a form of martial art, was a central place for sociability, the special area for the *javânmard*, who might either be skilled in the sport himself or, in his later years, a sponsor of it. Today, the tradition of the *zur-khâneh* has lost much of its lustre. Many 'houses of strength' have disappeared or been turned into sports centres. It is true that others have been started recently, but they are hardly visible at all, being submerged in the boom of modern sports. Most of them tend to become quaintly traditional, having ceased to be places of references in the neighbourhood or the bazaar; as *zur-khaneh* adepts say, they have hardly any 'authenticity' now, having sacrificed too much to the needs of public events and competition. Above all, that 'ancient sport' (*varzesh-e bâstâni*) cannot rival the attendance at mass sports such as football, even though it is an integral part of Iran's cultural heritage and in

3. *Keyhan*, 1.7.1375 (1996).
4. *Keyhan varzeshi*, 2125, 22.12.1374 (1996), p. 3.

international competitions Iran only does well in sports derived from the ancient one – weight lifting and wrestling – although the latter are only very modestly funded.

We can admit, following Norbert Elias and Eric Dunning, the differences between a traditional martial art such as the 'ancient sport' of *zur-khâneh* and modern sports: in particular, the latter have achieved independence from warlike confrontations, participating in the emergence of a secularised public space, and they are subject to uniform written rules – a difference to which we shall return later.[5] But at the same time, the sportsperson of our days is no less a modern-day *javânmard* in the qualities which he displays and which are expected of him – a further proof that that life style is adaptable and has room for change as well as continuity. It is as an incarnation of the spirit of *fotowwat* that Hashemi Taba celebrates the model of Imam Ali: 'Ali is the sum of all the virtues and all the strengths. Normally he who holds power uses it for his own ends. Ali is the only one who did not wield power to serve his own interests...such a person can be a model.' He added, 'It is not only for us Muslims that ethical questions are important. For example, I have heard that in the Italian football federation one player did not receive a single warning in 143 matches, and this is praiseworthy.'[6]

It is also as a *javânmard* that the great wrestler Gholam Reza Takhti, gold medallist at the Melbourne Olympics, who died in suspicious circumstances in 1967 – he was said to have been murdered by the Savak for being too popular and not being submissive to the royal power – continues to be the object of adulation, even of a real cult. Books and innumerable articles describe the epic of his life, subject of a film being produced by Hatami Kiya; a statue of him has been put up in Tajrish Square in the north of Tehran, a cup dedicated to 'Gholam Reza Takhti, national hero' is awarded every year to the best wrestlers, and on the anniversary of his death adepts of that sport assemble at his grave at Ibn Babvei, calling on the crowd to join them by means of leaflets and posters: 'He was not Puriyaye Vali [a legendary wrestler], he was not in the image of any other person, he was himself. Admit that others can be judged in accordance with his name and his presence. He is the base and the very meaning of greatness and nobility (*azâdegi*)', proclaimed a poster put up in the winter of 1995, reproducing words used to praise him by the essayist Jalal Al-e Ahmad.

The process of '*javânmard*isation' of Takhti is all the clearer as his biography is a succinct one. Little is known about his life, except his modest origins in the south of Tehran, his victories beginning with the first gold medal won by Iran at the Olympic Games, his commitment to the service of the disinherited and his sympathies for the national cause, illustrated by a photograph of him wearing a suit and tie, sitting cross-legged next to Ayatollah Taleghani. That does not stop hagiographers from waxing

5. N. Elias and E. Dunning, *Sport et civilisation. La violence maîtrisée*, Paris, Fayard, 1986.
6. *Keyhan varzeshi*, 2125, esfand 1374 (1996), pp. 4-5.

eloquent: 'Takhti often got up on podiums, he often raised his eyes to heaven, he became a credible and respectable figure in world sport. But what distinguished him and gave him his authenticity was his qualities as a hero, a *javânmard*, his simplicity. What makes a hero or a sportsman is not his rounded torso or his muscular arms, it is his lofty ethical and human qualities. It is they that make the difference between the champion (*qahramân*) and the true hero (*pahlavân*)', exclaims a brochure published by the Physical Education Organisation.[7] In the last few years the Khadem brothers have, with others, given new life to the ideal of the *javânmard* wrestler by their brilliant victories in a number of international contests. This is particularly true of Rassul Khadem who won the gold medal in his group at the world championships in Atlanta in 1995. But the conditions in which his brother Amir-Reza was defeated were still more eloquent; he preferred to lose against his Turkish opponent so as not to have to face the Israeli competitor, and this 'failure in a good cause' aroused the admiration of Iranian observers.[8]

Certainly one may think that wrestling, an 'ancient', 'traditional' and 'indigenous' (*bumi*) sport, is particularly suited to such a '*javânmard*isation' of athletes. But a footballer like Mehdi Abtahi, whose distinguished technique is admired, similarly forced the admiration of the public when he was able to acknowledge, in the purest *fati* tradition, a referee's decision against his team, Vahdat, in a match against Esteqlal in the autumn of 1990. He placed respect for the referee's decisions and the beauty of the game before the winning of victory; similarly he remained faithful to his club, which did not have much prestige, at a time when he could easily have let himself be acquired by another team. 'He is the greatest Iranian footballer, an exemplary sportsman, faithful to ethical principles; he has been nicknamed the "ethical sportsman"'[9] – a view largely confirmed by his supporters who emphasise especially his 'good behaviour', his 'technical brilliance', in short, his '*javânmard* playing'.

The leaders of the Republic are not behindhand in echoing this theme. Karim Fallâhi, second in command of the Tehran military district, equates taking of performance-enhacing drugs with anti-*javânmard* behaviour: 'We have placed ahead of everything else, as our watchword, the defence of heroism and *javânmardi*. Many times have we sacrificed our place on the podium to safeguard our values.'[10] The press regarded the anti-drug-taking days organised by FIFA in 1997 as 'international days for playing like a *javânmard* (*bâzi-ye javânmardâneh*)'.[11] When congratulating the Iranian athletes on their performance at the wrestling championships in Atlanta, Ali-Akbar Nategh Nuri approved their behaviour: not only did they pray, they

7. Bijan Rouintan, *Jahân pahlevân Takhti*, Teheran, Hamrâh, 1374 (1995-6), p. 45.
8. *Keyhan*, 21.5 and 22.5.1374 (1995).
9. *Keyhan varzeshi*, 1885, 25.12.1369 (1991).
10. *Keyhan*, 30.6.1373 (1994).
11. *Keyhan*, 26.12.1375 (1996).

also kissed the hands that gave them their medals, because 'that it is the *javânmard*'s way [the Speaker of Parliament used the synonymous word *mardânegi*], through which respect for the forerunners (*pishkesvat*), the masters, is shown in stadiums and in the circle of the *zur-khâneh*'.[12] Sport is accorded value because of its moral virtues; it is held to preserve the youth from 'corruption', it purifies society from its evils and stains. The leaders of the Republic seem to be unanimous in calling for *mens sana in corpore sano*, to use the Latin adage quoted by Hashemi Rafsanjani.[13] Behind these edifying speeches it is not difficult to see the regime's anxiety about unemployed youth – better for the young to devote themselves to the healthy pleasures of physical activity rather than the murky pleasures of disorderly conduct or even sex. But again these concerns are wrapped up in the language of *javânmardi*; what is recommended is to 'combat immoral practices as a *javânmard*';[14] 'what we want is sport that combines ethics with *javânmardi*'.[15]

However, one should not be deceived by the apparent traditionalism of attitudes or expressions. First of all, the *javânmard* sportsman operates in the modern world; his exploits are broadcast on television across continents, or take as models performances that he learns about in the same way. Furthermore, he follows internationally defined rules for the game without the political authorities crying 'cultural aggression!'. Significantly, he can symbolise success for the adventure of emigration, as in the cases of Andre Aghassi and Mehdi Zand, or even contribute to the migration process, if it is true that the large Iranian community in Tokyo originated from athletes from the south of Tehran. Lastly, the *javânmard* sportsman may have an engineering diploma, which is just what the footballer Abtahi has; he is praised for his knowledge, a guarantee of wisdom and fair play – 'If Abtahi became Abtahi even before becoming a well known footballer, it was because of its lofty ethical code, rational and based on principles (*osul*)', said one of his colleagues.[16] To respect the rules, one must first know them.

Lastly, and most importantly, the *javânmard* sportsman submits to those well known written and standardised norms of modern sport, which are universal, public, and produced (or applied) by bureaucratic structures. The rules of football are known to everyone, and are watched over not only by referees trained in specialised schools, but also by spectators at large, who are quick to approve or else shout abuse at referees' decisions during matches whose programmes are fixed by the Football Federation at the national level. In other words, we could repeat in this connection a good deal of what we have written about rationalisation in the religious field.

12. *Ettela'at*, 29.4.1374 (1995).
13. *Keyhan*, 19.1.1372 (1993).
14. *Keyhan*, 28.3.1374 (1995).
15. Statement by Hashemi Rafsanjani, *Keyhan*, 19.1.1372 (1993).
16. *Keyhan varzeshi*, 1885, 25.12.1369 (1991).

Sport is more and more obviously linked with science and technology. As such it is now taught in special establishments approved by the Ministry of National Education. It is organised in structures following a dual logic, bureaucratic and democratic – the leaders of the Federation of Clubs being elected, for example. It is certainly financed in part by public generosity donations, but also from the state budget, notably through a tax on cigarettes and another tax paid by businesses which do not have their own equipment. It plays an increasing part in the world of *sherkat*, which take charge of teams – if only for advertising purposes – or which have to release their employees for one hour per day, in working hours, for physical exercise. This process of bureaucratising and rationalising the sporting domain leads also to its commercialisation. Players sell themselves to the highest bidder, so much so that a sporting career becomes a real way of accumulating wealth; extension of the practices of body building, swimming, martial arts, even riding in Iran opens possibilities for acquisition of money by enterprising individuals, including women, especially in the informal sector. In addition, amateur sportsmen are also consumers who buy tickets, training courses, newspapers, equipment, sportswear and shoes, the last two items being all the more important in household budgets as the fashion for tracksuits and trainers has spread, especially among young people and children.

Sport is now the setting and the object of numerous conflicts. For example, building of sports facilities can be undertaken by public benefactors, and the state acknowledges this in its taxation policy. But their projects can clash at times. At Fariman, in Khorassan, a man named Haghighi wanted the complex sponsored by the Ministry of National Education to bear the name of his brother, a martyr of the war, in exchange for a gift. The Motahhari family, natives of the city, expressed the same wish to honour the memory of its illustrious deceased member Ayatollah Morteza Motahhari, assassinated by the extremist Forqan movement in 1979, and made a contribution accordingly. On the day of the ceremonial opening, the first donor, furious at being cheated, publicly slapped the cleric in charge of the project, with consequences that can be imagined: at first he managed to escape, but he was caught a few months later and imprisoned. Similarly enterprises, ministries, guilds, the armed forces and to a lesser extent foundations finance teams, especially football teams, through which they engage in symbolic combat: Sepah is the Revolutionary Guards' club, Keshavarzi the club of the Ministry of Agriculture, Saypa that of the Industry Organisation, Purâ that of the Skin-Dressing and Meat Casing Organisation, Polyekril-Tabriz is the club of the company of the same name, and so on.

It will be recalled that the sporting scene has also been a scene of severe battles, essentially over the proper place for women in it. In particular, the supporters of the Ansar-e Hezbollâh denounced the women cyclists of the

Park-e Chitgar in Tehran at the time of the 1996 parliamentary elections, to destabilise the leaders of the 'Reconstructors' – Faezeh Hashemi and Gholamhossein Karbaschi – and went as far as smashing the marble skating rink at Isfahan, the city that is a beacon for urban modernisation and that persistently votes the wrong way in the conservative Right's view. Under the pressure of these events and the complaints of a section of the clergy, television increasingly hesitates to broadcast competitions in which women take part. Meanwhile the large expenditure devoted to football arouses numerous criticisms inasmuch as the national team's performance for long left much to be desired.

What is essential for the moment is to note that Iranian society, or at the very least large sections of it, avidly watches regulated sporting competitions which are the same time opportunities for individual self-assertion and for public expression. But sporting contests are only particularly visible expressions of a much wider phenomenon. This regulated competition approach is found in many areas of social life. As in the sports sector, it mediates and promotes the individualising process and the relationship between that and the processes of rationalisation, bureaucratisation, commercialisation and the creation of a public space.

Competition and Self-Reflexivity

There are no activities left that do not provide opportunities for competition. Reading of the daily press is instructive. To give some examples chosen at random, not in order: *Ettela'at* reported in its 12 October 1994 edition a competition to choose the best shepherds in eastern Azerbaijan, with contestants filing past with their flocks not far from the Assâmatebn-e Zeyd shrine, under the aegis of the Reconstruction Crusade, while a jury of veterinarians and stockbreeders picked out the best of them. On 3 May 1997 President Hashemi Rafsanjani conferred on 15 university professors the title of 'exemplary tutor'.[17] He also honoured the best wives of disabled war veterans for having chosen their husbands from the ranks of the war disabled 'in consciousness of and in accordance with the values and principles of self-denial';[18] or else the best office workers – though without rewarding any woman on that occasion.[19] He suggested rewarding donation of organs as 'a humane, learned and fundamental solution (*sic*)'.[20] In February 1997 the Central Bank organised competition among note counters. In Yazd, on 5 April 1997, 20 exemplary senior officials of guilds were elected for their ability to satisfy the public, their respect for the rules and the quality of their service,[21] and on 19 April the towns of Kashmar and Ferdos won the

17. *Hamshahri*, 13.2.1376 (1997).
18. *Keyhan*, 24.11.1373 (1995).
19. *Keyhan*, 2.6.1374 (1995).
20. *Ettela'at*, 28.2.1376 (1997).
21. *Keyhan*, 16.1.1376 (1997).

Khorassan public health prize.[22] In July 1994 the equivalent of the Automobile Association, encouraged by the success of its 'Liberation of Khorramshahr' rally, was planning two new successive cups, 'Disabled War Veterans' and 'Holy Defense'.[23] And in April 1997 the Association for the Struggle against Diabetes invited young people from four to 16 to enter a painting competition with pictures on the following subjects: 'Prevention of illness', 'Diabetes and me', 'Diabetes and parents', 'Diabetes and school', 'The Anti-Diabetes Association and me', 'My diabetic friend'[24] (we are not in a position to assess the results).

The religious sphere is also affected by this thirst for competitive success. On 19 April 1997 110 people, natives of Seistan-Baluchistan, who were able to recite five *Hadis* tending to justify the succession from the Prophet to Ali were rewarded: they received household electrical equipment, industrial carpets, gold pieces and journeys to Mecca.[25] On 29 August 1994, in Karaj, a thousand of the faithful chanted the second Sura of the Koran and reciters who mastered the text from beginning to end received a Walkman each as prize.[26] In Gilan province prisoners who learned a *joz'* – i.e. one-thirtieth of the Book – were rewarded with a week's temporary release.[27] Similarly, at Sari, prisoners were given up to 336 days of freedom if they learned the entire Koran by heart.[28] On 16 March 1995 the Leader of the Revolution's delegate to the *bassij* announced that conscripts able to recite the Koran would have extra leave, be able to choose their postings and be promoted to higher ranks.[29] On 9 March 1991 girl students at the University took part in three Koranic competitions – quotation, comprehension and recital; ten of the 150 candidates won prizes, three receiving gold pieces.[30] On 30 September 1993 the armies of Iran and Pakistan engaged in a Koran recital contest.[31] But the 'children of the mosques' are not left behind; they also hold Koranic competitions in plays, drawing and poetry.[32]

So Iranian society is going through a real fever of competition, described daily in the media which can themselves provide a setting for it. The regular Thursday evening television broadcast 'competition of the week', a general knowledge quiz for about twenty contestants, has become one of the public's most closely followed programmes. It shows that this sort of competition is a real part of the general movement towards individualisation. The catch phrase used by the presenter, Manuchehr Nozari (already a radio star before

22. *Keyhan*, 30.1.1376 (1997).
23. *Keyhan*, 16.4.1376 (1994).
24. *Hamshahri*, 4.2.1376 (1997).
25. Ibid.
26. *Keyhan*, 7.6.1373 (1994).
27. *Keyhan*, 30.5.1373 (1994).
28. *Keyhan*, 3.4.1374 (1995).
29. *Keyhan*, 25.12.1373 (1995).
30. *Keyhan*, 18.12.1369 (1991).
31. *Keyhan*, 8.7.1372 (1993).
32. *Salam*, 26.9.1374 (1996); *Keyhan*, 11.5.1373 (1994) and 26.1.1376 (1997).

the Revolution), is revealing: 'Who do I ask?'. It has been well said that the winner of the game is 'distinguished': he stands out from the crowd by his personal qualities, his knowledge, his performance. This individualising process is widely mixed up with commercialisation; besides the honour which the 'distinguished' person receives, material rewards – gold pieces, household electrical equipment, pilgrimages to Mecca and Syria or journeys to Cyprus – generally complete his triumph. On essential points these competitions also contribute to rationalisation of society: they lead to assessments which give rise to discussions. In addition they go together with a proliferation of fairs, festivals, commemorations, seminars and colloquia which deal with the major problems of the moment or the practices that they highlight; such gatherings are also, in their turn, often an occasion for prizes and rewards. Continued public discussion on the major questions facing Iranian society, discussion that gives those questions their legitimacy, is mediated through such competition among individuals. However, the rationalising process in this area is not without ambiguity: the distinction achieved by competitors, although in accordance with precise rules, is still the result of chance when it comes from a raffle or drawing of lots, as often happens in the banking sector, in the interest-free loans fund network, and in the allocation of public housing.

The paramount field for these competitions is, revealingly, that of knowledge (or talent, as teaching gives a prominent place to artistic expression). Selection in schools is getting steadily tighter, especially as elite establishments are being developed, university places are extraordinarily limited (over a million candidates compete for about 400,000 places, half of them in independent or fee-paying universities), and admission to religious schools is also increasingly on the basis of tests. As a result of all this, schools are now subdivided, and thus placed in several hierarchical categories: 'non-profit-making' establishments, 'popular exemplary' and 'state exemplary' ones, establishments for 'sharpened or quick minds' and others for 'brilliant vocations', not forgetting schools for 'special needs', that is, the handicapped. Some qualifications need to be added again: the school and university systems are not exclusively meritocratic, in so far as the Republic has agreed to affirmative action in favour of some social categories – families of martyrs, prisoners of war, its own officials – and underprivileged provinces, through zoning and regional quotas in tests (which give extra opportunities for cunning students in the big cities who register for the last secondary school year in a school in an economically underdeveloped zone). In addition, the regime excludes Baha'is from higher education. However, the new elites forge ahead through this system of heightened competition which sometimes reaches 'Japanese' proportions in the cities; more and more children are taking additional private lessons after school, the better-off families being naturally the ones best able to take advantage of this development.

At the same time institutionalising of competition among individuals expresses the special local variations in the public space: the tests are often organised at the provincial level and are reported in that way in the press, before final examinations at the national level. Their results inspire utterances praising the qualities of the Khorassanis, the Gilanis, the Kurds, or others, and this arouses more general debates about the state's public policies. For example, the sports weekly *Pahlavan*, reporting a football match between the Malavan team of Bandar Anzali in Gilan and the Piruzi team of Tehran, praised the 'worthy playing' of the former and criticised the 'dark aspect' of the second, while also wondering about the soundness of the spending on the capitals' clubs and about the clubs' 'mercenary' tendency: 'The past year illustrates the Football Federation's negative results. Its propaganda and the self-interested complacency of those who profit by the system, by selling their honour for tickets allowing them to buy household electrical goods cheap, have succeeded in concealing the responsibility and mistakes of the leaders of Iranian football.' It went on to mock the defeated captain of Piruzi who had vainly promised his players a washing machine, a watch, a gold piece and a thirteenth month![33] Behind comments of that sort can be seen the symbolic playing out of the relationship between the 'brave' but poor provincial and the Tehran city dweller softened by all the advantages the Republic gives him – though this latent tension cannot of course be interpreted as a challenge to national unity.[34]

This interaction between competitive practices and the processes of rationalisation, commercialisation, individualisation and creation of a differentiated public space, both in the geographical sense and from the point of view of social categories and the two sexes, reveal the emergence of what Anthony Giddens calls 'life politics', and Michel Foucault 'bio-politics', to describe 'what makes life and its mechanisms enter the domain of explicit calculations and makes ability and knowledge an agent for change in human life.'[35]

Through regulated competitions *Homo Iranicus* builds up his personality in difference, tries to programme his life, makes an effort to overcome his weaknesses, and finds in knowledge a basis for confidence.[36] This is how one should interpret Iranians' burning hunger for encyclopedias, manuals and brochures, all those 'prescriptive texts'[37] intended for modern-day autodidacts. There are books like *Long Live Me, Change Your Thinking and*

---

33. *Pahlavan*, 106, 1369 (1991).
34. See for example *Keyhan varzeshi*, 1872, Azar 1369 (1990), p. 31.
35. M. Foucault, *Histoire de la sexualité, I: La volonté de savoir*, Paris, Gallimard, 1976, p. 188.
36. A. Giddens, *Modernity and Self-Identity*, Stanford University Press, 1991.
37. This term is used by Michel Foucault for texts that 'claim to lay down rules, opinions and advice to behave in the right way' and are 'themselves the object of "practice", insofar as they were made to be read, learned, meditated, used, put to the test, and aimed at eventually constituting the framework of daily behaviour'; 'The role of these texts was to act as operators allowing individuals to ask themselves questions about their own behaviour, to watch over that behaviour and train it, and to fashion oneself as an ethical subject'. *Histoire de la sexualité, II: L'usage des plaisirs*, Paris, Gallimard, 1984, pp. 18-19.

Your Life Will Change, How to Have Self-Confidence, Self-Confidence in Ten Days, The Power of the Brain, a Programme for Cultivating your Thought and Mind in Twelve Weeks, The Art of Good Thinking or *Welcome to Desires, How to Change Failures into Successes and Walk Like a Guide, Power and How to Get it and Use it, The Powerful and How they Think** – generally American booklets translated from English. These are all the rage and sell in impressive quantities. Their distribution in the best bookshops in the city, even in front of the University of Tehran, is accompanied by the holding of numerous training courses which contribute towards popularising them among the middle and upper classes. In fact, the vogue for that literature affects first of all the better educated circles, if only for financial reasons, and clearly fits into the dream of modernity, even in its more irrational aspects. This does not mean that it has no precedent in *sonnati* (i.e. traditional or classical) tradition in Iranian society; the Sufi and the *javânmard* also found their own strength in their inner selves and forged their characters through initiation which revealed them to themselves. But now this work of self-mastery is mediated through knowledge which claims to be scientific and is committed to writing; thus it is a part of the 'public use of reason', in the form of a 'process by which private individuals analyse and criticise among themselves the personal experiments they make in their new private sphere.'[38]

This propensity of Iranian society for what Giddens calls 'self-reflexivity' is found easily in the numerous manuals dealing, for example, with food, marital relations, the benefits of physical education or the upbringing of children. Through the pages the reader is supposed to attain self-knowledge, understanding of his or her own deeds and those of his entourage, the improvement of his condition and that of his close kin, in short, the development and expression of his or her Self. In this way he integrates into his own life the procedure of choice among several possibilities, and he acquires ability to plan his existence according to particular 'agendas'.

Let us take for example the work *Teaching Yourself to Know Meals and Cookery*, published by the women's section of the Islamic Cultural Foundation at Qom. Starting from the observation that mediocre diet can damage the stability of a marriage, the health of the children, and the psychological balance and intellectual faculties of members of the family, the authors comment that 'if a housewife makes worthy use of food products and prepares varied and appetising meals, she is doing her religious, human, ethical and social duty' – the word *ejtemâ'i* being used to denote the latter, and subtly referring back to the questions relating to the 'social being'. They divide their book into three parts, respectively devoted to knowledge of food

---

**Translator's Note*: These titles are translated from Persian via French and may differ from original US titles.

38. J. Habermas, *L'espace public*, Paris, Payot, 1993.

Looking After Number One   151

and the real needs of the human body, indispensable products and cooking methods, and various recipes. The authors' key ideas are a certain theory of the body and its well-being, a certain idea of sociability among members of the family and their guests, and a certain rationalisation of food which is now interpreted according to utilitarian principles, relating notably to the composition of food items and the ways of preserving and cooking them – rather than traditional categories of 'hot' and 'cold', for example.[39]

The objective is to keep one's body in balance between leanness and fatness, between immaturity and ageing, avoiding under-nourishment and perhaps above all malnutrition: 'One single principle: eat little but well.' The reader is called upon not to submit passively to the attacks of age any longer, but to resist them by appropriate means, preferably natural ones, every organ becoming a battlefield. For example, manganese and garlic maintain the blackness of hair, calcium is good for the bones and fluorine for teeth, Vitamin D makes it possible to fight against rickets and Vitamin A strengthens sharpness of vision. A variety of dishes is an essential element in this strategy which for this reason brings in the procedure of choice in dietary practices – man is superior to the animals because he has the right to choose, recalls another book of recipes, The Culinary Art and Housekeeping – and turns cooking into a real art of living: dishes and the table must be attractive to entice guests and strengthen the family's unity. This philosophy recurs in the best-seller in this genre, The Culinary Art by Roza Montazami, whose first edition was published in the early 1970s; it is the reference work for all good housewives, and is often offered to young married couples. Its success has been such that it has been completely revised to fit 'the fashion of the day'. In this hefty tome of nearly a thousand pages is recorded the practical experience of the author and her pupils, embellished with illustrations and enriched with recipes from 'various nations': again the accent is on diet, with the idea of a meatless diet introduced (a truly revolutionary one in Iran), and on the economic rationalisation of menus, with a determined attack on waste.

Similarly, a work devoted to Health and Beauty of Skin and Hair, while placing itself under the protection of a Hadith – 'God is beautiful and loves beauty' – proposes 'the best and most modern scientific methods for every woman to preserve the beauty and freshness of her skin and hair so as to appear beautiful and lively at different stages of her life.' It assures readers of answers to all skin problems, based on 'prescriptions of doctors and experts [motekhasses – them again!] of the whole world, to avoid recourse to incompetent people.' It takes account of economic constraints and gives prominence to less costly methods which will allow girls and women to be more attractive at the least cost. Once again the body is presented in its various parts, each of which can be subjected to specific action in the form

39. C. Bromberger, 'Les blagues ethniques dans le nord de l'Iran. Sens et fonction d'un corpus de récits facétieux', Cahiers de littérature orale, 20, 1986, pp. 73-101.

of treatment, diets, courses of treatment, tattoos, even surgical measures. The individual is depicted as actively involved in her own physical future.

While American manuals of parapsychology are frequently translated from English, most books about housekeeping or beauty are written by Iranian authors. The clergy are involved in this craze also: an Ayatollah as important as Abdolkarim Biazar Shirazi did not disdain to devote a theological treatise (*resâleh*) in two volumes to 'Hygiene'; subjects covered include fats in the Koran, baths, washing machines and their 'lawful cleanliness', blood, the sex act, artificial procreation, contraception, abortion, and (with illustrations) the best way to brush one's teeth: not horizontally but vertically.

Obviously there still remains the question of how far manuals of this sort, sold on a massive scale, are really read beyond the immediate recipes that they provide. But that is a relatively secondary question. On the one hand, the titles of these books speak for themselves and are sufficient to preach a fairly precise philosophy of 'caring for oneself'. On the other hand, their ideas are relayed by radio, television, the press, and a plethora of conferences, training courses and other seminars, not counting family conversations and religious meetings. A housewife may even hear talk of hygiene, health, balanced diets, care of the body, pedagogy and psychology throughout the day: listening in the morning to radio broadcasts meant for her, like 'Home and Family' and 'Science and Life', whose presenters are very popular; taking part in a *jaleseh* meeting in the afternoon; taking the children to a municipal park and using the opportunity to test her weight and blood pressure at one of the appliances provided for the purpose by the benevolent Gholamhossein Karbaschi; receiving women neighbours or relatives before dinner; watching television in the early evening.[40]

On the other hand, it should be clearly seen that these expressions of self-reflexivity are only important through the social practices to which they are linked, according to the logic of 'reinvention of difference' inherent in globalisation, as argued by Clifford.[41] They provide pretexts or motives for strategies giving roles to the various actors in society. They provide terminology used by the latter to negotiate their relationships within the family, the neighbourhood and the village, circles of comradeship and places of work. Not that they are simply adopted in their entirety; obtrusive advertising encouraging children to consume this or that object is readily criticised for showing too little concern for the children's health – or their

40. It should be noted that advertising only plays an unobtrusive role in the promotion of self-reflexivity, at least where women are concerned: the revolutionary period's refusal to use image of women to advertise the sale of commercial products – a combination of Socialist criticism of capitalism and Islamic prudery – remains in force. The impact of films broadcast on television is more obvious; in 1996 the film *Sheltering from You* brought a special way of wearing the *chador* into fashion.

41. James Clifford, *The Predicament of Culture. Twentieth Century Ethnography, Literature and Art*, Cambridge, MA, Harvard University Press, 1985.

parents' purses! But the expressions of self-reflexivity offer moral support, references and a vocabulary which anyone can draw upon to define himself, assert his 'life style', defend his interests – in short, enter life's contest.

The attitudes toward television broadcasts are a very good example, which in addition, shows well how the extremely family-oriented ideology so strongly preached by both the political authorities and the clergy, as well as the media and self-help books, is in no way contrary to the process of individualisation. This is illustrated by the television series *Patriarch* (*Pedar sâlâr*) which was extremely successful in 1995-6. In this soap opera the father plans to gather his three married sons under one roof in his own house, allowing no argument. One of the daughters-in-law, the youngest, who is also a cousin and whose marriage takes place before the passionate gaze of the viewers, refuses to agree to this, and steadily the family comes apart; appalled, the patriarch throws his children out, cuts off all contact and withdraws all his economic support. The mother, the main binding force who makes it possible to feel the pangs of such a conflict between father and sons, uses her resources of diplomacy in vain to reconcile the household. Only an illness opens the patriarch's eyes, makes him 'get off Satan's donkey' as his wife and a Persian expression put it, and shows him that the world has changed. His distressed children readily forget the past and their ambitions, return to the home, sit around their father as they used to do by the dinner tablecloth which, as it is unfolded, symbolises a pole of stability and solidarity, an incomparable haven of peace in the social landscape. But it is the father who, beside that tablecloth, in giving a bunch of keys to each of his sons seizes the initiative of turning over a new leaf with his new proposal: from now on they will live next to each other, no longer in the same house as in former times, but in neighbouring flats within the same dwelling.

The moral of the story is clear: there is no salvation outside the family, but there will be no more family without respect for the autonomy of individuals and couples. Again, we should not underestimate the emotional power of messages of this sort. The broadcasting of the Japanese series *Oshin*, in 1987-89, had previously been a major event. It appeared on the Iranian broadcasting scene at a time when the regime planned to give pledges of political relaxation without thereby renouncing its principles of Islamic and revolutionary legitimacy. From that viewpoint the series had the merit of being produced by a non-Western but powerful country, whose investments and technology it was hoping to attract, and which was becoming a welcome outlet for emigration. Its heroine had the advantage of showing in her dress and behaviour a modesty in sympathy with Islamic morality, though without being veiled. Above all, she embodied the outstanding qualities of the social being. Far from being confined to a supposedly traditional sphere of private life, Oshin takes part in social life through her work. She shows herself to be determined, strong, responsible, dynamic, independent, no longer just long-suffering. She is a fighter, and it is definitely this quality that wins the unanimous sympathy of the public. By wearing the same clothes at home and in her working life, she expresses one of the essential features of the social being: the continuity between the private and public spaces.

Throughout its run this 'foreign' *(khâreji)* series gave Iranian viewers a chance to rethink the tensions inherent in the private space in their society by suddenly finding a universal aspect to them. The phenomenal audience attracted by the series was partly due to the fact that it depicted the classic antagonism between mother-in-law and daughter-in-law, while revealing the split between two family worlds allied in marriage. Every episode affecting Oshin aroused long commentaries in people's homes, on public transport, at the workplace and at school. During these often passionate discussions, various people expounded comments and interpretations concerning the various family roles, praising the heroine's sense of responsibility or criticising the husband's recklessness. The series thus brought on to the public stage conflicts traditionally belonging to the enclosed world of the family. In some ways it seems to have strengthened social cohesion by providing different generations with common rituals and topics of interest. Still more important, *Oshin* gave new topicality to time-honoured qualities such as courage, by giving them a 'modern' connotation suited to the 'twentieth century'.

To the extent that the central character was a woman, this broadcast series seems to have voiced the social aspirations of Iranian women today, in accordance with a theory that has been suggested concerning Asian TV melodramas and soap operas.[42] It would be an exaggeration to say that it subverted the Republic's patriarchal and Islamic order, although one woman, questioned on television, aroused the wrath of Imam Khomeyni by saying she identified with Oshin rather than with the Prophet's daughter Fatemeh. But in that connection *Oshin* is clearly distinct from *Dallas*. For obvious 'Islamic' reasons, the latter series has not been broadcast in Iran. Nobody doubts that it too would have been a definite success there; but its message would have been very different from that of *Oshin*. It would have transmitted a world of dreams and fantasy about sex and money, and not the mirror effect which characterised the active response to the Japanese broadcast series and gave legitimacy, in a roundabout way, to the redefining of relations among family members.

The extent of public response is thus explained by the urgency of issues within Iranian society that *Oshin* crystallised. It also echoed national film production which has created female roles comparable to that of the Japanese heroine. Western cinema-goers have been able to applaud the courage and generosity of the Gilan peasant woman who welcomes Bashu, 'the little foreigner', in the absence of her husband, mobilised for the war

42. W. Dissanayake (ed.), *Melodrama and Asian Cinema*, Cambridge University Press, 1993.

front, despite the hostility of her family and the village, and makes her husband accept this decision when he returns disabled from the war (*Bahram Beyzai*, 1987). But *What Else is New?* by Tahmineh Milani (1992) and *Sara* by Dariush Mehrjui (1993) obtained much greater success in Iran itself. They portray identical figures of 'fighting' women whose independent spirit and behaviour are in contrast to the more retiring characters of television series in the 1970s.

In short, the country does not receive cultural and social expressions imported from abroad in a passive way. It takes them over and builds them up in accordance with many individual initiatives and sometimes real collective mobilisations. Literature on 'caring for oneself' is put into practice and brings about real social facts in suitable conditions. For example, cultivation of a mushroom imported from America in 1996 and said to have miraculous healing properties became *de rigueur* in families after a few months, the water used for its growth and proliferation being drunk by the litre. In recent years, consumption of various sorts of *arak* (*araq*) made from plants and industrially packaged[43] has spread in a similar way for self-medication purposes, while beauty treatment and sporting services have multiplied, such as body building and gymnastics halls, swimming pools, hairdressing and beauty salons, whose customers are no longer only from the well-to-do classes; numerous women from the underprivileged districts and residential suburbs such as Mehrshar, Karaj and Islamshahr go swimming at the Bahman cultural centre in the south of Tehran, and the use of cosmetics is now general among women of the cities,[44] the purchase of a vanity case being a suitor's first duty to the lady of his heart.

This 'care for oneself' also involves attention to one's appearance: the choice of clothes can show one's physique to advantage or conceal certain areas of plumpness, and the permanent reinvention of Islamic dress imposed by the authorities is not the least of the ways in which women work out their identity in relation to themselves, their families, and society where they play more and more active roles, as we have seen in the preceding chapters. We could trace the clothing and cosmetics itinerary followed by such and such a person during a day or a week, in accordance with her activities or obligations of a family, occupational, administrative, religious, sporting or other nature. A woman of about 60 will thus move on from the *châdor namâz* or headscarf which she wears indoors to the black *châdor* which she puts on to cross the city and takes off once she arrives among her family. A female employee of about thirty may or may not wear a headscarf at home,

---

43. In this case the reference is to plant essences which must not be confused with the Lebanese *arak*, an aperitif flavoured with aniseed, or with vodka which is also called '*arak*' in Iran.
44. Masserat Amir Ebrahimi, 'ta'sir-e farhang-sarâ-ye bahman bar zendegi-ye farhangi va ejtemâ'i-ye javânân va zanân-e tehran', *Gotf-o-gu*, 9, Autumn 1374 (1995), pp. 17-27; M. Habibi, 'Islamshahr, un nouveau type de banlieue à Téhéran', *Cemoti*, 21, 1996, pp. 251-71.

depending on who is present; she will slip on a coat and *maghna'eh* (a sort of hood) to go to her workplace; she will go to the park with her children or her women friends wearing a headscarf; she will go to the mosque in a *châdor* – which will not stop her going to bed in a nightdress and without headscarf, or taking a shower completely naked contrary to what the Westerner watching Iranian films might think.[45]

These micro-practices of self-reflexivity, on the individual level, are bringing in general transformations in Iranian society and are also involved in a public debate of national relevance. It is, for example, noteworthy that fertility has fallen by half in less than ten years, from seven children per woman in 1986 to 3.5 in 1993. The country had already gone through a slowing down of demographic growth between 1966 and 1979, but this seemed to have been halted between 1979 and 1985. However, the trend resumed even before the authorities again gave active encouragement to birth control from 1988. This spectacular demographic change is due, according to Marie Ladier, to a whole series of factors including the rise in the average age of marriage despite the lowering of the legal minimum age, the spread of contraceptive practices, the fall in infant mortality, the progress of literacy and school attendance especially in rural areas, and entry of women into active life.[46]

Self-Reflexivity and Relations with Others

We already know that this individualising process does not exclude belonging to a village, a district, a guild, a network of sociability or friendship, and above all a family, which remains the cornerstone of Iranian society and the major reference point against which subjectivity is defined. In other words, the vigour with which individualities assert themselves, according to specific 'life styles' in no way excludes their acting according to collective interests, and does not necessarily assume that their strategies are of an individualistic type. This is just the lesson given by our *javânmard*, on the lines of the 'individualities of eminence' studied by Mattison Mines in Madras in southern India.[47] Conversely, a practice derived from community ethics does not necessarily contradict the process of individualisation; a gift from a public benefactor or a well-off relative can help the individualising of the recipient, who is given more financial autonomy in relation to those around him, or social prestige – especially as this practice now meets the needs of a consumer yearning for distinction, and not only the pauper, for example when it comes to offering a washing

45. For these different forms of Islamic clothing, cf. F. Adelkhah, *La révolution sous le voile. Femmes islamiques d'Iran*, Paris, Karthala, 1991.
46. M. Ladier, 'La transition de la fécondité en Iran', *Population*, 6, 1996, pp. 1101-28.
47. M. Mines, *Public Faces, Private Voices. Community and Individuality in South India*, Berkeley, University of California Press, 1994.

machine to a young wife, a denture to an aunt or, with dollars in hand, a pilgrimage to a sister. The recipient also has the feeling of doing a service to the donor from whom he accepts the gift, since he helps to sanctify the donor's wealth and bless his reputation: the real beneficiary of a gift is not always the person one supposes!

The Iranian family, which has been thoroughly reshaped since the 1960s, is becoming nuclear and taking note of the individualising of its members, which is favoured by the changes of modern life: the spread of flat dwelling and Western furnishings, car use and air travel as everyday features of life, social expressions given importance by the media (including the American cinema, still very popular). Self-reflexivity often owes less to ideological pronoucements than to changes in the framework of life, sometimes imperceptible but often, nonetheless, very widely debated within families. In this respect, the Islamic Republic has in no way interrupted the changes in private space started in the 1970s. It created a new political and ideological context for those changes, and this reoriented certain practices but, above all, gave powerful backing to the nuclear family, with which the aspiration to be a social being is particularly concerned. In addition, the influences of globalisation have continued to be involved in these changes. For example, Western furnishings, now a mark of social distinction which it is important to show off to visitors – including women, of course – have contributed to the mingling of men and women in receptions. The functional specialisation in use of space in new houses, with the appearance of bedrooms for parents and children in particular, is strengthened by 'modern' furnishing and especially by beds. It has led to the disappearance of the private space reserved for those intimately linked (*khodi*) and the emergence of individualised spaces. Thus it is both one of the causes and one of the consequences of the growing autonomy of the nuclear family in relation to the extended family. Similarly, this conjugal family gathers around the television set – men, women and children together – and programmes and commercials do not fail to celebrate in their turn the enviable happiness of that life 'in the fashion of the day'.

But every one of these changes gives rise to an infinite number of micro-conflicts or micro-negotiations, especially between generations or between parents from different backgrounds. For example, the Western-style dining table may be abandoned for the traditional tablecloth laid out on the ground so as not to upset an aged guest, while the coverings normally placed over armchairs may be removed for the visit of a family member whom one wishes to impress, or else to spoil. It is obvious that the views of different family members are not necessarily in agreement in these circumstances; children may be upset by the old-fashioned furnishing of the family home, the mother may come to terms with it but go to borrow an armchair for use by the religious authority presiding over the *jaleseh* gathering that she is organising, the father will be all the less inclined to lay out lavish expenditure on furnishings because he thinks of his grandchildren's destructive energy. Through these domestic mini-dramas, daily reshaping of family relationships goes on, with the element of power involved. The big debate of the day is about this 'flat culture'[48] and especially the advantages and drawbacks of 'open', that is 'American' kitchens. For example, one university don in a provincial city, organiser of Mohammad Khatami's 'propaganda front' in 1997 and married to a secondary school teacher, was faced with a serious dilemma in a house which he built according to 'the fashion of the day' so as to resell it more easily; the 'open' kitchen deprived his wife of all intimacy when guests came, but it would be unfitting to have the guests going into one of the two bedrooms where they would be able to look at the candlesticks and mirror which symbolise the ties of affection between the husband and wife, just as it is disagreeable for a housewife to be confined in a room reserved for rest, where she cannot carry on her usual activities.

Amidst everyday life the arrangements between the individual and his or her family lead to more or less open rivalry among members of the family, especially in the classic conflict zone of social distinction, and, on occasion leading to real conflicts; the strength of family ties does not necessarily ensure harmony. More or less scrupulous adherence to the norms of subjectivity laid down by the political and religious authorities is a favoured field for rivalry within the household. At a marriage feast, acceptance or, alternatively, refusal of music can provide an opportunity for the bride's different sisters to part company and proclaim in one case her attachment to 'technological-age' pleasures, in another her devotion to the teachings of Islam.

The process of individualisation within the family is at the heart of 'bio-politics' in the Islamic Republic. The report by the newspaper *Keyhan*[49] of an inquiry carried out by the Women's Sport Delegation among women doing gymnastics regularly for three months reproduces the logic of this well. Recalling that mechanisation compromises health by reducing physical activity, and that the 'mobile man of yesterday has become a shrivelled up being', the study showed that 91 per cent of the women in the sample did their household tasks faster, 86 per cent slept better, 70 per cent had lost their excess weight, 95 per cent no longer had back pains, 87 per cent no longer had leg pains, 79 per cent no longer had heart problems, 84 per cent had no more breathing problems, 94 per cent had more self-confidence, 88 per cent had better morale, 60 per cent spent more time reading, 91 per cent took more interest in their children's sporting activity at school and at home. The greater well-being obtained through gymnastics helps both a woman's ability to control her body, according to the norms of self-reflexivity, and her performance of her duties as a housewife and mother, in accordance with the

48. M. Rouholamini, 'Ravand-e 'âpârtemân sâzi, ve farhang-e 'âpârtemân neshini', *Ettela'at*, 28.7 and 29.7.1375 (1996).
49. *Keyhan*, 4.10.1374 (1996).

expectations of the regime's ideology and an ethical code widely shared in society. The journalist concluded that the practice of sport by women favoured their social progress (*ejtemâ'i shodan*) in making them escape from their daily routine and widening their vision of the world. He adopted the common distinction between 'sport for everyone' (*hamegâni*) and competitive sport (*qahramâni*); only the first seemed to him favourable to women's breaking into the open in an Islamic society as social beings in the service of the family.

As we have seen, nostalgic populists, for whom *Keyhan* is a spokesman, and conservatives take a low view of women appearing in stadiums. This is definitely not the attitude of Faezeh Hashemi: 'We cannot separate sport for all from competitive sport. Of course the first is our aim. But the second is the pillar of the first. Sport for all and competitive sport are complementary and inseparable. Sport without competition loses its meaning and its ambition. A quick look at recent years shows that the honour of that heroic presence of sportswomen in stadiums has done more than any organisation to show the true face of the women of the Islamic Republic. So competitive sport has benefited the Republic.'[50] She was supported in this by Hojjatoleslam Mostapha Raisi, who sees in sport a factor for education and strengthening of both body and spirit, so as to be better able to face...the menopause.[51] Earlier, in 1993, Hashemi Rafsanjani, in his inaugural speech for his new term of office as President, had said of his daughter that she was devoting herself to 'oppressed female sport', adopting the term used to describe the martyrdom of Hussein.[52] On her side the lady editor of *Zanan* protested unceasingly against the lack of facilities provided by the government for female sport and the harassment that its adepts endured from a number of pressure groups.[53]

So there is, in this subject, material for public debate, even electoral polemic. It will be recalled that the commitment of the Servants of Reconstruction in favour of sport incurred fierce attacks from their opponents. But the conservatives are having to take note in their turn and in their own way of the sporting boom of the 1990s. A personality like Ali-Akbar Nategh Nuri did not spurn the support of athletic associations, in the form of a marathon on the feast of Qadir, during the last presidential election.[54] Did the Leader of the Revolution not himself offer congratulations, the day after that election, on the way in which the political class, the media, the clergy, the university staff, the believers and the 'revolutionary people' had set the 'stage for a public competition'?[55] Was the

50. *Keyhan*, 19.12.1375 (1996).
51. *Jâygâh-e varzesh-e zanân dar eslâm* (The place of female sport in Islam), Tehran, Shorâ-ye hamâhangi-e varzesh-e zanân-e mosalmân, 1374 (1995), pp. 19 and 72.
52. *Keyhan*, 13.5.1372 (1993).
53. *Zanan*, 30, Mehr 1375 (1996), p. 2.
54. *Keyhan*, 2.2.1376 (1997).
55. *Hamshahri*, 4.4.1376 (1997).

high point of the campaign not the televised contest organised in three successive evenings among the four candidates, so that citizens could make their choice in full awareness? Was not the winner of the election the one who was most a fighter, the outsider?

So it can be seen that 'subjectivity which originates in the intimate sphere of the limited family has...so to speak created its own public': 'the process by which private persons analyse and criticise among themselves the personal experiments they make within their new private sphere' appears like 'the exercise ground of public reasoning'.[56] The transition from subjectivity to the public domain is very obvious, for example, in the step taken by Ayatollah Biazar Shirazi when he wondered whether a women having her period could enter the mosque to perform her duty of voting; in his view she is not allowed to do so 'according to what is written', but this reply is not understood as a categorical negative opinion insofar as it does not use the word 'unlawful' (*harâm*). In any case, fewer and fewer women are deciding on their behaviour in this respect in accordance with traditional principles. They want to be guided by conscience – taking care not to show lack of respect for the sacred – but by critical conscience, bringing in rational considerations and realising that a number of prohibitions of this sort have fallen into abeyance in the last few decades. In this particular case the use of a mosque for civic purposes on polling day probably calls for another sort of attitude than the observance of religious rituals, from which women must stay away when they have their periods. It is in that sense that individualisation in the family, according to the pattern of self-reflexivity, intervenes more and more in public consciousness. It is becoming at the same time the issue at stake in political conflict and that conflict's vocabulary, expression and experience.

However, it should be made clear that the field of subjectivity has been differentiated at the same time as society, both geographically and socially. On the one hand categories of class, status, age and gender have been asserted and have gained in autonomy. They now have specific 'life styles' from the viewpoint of material culture – dress and leisure, for example – and from that of the values they claim to embody, even if those values all tend to claim affinity with a form of Islamic-Persian humanism. From that point of view one should not underestimate the ability of the political class of the 'Thermidor' phase of the Revolution to propose a model of subjectivity. This is probably one of the roots of the undeniable popularity of Ali-Akbar Hashemi Rafsanjani: by speaking openly of young people's sexual desires in a memorable speech in November 1990, enthusiastically applauding the Iranian wrestlers grappling with their foreign opponents in June 1995 (to the great annoyance of conformists), letting his daughter Faezeh (as is well known) appear in the public arena, taking his wife with him on official journeys overseas, not hiding his tears at his mother's funeral, the former

56. J. Habermas, op. cit.

revealed another image of the revolutionary leader and cleric. It is probable that those around him worked to organise that image, notably by relating difficulties he faced: had his wife not thrown a shoe at his face when he took a stand in favour of temporary marriage? (He saw this traditional form of temporary arrangement between a man and a woman, *sigheh* or *mot'a,* as a way of resolving young people's sexual problems.) But that does not detract from the echo which his behaviour and utterances found in society.

Mohammad Khatami played similar tunes throughout his election campaign, winning people over with his radiant smile and his prestige as a polyglot intellectual; having the idea to show on most of his photographs not the ring with an *aqiq* or *firuzeh* precious stone which would be expected of a man of religion, but his signet ring, a sign of his belonging to the new middle class, his affluence and his adherence to a certain idea of living as a couple. These signs backed up very clear statements on the promotion of women and youth and the liberalisation of political life, and were not without effect in the tidal wave that brought him to power; 'He has arrived. Spread your wings, draw back your curtains', proclaimed his election posters, in the dynamic and intimacy-oriented style of modern poetry which definitely owed very little to revolutionary or religious language. In fact those two categories of women and young people, which seem to have voted massively for the joint candidate of the Islamic Left and the Servants of Reconstruction, are contributing decisively to define reflexive subjectivity, in both its material and ethical aspects.

On the other hand, this differentiation of subjectivity also occurs in space, since most social practices and organisations are mediated through province, city and district identities. There are hardly any religious associations, networks of public generosity or groups (*jam'iyat*) that do not relate to that dimension, possibly as sub-groups in the midst of other structures such as bazaar guilds. The clergy itself is linked together around regional poles such as Qom, Isfahan and Mashhad. Spatial differentiation of society is reflected in the field of material culture, especially in customs relating to clothing and food, and gives rise to particular forms of sociability that help to map out the public space. Thus the deputy for Sabzevar in Khorassan province took the initiative in founding Sabzevar House (*Khâneh Sabzevâr*) in Tehran, intended for people from that town; it was not one of the *hoseynieh* that we mentioned in the last chapter. This example is interesting because it projects into the public space, for political purposes – the development of Sabzevar – a feature of private space, the 'house', following a growing trend of using that word (increasingly people talk of houses of culture, the Koran, science, the cinema, etc.). As a good politician one member of parliament even offered himself an environment-friendly play on words; as *sabz* means 'green', people speak of the 'green house'.[57] In the reverse direction, active members of local-interest bodies are liable to take over national political or ideological tendencies, like

57. *Keyhan,* 6.11.1375 (1997).

the Association of the Friends of the Green Open Spaces of Hamadan, whose creation allowed the Mayor of that city to make a celebration of the flower that has given the city its fame.[58]

Faced with this double process of differentiation of subjectivity, the social being is in a position to choose his life style, a major characteristic of contemporary modernity according to Anthony Giddens, especially as 'the existence of multiple milieux of action' allows him to operate 'segmental' choices according to contexts, and to adhere temporarily to 'life style sectors' according to circumstances.[59] He is not situated exclusively in relationship to identity resources provided once for all – Persian civilisation, local culture, Islamic principles – but works on those resources constantly, sometimes referring to other sets of concepts, newer ones or even ones from outside. For example, a young woman can at the same time give aerobics courses, be a wife and mother of a family 'in the fashion of the day' taking part in the school parents' association, and be an assiduous Muslim; each of these activities corresponds to a different category of subjectivity whose expression in clothing is clearly different, ranging from the body stocking to the *châdor*. It is probable that the present time has increased the variety of choice available to individuals, as Giddens says. But it is interesting to emphasise that a 'milieu of action' does not really mean only a fixed 'life style'; the young woman in question gives her aerobics classes to keep in good health herself, to increase the household's income, to reduce her dependence on her husband, to obtain professional recognition, to meet women friends, all without depriving herself of the pleasures of sport as a spectator; to put it briefly, on the scale of that sporting 'milieu of action', she carves out her own subjectivity from composite elements, both unconsciously and by bringing her critical faculties into play.

Certainly the competitive nature of society of which we have been speaking comes to a great extent from that double differentiation; it focuses on rivalries among regions, cities, districts, families, sexes, age-sets and state, economic and clerical institutions, while Iran waits for the problematical recognition of political parties, debated for a number of years; Mohammad Khatami has said this must come. From this point of view one important change relates to the increasing institutionalisation and rationalisation of conflicts in social life; 'Even prohibitions must be regulated', the new President felt it necessary to declare the day after his cabinet was sworn in.[60]

From Social Relations to Social Regulations?

Iranian society – it is almost a cliché to say so – operates readily on the basis of informal activity and string-pulling (*pârti*). It is based on the idea of

58. *Keyhan*, 16.1.1375 (1996).
59. A. Giddens, op. cit.
60. *Hamshahri*, 30.5.1376 (1997).

'connections' (*râbeteh*) between individuals and families. These ties are created by blood relationship, but also by common origin or between schoolmates, economic partners, neighbours or simple friends. Even such a structured institution as the clergy is bound together by networks of this sort, and the notion of household (*beyt*) precisely recalls such *asabiyya* – the word used by the Arabs – with a sense of flexibility and permanent reformulation.[61]

We have noted at several points that the operation of 'connections' is more and more undermined by expectations from the alternative ways based on rules known to all. To describe the latter, people generally talk of *zâbeteh*, *nazm* or *enzebât*, but the words *osul* (principles), *qânun* (laws), *'elm* (science) and *hesâb-o ketâb* (arithmetic and book) derive from the same set of ideas. Such a demand for rules assumes the use of reason and also, more and more often, recourse to elections as the legitimate procedure for evaluation and choice, precisely in accordance with rational or 'scientific' criteria. Mir-Salim, Minister of Culture and Islamic Guidance in the last Rafsanjani government, thus expressed in 1997 the hope that young people would be mobilised in a 'scientific' way for the presidential elections.[62] One of the leading figures on the Right, Dr. Abbaspur, deputy for Tehran, announced that in the event of victory for Ali-Akbar Nategh Nuri there would be 'management no longer based on effort and error, but on scientific principles' – apparently science does away with effort![63]

Concretely, in daily life, the demand for rules takes on a number of aspects. A school parents' association may ask candidates for its management committee to declare themselves, to introduce themselves to a meeting, to set out the plans they may have in mind, so that members can decide among them by secret ballot to choose representatives to deal with the school authorities. What is even more remarkable is that the secret world of the bazaar is now confronted by a call for rules on the part of some of its operators, obviously the younger and more educated ones: on the one hand because the latter can be tempted to bypass the dominant position of the best established traders within their guild by setting up a cooperative; on the other, because they can set out to attain leadership positions in the guild through periodic elections that are traditionally controlled by the team in place (often in place for several decades). The famous 'flat culture' mentioned by the ethnologist Rouholamini is not exempt from this development; in the spring of 1997, parliament voted a law regulating the rights and duties of joint owners, placing them under an obligation, for example, to take out fire insurance, and providing for measures against recalcitrants.

The trend extends to the Siyâh Bâzi satirical theatre, rather like Italian

61. O. Roy, *Groupes de solidarité au Moyen-Orient et en Asie centrale*, Paris, Les Cahiers du CERI, 16, 1996.
62. *Keyhan*, 5.1.1375 (1996).
63. *Keyhan*, 11.2.1376 (1997).

164 Being Modern in Iran

comedy, which puts on stage an absurd servant, a sort of macabre clown; contrary to what is often thought, the Republic's censorship has no more altered the repertoire than the Empire's censorship or the environment of moral conformity, and according to one of the most famous actors it has at least the advantage of seeking to protect relatively clear norms. The Ministry of Culture and Islamic Guidance has distributed a booklet laying down criteria of what is lawful and unlawful in published matter, entitled a 'manual for filtering' (*momayyezi*), the term used for censorship (*sânsur*) in good Persian. The satirical weekly *Golagha* poked fun at this, saying that the Culture Minister's concern to purify the language of neologisms of foreign origin had not stopped it distributing a handbook on '*sânsur*'!

The connection between this question of rules, the rationalising process and individualisation in accordance with self-reflexivity is obvious. It can be understood from three angles. First, the bureaucratising of 'bio-politics' is plain to see. A Centre for Medical Ethics Studies and Research was founded in 1997, formally opened by Dr. Habibi, Vice-President under President Rafsanjani. Promotion of contraception comes under the Ministry of Public Health. Youth and family counsellors are proliferating to help the public. 'If you are in a difficult psychological situation, if you need help to get married, if you have marital problems, if you have difficulties with your children, you can call us from 8 in the morning to midnight', the Khavaran Cultural Foundation says in a press advertisement. Morteza Mir-Bagheri, Chairman of the coordinating bureau for the specialised counselling centres for the youth set up by Hashemi Rafsanjani in 25 provinces in 1996, declared that his services were meant to help people in psychological matters, but also in affairs of the faith, studies and general information.[64] A year earlier, twelve thousand medical students took responsibility for a 'counselling mobilisation' (*bassij-e moshâvereh*) project, to spread basic knowledge of birth control – which is, in an eloquent fashion, called 'family regulation' (*tanzim-e khânevâdeh*) in Persian – and nutrition for children and expectant mothers, as well as cancer detection.[65] Iranians' daily existence and their rational and 'scientific' management of life are now permeated by a massive framework of such administrative structures, which, of course, cannot be seen as mere instruments of ideological control.

Secondly, definition of the Self has become a major subject of public debate not only in the media, as we have seen, but also in the political arena, during election campaigns, in Friday prayers sermons and in parliament. One of the debates today, for example, is about the question of the marriage gift in cases of divorce or the husband's death. Under the Empire a Western-inspired civil code was adopted which more or less recognised equality between men and women. In this, it had the backing of a section of the Shia hierarchy, especially Ayatollah Hakim who lived in the

64. *Akhbar*, 29.11.1374 (1996).
65. *Keyhan*, 20.8.1374 (1995).

Holy Places in Iraq.[66] But this 'progressive' legislation was in fact largely disconnected from the realities of society, and remained a dead letter for the vast majority of women, if only for economic reasons. The Republic annulled those texts and adopted so-called Islamic laws which brought in a number of inequalities to women's disadvantage, though without going back on all the achievements of the Pahlavi era because of the mobilisation of women militants who took part in the Revolution, the most Islamist among them being not the least determined to defend the cause of women. Very considerable legal confusion resulted. Before the courts the evidence of a woman is equivalent only to half of that of a man, and it is similar with the 'blood price';[67] a girl is considered legally responsible, and thus able to be married at the age of nine while she only acquires the right to vote at 15 like boys, and she must ask for her father's permission to take a husband or get a passport even when adult. Even so, once elected to parliament she has a vote equal to that of her male fellow deputies, and under the Constitution there is nothing to stop her reaching the highest positions in the Republic.[68]

These contradictions are more or less managed and resolved by the Expediency Council, of which Hashemi Rafsanjani was appointed Chairman in March 1997. Meanwhile, they lead to arguments and conflicts over interpretation which do not coincide with a simple antagonism between men and women, or between modernists and traditionalists, or between the laity and men of religion. Thus a bill has been submitted to parliament concerning the rights of widows and divorced women. As the economic crisis has bankrupted many heads of families, should the state not take their place to pay women a subsistence pension or repay their marriage gifts? But in that case, how should those gifts be assessed in view of the depreciation of the currency since the early 1980s? Some women emphasise the ravages of inflation and plan to seek compensation in constant rials or have their dowry indexed on the dollar exchange rate. To that a cleric gravely objected that the wife may herself have depreciated during the marriage! Other women revolt against financial calculations in doubtful taste and prefer to raise the more fundamental question of their legal status in society, which only the state can guarantee, on the financial side among others. This proposal obviously encounters criticisms from other men of religion who say that such matters are within the multiple and diversified competence of the 'sources of emulation', not the legislature.[69]

66. Shireen Ebadi, 'Nerkh-e ruz: piry-e zan yâ tavvarrom-e eghtesâdi', *Zanan*, 33, 1376 (1997), pp. 62-3.
67. According to the penal code the murderer of a woman is not liable to the death penalty because his life is considered to be worth double that of his victim, while conversely a woman who murders a man is liable to the death penalty, to which is added payment of financial compensation owed by her to the victim's family. In fact legal practice is different; courts have already sentenced two men to death for the killing of a woman.
68. For more about the legal ambiguities in Iran see Shireen Ebadi and Mohammad Zeymaran, *Sonnat va tajaddod dar hoquq-e iran*, Tehran, Ganj-e dânesh, 1375/1996.
69. Cf. the opinion of Ayatollah Mohammad Reza Fakar, deputy for Mashhad, in *Zanan*, 33, 1376 (1997), p. 63.

It can be seen from this example that the regime's public policies cannot be seen simply as a coherent totalitarian programme. Their implementation has to take account of the complex interplay of a combination of social forces, not excluding women. In these circumstances, this battle over the Self is mediated through an institution, parliament, which is one of the referees with other constitutional bodies under the supreme authority of the Leader of the Revolution, such as the Expediency Council and the Guardianship Council. It brings in a 'capital calculation' which is very revealing of the 'economic orientation' of contemporary Iranian society. It is expressed in laws which in turn give rise to debate among judges and to jurisprudence and its interpretation.

The conflict over satellite television in 1994 was also a good illustration of the relationship between the question of regulation, legal and institutional, and the individualising process. There is just as keen interest in receiving foreign programmes as in watching national television broadcasts: they are the object of choice and critical comment. Broadcasts relaying sporting events (football and, a more recent phenomenon, tennis and figure skating) are especially sought after, as are cartoons which are seen as a way to start children off in English. CNN news broadcasts, in the absence of BBC news, are also well regarded. On the other hand, the most daring broadcasts do not seem to be favoured by the public, another point on which conservatives are mistaken, and violent scenes are rejected firmly. The role played by appropriation and reinvention of difference is all the greater in that the Iranian public, for the most part, does not understand English. This does not stop housewives from dilating at length on the clothes, poses, hairdo and inner nature of characters in the series that they follow, or children from identifying with classic heroes of the global village. Similarly, practices relating to television fit into the context of the social scene. Access to satellite television is a mark of distinction between families or between individuals. It has a gender aspect, men having the leading role in getting round the ban by hiding the dish and exchanging information about the best way to outwit the vigilance of the forces of order, while women argue endlessly about the previous night's melodrama. But it tends at the same time to unite families, overcoming differences of sex and age, around a common cultural object – except in the specific cases of certain communities, such as the 'Arabs', more attached to the traditional division of roles; among them the room reserved for satellite television is barred to women, and is like a reinvention of the man's exclusive space where he could cultivate his own privacy, receiving friends to chat, drink or smoke.

Like the watching of soap operas broadcast by national channels, watching satellite broadcasts is part of the process of individualisation within the family. It has reverberated in the public space according to the theme of regulation. The common sight of satellite dishes on the roofs of the big cities naturally aroused the indignation of the most conservative faction of the regime. But the actual extent of this opposition must be assessed. In 1994 only about twenty members of parliament took the initiative of introducing a bill to ban 'the importing, sale and use' of those dishes.[70] But the reservations and criticisms that this provoked need to be stressed, as well as the stand those deputies took. A number of ministers, parliamentarians and even clerics – for example Hojjatoleslam Mohammadi Araghi, Chairman of the Organisation for Propagation of Islam, and Hojjatoleslam Dorri Najafabadi – considered that satellite television, while 'harmful', 'corrupt' and a vehicle for 'cultural aggression', was nonetheless a great human achievement of which Iranian society could not deprive itself, and that its use must simply be regulated to be placed at the service of the country's cultural, technical and economic development.[71] In their eyes, measures of coercion were a cure worse than the disease. For example, the daily *Jahan-e eslam*, whose editor was Hadi Khamenei – the Leader of the Revolution's brother, and a spokesman for the Islamic Left – pointed out that the ban would quickly become unenforceable through the introduction of miniature dishes, that it would drive the public into clandestine activities more harmful to their morals than the reception of the despised broadcasts, and that it would eventually give value to the forbidden fruit.[72] Other politicians suggested that the Islamic Republic should retaliate in kind against 'cultural aggression' and transmit its own television programmes by satellite.[73] Opponents of the twenty deputies' bill also insisted that the authority of the state would not be enhanced by the adoption of a law which it would find difficult to enforce. The Leader of the Revolution himself, busy with his recognition as a 'source of emulation', then under discussion, reserved his position in the dispute, even though it related to his favourite theme of 'cultural aggression'. One may in addition wonder whether the final victory of the supporters of a ban in December 1994, after more than a year of political battle, was not a concession made to the conservatives to soften the blow to them of the elevation to the *marja'iyat* of a man to whom they had given only qualified support since he succeeded the Imam without having the necessary theological qualifications.

The conditions in which the bill was finally adopted by the Majles reveal the new concern for regulation. The Minister of the Interior, Mohammad-Ali Besharati, who had taken the side of prohibition at a very early stage, seems above all to have followed classic bureaucratic logic; he intended implementation of the law to be entrusted to his department. But he did not, even so, go beyond strictly legal reasoning. He quickly had to accept that it was impossible to confiscate dishes on roofs without a proper legislative

70. *Salam*, 22.2.1373 (1994).
71. *Basaer*, 9, tir 1374 (1995), pp. 23-27; *Keyhan*, 28.2.1373 (1994).
72. *Jahan-e eslam*, 25.2.1373 (1994).
73. Cf. for example the statements by Dr. Kharrazi, future Foreign Minister under President Khatami, in *Ettela'at*, 7.3.1373 (1994), and Ali Larijani, Chairman of the television authority, in *Keyhan*, 4.7.1373 (1994).

instrument, and he continually emphasised the virtues of persuasion rather than force.[74] 'Everyone is free to have his own opinion as long as it concerns him alone. But the expression of that opinion in public places is subject to principles. For example, we do not accept unveiled women or alcohol consumption. Those facts are reprehensible in public. But nobody has the right to go to people's houses to check whether they are behaving in that way. That principle applies to satellite dishes. Parliament has voted to ban displaying of them on roofs. However, if someone installs a dish inside his house, that does not concern anyone', declared Ali-Naghi Khamoushi, President of the Chamber of Commerce and one of the leaders of the conservative Right.[75] In fact, the polemics around satellite dishes indicated how long a road had been travelled in the sphere of public liberties since the dark hours of the 'Cultural Revolution' (1980-83) – the Constitution Guardianship Council even sent back a first draft of the law for being unconstitutional, since it did not provide for financing for the new expenditure arising from it – and the persistent strength of private space in Iranian society was revealed.

In practice the law has naturally remained a dead letter, or almost so: it has provided the forces of order with a pretext for reasserting control over the districts considered *tâquti* in the north of Tehran – for example Shahrak-e Gharb, the 'suburb of the West' as people continue to call it even though the district was renamed Shahrak-e Qods, 'suburb of Jerusalem', after the Revolution, and more precisely the residences surrounding the Golestan commercial centre – but, just as opponents of the ban had forecast, it has not really eradicated the phenomenon of dishes in the city as a whole. The thousand and one tricks through which households have remained open to the world audiovisual landscape have become a favourite topic of conversation, and so has the content of the cultural aggressors' broadcasts.

In the same way, lastly, the world of business – which we know to be increasingly under siege from companies (*sherkat*) that are, to use Max Weber's terminology, bureaucratic organisations – has become a favoured area for self-reflexivity, in the form of 'professionalisation' (*herfehi shodan*) of skills and of the economic ethos. The main model in this regard is Asian – Japanese, of course, but also Malaysian, Korean, Singaporean and Chinese. A whole literature, in the form of pamphlets and newspaper articles, praises the qualities of a good manager. For example, according to *Keyhan*, the key to his success lies in his capacity to control himself and to 'manage himself before managing others'; 'The "successful" manager has control of himself. He knows his strengths and his limits. He knows how to adapt to circumstances...He knows himself and chooses his trade according to his objectives. He uses his abilities for management of his affairs and

---

74. *Keyhan*, 1.6.1373 (1994); *Resalat*, 21.1.1373 (1994).
75. *Akhbar*, 26.1.1375 (1996).

never expends his energy for nothing...The manager must know himself.'[76]
The press is filled with articles of this sort, often translated from English,
especially from the *Reader's Digest*. It is also worth noting that left-wing
newspapers, such as *Salam* and *Keyhan*, are not the last to purvey this
ideology. Iran's industry is even depicted as a Sleeping Beauty whom
determination and self-control on the part of her management staff should be
enough to wake up. This at any rate was the message – supported with
quotations from Bertold Brecht! – of the opening speech at one of the
seminars regularly held by the Association of Company Chairmen, on that
occasion at the Homâ Hotel in Mashhad, in November 1996.

At the same time, the consumer, the companies' target, is invited to
rationalise his behaviour by the authorities and the media – to avoid waste,
to spend advisedly, to choose the best products, to recycle paper, to
economise on water and electricity – while he defines his subjectivity and
gives it his own style through access to goods. 'The history of attitudes to
objects and goods...is a way of reconciling subject and object, internal and
external facets of character,' wrote historian Daniel Roche.[77] On their side
more and more anthropologists are rejecting the idea that goods are purely
and simply a factor for alienation; they can also be a factor for
individualisation, even emancipation.[78]

In Iran, as elsewhere, working on one's body through sport or beauty
treatment involves buying of clothes and *ad hoc* accessories or cosmetic
products. In particular, the use of cosmetics is expanding rapidly among
women – not only as attire appropriate to going out in the public space,
following what happens in Western societies, but also as a practice
enhancing worth in the private space. Women put on makeup at home and in
the company of other women, among other occasions at their religious
meetings (*jaleseh*) – perhaps especially there. The absence of 'marriageable'
(*nâmahram*) men makes the cultivation and celebration of the female body
lawful, and the husband's presence makes them desirable insofar as they
correspond to the values of a modern couple. 'God is beautiful and loves
beauty,' provided that the beauty is reserved for the right person. This
privileged relationship between cosmetic use and the private space appears
clearly in the way in which women guests are welcomed in well-off circles:
they are directed towards a cloakroom and a bathroom so that they can
remove the Islamic coat and headscarf, even thick stockings, and put on
makeup before joining the gathering. Obviously the way of dressing – or
rather, often, underdressing – is in harmony with the face makeup; women's
meetings offer the best opportunity for striking décolletés and bright colours.

76. *Keyhan*, 28.5.1374 (1995).
77. D. Roche, *Histoire des choses banales. Naissance de la consommation, XVIIᵉ-XIXᵉ siècle*,
Paris, Fayard, 1997, p. 14.
78. D. Miller, *Modernity. An Ethnographic Approach*, Oxford, Berg, 1994; C.A. Breckenridge
(ed.), *Consuming Modernity, Public Culture in a South Asian World*, Minneapolis,
University of Minnesota Press, 1995.

In contrast, in the public space, cosmetics are, if not banned, at least frowned upon. They are synonymous with 'corruption' (*fesâd*) and commercialisation of the other sex in the eyes of defenders of the revolutionary moral order, and are always an adequate reason for arrest by the police. They are banned in schools and universities. At the entrance to government offices, agents watch over the proper dressing of women employees or members of the public – even, when necessary, opening bags which may contain despised products: 'Lipstick!' cries the official, holding up the accursed tube as with a look as grave and severe as if it had been a sachet of drugs, a revolver or a bomb!

As consumer products, cosmetics form the dividing line between different ethical ideas, between life styles or sections of life styles, between public and private, even if those products have ceased to be illicit and anti-Islamic for several years, and especially since the institution of Islamic norms in the lives of the citizens.[79] They are a major element in medical attention to the body – their sale and application are increasingly often carried out in pharmacies or at dermatologists' clinics – and they now intervene in general discussion about nature, from which they are considered to be derived. They can even allow *Homo Oeconomicus* to use his/her talents as a sensible consumer – concerned to know if the cream purchased is the genuine article and has not passed its expiry date – or even a vocation as a businessman, since beauty products are, with household electrical goods, the principal goods sold in the country's Free Zones or brought back from journeys and pilgrimages, and are now a not negligible export of Iranian industry.[80] Lastly, cosmetics can be made a subject of criticism of the Islamic Republic: this country, it is said, bans lipstick in government offices but derives substantial profits from its sale; it shows films whose actresses are outrageously made-up, but forbids Iranian women to appear like that in the streets of Tehran.

Similarly, the relationship with the main stages of one's life is now widely turned into something objective, through use of images, in the form of photographs and videos, which assumes of course acquiring the necessary appliances. Without returning to the filming of feasts of reason and funerals, we can stress how it has become impossible to think of a child without visual representations of him or her. This is true in families where, as soon as you cross the threshold of a house, you are assailed with the inevitable album showing the offspring in all their social-being postures: by the sea, on a neo-Louis XV armchair, in front of the birthday candles, in a park, dressed as Zorro or as a Kurd or a Gilan dweller or an Indian girl, on the telephone, in the classroom, with brothers and sisters, or in a scarlet-coloured modern

---

79. Cf. for example the proceedings of the international seminar on 'the cosmetics industry and health products', organised by a delegation of the Ministry of Industry in October 1995, *Sanaye' behdasht va arayesh*, 10, 1374 (1995), pp. 4-5, 10-13.
80. Ibid.

high chair, preparing for the highest stage of individualisation. But it is even more remarkable that magazines and even daily newspapers have taken over in this area and have whole pages filled with portraits of children, in passport photograph format, sent to them by marvelling parents, especially to celebrate their children's success at school. Thus the daily *Salam*, under the heading 'The First', has for two years been rewarding the best primary and secondary school pupils of the whole country by announcing their final marks, adding their photographs and, in certain conditions, those of their teachers.[81]

The child is king in Iran, so much so that people talk of 'bambinocracy' (*bacheh-sâlâri*), but it is partly thanks to Canon and Agfa. By definition, a photograph is an individualising process, especially as the family photo albums are often made up in the form of one per child. It is also a way of fitting this process into the family setting, according to the logic that we analysed earlier: it is not unusual to see in inside rooms old photographs from the 1930s, signs of continuity and the family's distinction. But this 'family orientation' of the individual now has to do with the nuclear family, although there is no contradiction between this and the ancestral logic of private space: the photographs stuck on the wall of the living room are not as intimate as those placed at the bedside, the preferred place for the wedding photograph; in other words, *andarun* – the private sphere – today means married life. The eye of the photographer also contributes to a change in the way childhood is regarded. As prevailing Islamic norms prohibit representation of women without headscarves and photographers are anxious to display their talents, the habit has developed of showing portraits of small girls with makeup, dress and hairdo like adults, adopting attractive poses and giving appearances of seduction before the eyes of all, in place of their mothers.

Drinking straws and plastic utensils and plates and cups, which are disposable, allow public benefactors to honour their guests in their individualities and their qualities as social givers while respecting elementary rules of modern hygiene. Family members no longer have to share the same glass or the same portion of the dish offered; every one of them, however young, has the right to receive his or her share of the gift thanks to the successes of Iranian industry. There is thus a real market in crockery for 'one-off' use, as people say in Iran; public generosity and religious usage, even more than rapid catering, have caused that market to flourish. Similarly, freezer bags allow the faithful to take home the remains of blessed food. In short, the object and its consumption take part in the formation of the 'ethical subject' and the new updating of his/her practices, rather than in the 'disillusioning' of his world. Is not Coca-Cola, in the Iranian version or the authentic one imported from Cyprus, the obligatory drink served at *hey'at*?

81. *Salam*, 18.4.1376 (1997).

As understood in this triple aspect of bureaucratising, 'advertising' and commercialisation of 'bio-politics', the generalisation and also the rationalisation of competitive practices in Iranian society lead eventually to a profound change in the relationship between private and public. Too often those two dimensions are understood as being related in a way that means one of them being external, or even being excluded in relation to the other – as if more private meant less public and vice versa. In reality the dynamics of individualisation as we have analysed them straddle the two spheres, especially as they follow the way of self-reflexivity. The social being restores precisely that continuity between the two spheres, by seeking a new connection and a new harmony between them. This, for example, was the meaning – paradoxical for many Westerners – of the wearing of the veil by many women who identified with the ideal of the Islamic Revolution.[82] This is also the way in which one can interpret the use of the car which is for driving, by definition, on the public highway, but partly to show one's 'distinction' in private life; this is not the least of the ways in which women assert their role in society. So there is not necessarily any contradiction or psychological imbalance, contrary to what is often said, in observing certain practices in families and the rules of Islam in public, even though a father like the film producer Abbas Kiarostami may show concern at the gap betweeen them and prefer to take down his satellite dish: 'We live in two worlds, internal and external, which do not fit together, this is a schizophrenic situation whose effects I dread, especially the effects on the young. I did not want television to be showing my son without a break things that he cannot have.'[83]

What matters is to understand the permanent renegotiation, through daily behaviour and recourse to reason, of the frontier that is supposed to separate public from private, a renegotiation that also involves the definition of the lawful and unlawful, in accordance with changes in knowledge and habits. Looked at from this angle, the growing autonomy of the private sphere and the individualising process that we have noted often go together with strengthening of the public sphere. Thus divorces are no longer managed by the families alone, but there is also, at the request of one or both of the couple, settlement by courts in accordance with the laws and the legal system. In this case individualisation is inseparable from the individual initiative of the husband or the wife, from his entanglement in his family network and his enrolling in the order of the law and the state. One can foretell, in observing Iranian society, that the celebration of the private sphere to which the prevailing family-oriented ideology lends itself could quite well lead to its strict delimitation and the reduction of its domain. But at the same time the family is being undeniably strengthened. More than ever it is the cornerstone of the process of individualisation and, to

82. F. Adelkhah, op. cit.
83. *Le Monde*, 4 Aug. 1995.

paraphrase Jürgen Habermas, it commands the reasoning of the public.[84] Historians of the French Revolution have shown well this interaction between growing autonomy of the private sphere in relation to absolute power, the formation of a public space, and the emergence of the idea of citizenship.[85]

Meanwhile the principle of competition, in Iran's social conditions, is giving rise to solid conformism. We have seen that rationalisation of the individualising process owes a good deal to its relationship with commercialisation. The result, despite the severity of the economic crisis, is a feeling of bourgeoisification, a real frenzy of consumption which is in contrast with the revolutionary romanticism of 1978-79 and even with the patriotic austerity of the war years. Things have gone far since the period when a young married couple was content with marriage gifts consisting just of a red rose, a Koran and a stick of sugar candy! Individualisation concerning weddings requires as an absolute 'must' the bridegroom offering a number of gold pieces corresponding to the beloved's year of birth. It is fortunate for engaged couples that the solar Hegira calendar[86] is used in these circumstances rather than the Gregorian calendar, used for example for identifying models of imported cars; this means a saving of 621 gold pieces! In a few years the Islamic Republic seems to have passed from its Thermidor period to Guizot's watchword '*Enrichissez-vous!*' In the eyes of its leaders, it is certainly a good idea to be thrifty, but not to disdain 'gifts from God': 'God the Merciful does not want a poor society...he calls for fertilising of the earth, the increase of wealth in society', the Leader of the Revolution declared in his new year speech in 1997.[87]

It would be an oversimplification to confuse this conformism with rejection of social change, even though its most important political expression has been the conservative Right since the early 1990s. First of all because the supremacy of that tendency is not unlimited, as was proved by Mohammad Khatami's victory in June 1997; secondly because this bourgeoisification and conservatism in Iranian society are not in themselves factors of stagnation or regression – they are in many respects innovating forces, whatever may be the feelings aroused by the innovations. For example, the economic ideology of the spokesmen of this idea of modernity poses in an increasingly explicit way the problem of the necessary distinction between unlawful interest (*rebâ*) and interest (*bahreh*) which should be legitimised by depreciation of the currency or the requirements of investment: rather as Catholic theologians of the Middle Ages contrasted

84. J. Habermas, op. cit., p. 40.
85. R. Chartier, *Les origines culturelles de la Révolution française*, Paris, Le Seuil, 1990.
86. Iranians follow the lunar Hegira calendar like other Muslims for religious festivals, but they use the solar calendar in the civic domain (for registration of births, deaths and marriages, for education, salaries, etc.) and the Gregorian calendar for everything relating to the 'twentieth century' (*gharn-e bistom*).
87. *Keyhan*, 16.1.1376 (1997).

'real exchange', which was acceptable, with 'dry exchange', the fruit of financial speculation, which was seen as almost incestuous dealing.[88]

To describe this development in the Islamic republic, some people do not hesitate to talk of 'Saudisation'. They suggest that the Thermidor phase was the death knell of political Islam, whose failure has meant withdrawal into the family, the individual and his personal moral problems. One may however wonder if the changes in the Islamic Republic are not rather instituting a form of 'bio-politics' now inseparable from the Islamist programme – after twenty years of institutionalising of the Revolution and turning it into something routine – and responsible for all its modernity.

88. B. Clavero, *La grâce du don. Anthropologie catholique de l'économie moderne*, Paris, Albin Michel, 1996, p. 113.

CONCLUSION

We have sought to show in this work how a 'life style' recurring through Iran's history, that of *javânmardi*, has been continually brought up to date in accordance with changes in society due to oil exploitation, urban growth, increase in population and political changes. Over the years, *javânmardi* has gradually become inseparable from the issue of the social being, and has allowed individuals – not only men but also women – to become part of the public space being formed. This public space is being developed from numerous social practices – political, religious, economic, and relating to the media and sport – to mention only the major phenomena we have analysed. In all these practices individuals, with their progress, rights and duties, are coming to be the object of their own questioning.

A sort of 'bio-power' is thus emerging, one of whose manifestations is individualising in accordance with self-reflexivity: 'Modern man is an animal in whose politics his life as a living creature is at issue.'[1] The rationalisation, bureaucratisation and commer--cialisation of Iranian society are facets of this development. Our theories thus involve the appearance of a 'type of man created by the conjunction of elements of religious and economic origin.'[2] The social being, as we have observed him, stands at the meeting point of changes in Iranian society and a programme that is both ethical and political, possibly involving religious conviction, which it has become customary to call Islamist in the 1980s.

Without denying the changes that have occurred since 1979, it should be clearly seen that the foundations of republican bio-power were laid in the writings of people like Mohammad Bagher Sadr – especially in his treatise *Our Economy*[3] – and Motahhari, for example in his articles published in the 1960s in the monarchist weekly *Zan-e ruz* (Modern Woman) on family problems, to defend the Civil Code insofar as it was compatible with *fiqh*. The issues concerning the social being relate first of all, if not to a middle class, at least to relatively homogeneous urban social strata which in a certain sense 'uphold' that class (to quote Max Weber). Historically, and in a contingent way, it overlaps partially with the socio-political policies of the Islamist movement, certainly in a minority in the 1960s but alone in formulating, with the backing of legal thinking, the bases in law for republican demands in the first period after the Revolution. In contrast, the

1. M. Foucault, *La volonté de savoir*, Paris, Gallimard, 1976, p. 188.
2. M. Weber, *Sociologie des religions*, Paris, Gallimard, 1996, p. 138.
3. C.Mallat, *The Renewal of Islamic Law. Muhammad Baqer as-Sadr, Najaf and the Shi'i International*, Cambridge University Press, 1993.

active elements in the secular anti-imperialist Left from the 1970s, while they added plenty of value to the conscious mobilisation of the militants and their commitment, often had to be satisfied with denunciation of the people's alienation in high-flown language, hardly caring about giving a concrete dimension to their utterances.

However that may be, the social strata bringing forward the issue of the social being want the political city to be in their image. In this way one can see how the new form of *javânmardi*, following the mode of self-reflexivity, is distinct from former life styles which were considered as 'arts of existence'. The issue of the social being concerns every single person, whatever his or her condition, age and sex, and it concerns a public space, while the classic style of *javânmardi* was defined by the very singularity of the personal itineraries of eminent individuals who, by definition, were almost always men. It is the ethic of an urban mass society, relatively prosperous in spite of the economic crisis. This makes the extent of a certain misunderstanding clear: the public policies of the Republic relating to the body and life, for example regarding sexuality and dress, are not the expression of an obscurantist return to the past, as is often said, but of modernity as seen by Foucault, as they cause 'life and its mechanisms to enter the domain of explicit calculations and (make) ability and knowledge an agent of change in human life'; '...what could be termed the "threshold of biological modernity" of a society occurs at the moment when the human species becomes a stake in its own political strategies.'[4]

Similarly, the idea that the Republic's insistence on ethical questions is due to a 'failure of political Islam' has to be qualified. Political Islam, in its revolutionary aspects, may be toned down, may become routine and be unable to define an original 'third way', especially in the economic field. But the creation of a moral being is at the heart of its programme, not a fallback solution or an admission of failure. In Olivier Roy's view 'there is failure because Islamic thought, at the end of an intellectual journey which makes an effort to think of modern life, is finally returning to "the Islamic political *imaginaire*" of tradition and its essential paradox: that the political sphere can only be founded on individual virtue...The essential paradox of the Islamist movement is that the political model that it puts forward presupposes individuals' virtue, but that this virtue can only be acquired if society is truly Islamic.'[5] This well describes the thought of the 1970s, not only among Muslim thinkers of all tendencies, but also on the revolutionary Left. Such a theory is no doubt a characteristic of all avant-gardism. It has also clearly that it has been perpetuated in modern political discussion.

But the event of the Revolution, the institutionalising of the Republic, the creation of a public space, and changes in the fabric of society have profoundly redefined the problem. On the one hand, Imam Khomeyni did

4. F. Foucault, op. cit., p. 188.
5. O. Roy, *L'échec de l'islam politique*, Paris, Le Seuil, 1992, pp. 36 and 42.

not see the Islamic Republic as the ideal city, a city of virtue; as he replied to conservative critics at Qom, it aspired to prepare for the coming of the ideal city. He definitely followed the agenda of social action, meaning arbitration and compromise, going so far as to drink the bitter cup of the truce with Iraq in 1988. On the other hand, this agenda of action has involved precisely the relationship between ethics and the social domain. By definition, a social being is not a mystic, he does not abandon the civic stage, he intends to move actively into it as a moral being. Ethics, in any case, is not something fixed and timeless; it is constantly being reinvented in precise historical contexts, as we have seen through actual practices regarding the *hejâb* and the continual reformulation of *javânmardi*.

This was the real significance of Mohammad Khatami's election victory, however his government may perform; the voters' choice approved a 'type of man', a social being who is also highly qualified, regards application of the law as important and calls for a state based on the rule of law. Once again, there is no question of forecasting the 'success' (or 'failure') of what seems to be a movement to liberalise and open up the regime; one should rather seek to understand the problems at the heart of political – albeit Islamic – debates. Certainly no politician today has the charisma of Imam Khomeyni or the major leaders of the nationalist movement, but 'disenchantment' is the sign of a modern society, i.e., the autonomy of the social sphere. There are many more actors involved, they have given birth to a real pluralism though not real democracy, and life-styles have been diversified. One should not be misled by the continuity in the regime's ideological language and of some features – such as the handful of intellectuals of the pre-revolutionary years who continue to be revered: Ahmad Shamlu, Mehdi Akhavan Sales, Nima Yoshij, Forugh Farrokhzad, Ali Shariati. Society has become differentiated and more complex, and none of the actors can hope any more for a monopoly over it. The hotly contested elections of 1996 and 1997 illustrated this. The main loser in the presidential elections, Ali-Akbar Nategh Nuri, won 7 million votes, and even a candidate as marginal as Mohammadi Rey Shahri obtained some votes over the country as a whole, including rural constituencies and peripheral provinces.

Iran's modernity comes precisely from the formation of the moral being, the social being, to the extent that he is constantly and critically renegotiating the relation between private and public. It corresponds well to the definition given by Jürgen Habermas of the public space: it means 'public use of reason' which often involves the definition of subjectivity in the private sphere, but which also has repercussions on the political scene – according to a revolutionary theme yesterday, to the issue of regulation today.

But the creation of that public space, though derived from universal phenomena, is obviously not a simple carbon copy of the process that has prevailed in the West. For example, it is revealing that Iranians readily connect it with 'fertilisation'; Tehran's inhabitants express satisfaction that their Mayor has made their city 'fertile' by creating new parks, and Mohammad Khatami promised voters a 'fertile Iran' (*Irân-e âbâd*). If there must be a public space, it will be in the image of a garden or an oasis. Similarly, the distinction between public and private very probably recalls basic ideas of appearance (*zâher*) and the inner being (*bâten*); in answer to a question from a BBC journalist on the difference in behaviour between women in the street and at home, Hashemi Rafsanjani made a reply suggesting that at home their attitude concerns only their own convictions, not the state.[6] The diversification of Iranian society is not only political, socio-economic or geographical. It is also historical and cultural in nature, as the philosopher Abdelkarim Soroush recalls when he speaks of 'three cultures'.[7] The country relates just as much to its pre-Islamic past and its borrowings from the West as to Islam.

In short, to be modern in Iran is to set oneself up as a moral being in a relatively precise context, according to ideas of self-reflexivity and in relation to a public space of a rational-legal type. It is impossible to stress strongly enough that Islam is not really a relevant parameter in this matter, or more precisely that it is important only in relation to a whole series of other social, political, economic and cultural factors. However, it still remains at the heart of the modernity question twenty years after the 1979 Revolution. That Revolution triumphed over an illusion: the illusion of a modernity that would have confined religion to the private sphere. In fact Islam, as a set of practices, as an institution of knowledge and as an intellectual product, is directly involved in the creation of a public space – and, as we have seen, not only because the ideology of the regime aspires to be Islamic. But we must not fall into another illusion which would make Islam the conveyor of modernity *par excellence* or even the alpha and omega of socio-political change. It is more prosaically a part of Iran, certainly a central part, but not necessarily more important from the social point of view than, say, the reality of cities, the search for knowledge, the economic crisis, the upward thrust of youth, the regional environment and family obligations.

The anthropologist is often tired of seeing a country of sixty million people summed up in a few clichés epitomised in the endlessly reproduced photograph of women wearing the *châdor* in the streets of Tehran, supposing to symbolise the totalitarian nature of the republic of the Mullahs. The preceding pages are not intended to give legitimacy to that Republic, whatever some readers determined to slay the monster may think. The only object has been to analyse a society whose development remains very uncertain. While it is certain that Iranian society is not defined solely in terms of desperate resistance to an omnipresent and coercive power – to adopt the tone used in a good deal of writing – its capacity to set up a form of democracy remains to be proved.

6. *Keyhan*, 6 Jan. 1375 (1996).
7. A. Soroush, *Râzdâni, roshanfekri va dindâri*, Tehran, Sarât, 1370 (1991), pp. 105-29.

GLOSSARY

Note The Persian letter commonly transcribed as '*q*' is pronounced '*gh*' and is often alternatively transcribed as '*gh*'. In this Glossary '*q*' is used.)

'abâ	garment covering the body from shoulders to feet, with opening at the front
âbâdâni	fertility
âbâdi	oasis
âberu	honour
adabiyât-e masjed	mosque literature
âdam	human being
âdam-e bi kheyr	a 'man with no good in him', not capable of helping another
âdam-e ejtemâ'i	a social being – characterised by his commitment towards others, extending into the public domain, based on redefinition of his relations with others and with his own people
âdam-e hesâbi	person of integrity
ahel-e takhassos	expert
ahl-e mahal	residents, locals
a'lam	the wisest
'alâmat	emblem made from a blend of metals, carried during Âshurâ processions
'âlem-e motejazzi	learned man with specialised knowledge
'amal-e kheyr	good deed
'amaliyât-e zarbati	lightning operation
andarun	the private sphere
anjoman	association
aqiq	precious stone favoured by men of religion
ârâmesh	peace, calm
araq	plant essence
arâzel	delinquents, street boys
asabiyya	solidarity group
Âshurâ	the tenth day of the month of Moharram, anniversary of the dastardly murder of the Prophet's grandson, Imam Hussein, the third Shia Imam
aslah	the most suitable
asnâf	the guilds
Âstân-e Qods	'sacred threshold': the Imam Reza mausoleum complex

179

ayatollah	lit. sign of God; title in the clerical hierarchy
ayatollah ozmâ	supreme sign of God
'ayyâr	'social bandit' like Robin Hood
az khod gozashtegi	having the notion of selflessness, altruism
âzâdegi	grandeur, nobility
bâ mardom neshast-o barkhâst dâshtan	'sitting down and getting up with the people', 'sitting down and getting up with the people', liking to socialise in meaningful way
bacheh mahal	child of the neighbourhood
bacheh bâz	paedophile
bacheh-sâlâri	bambinocracy
bahreh	interest
bahreh banki	bank interest
bâjgir	racketeer
bânu-ye nikukâr	woman of good deeds
bâqcheh	small garden, small square patch laid out as a garden in courtyard of a house
bassij	originally, the mobilised volunteers on the Iran-Iraq war front; then, after that war, ex-volunteers forming an institutionalised body since 1994
bassiji	member of the *bassij* body
bâten	interior being
bâzâr-e entekhâbât	the electoral market
bâzargân	merchant
bâzâri	member of the bazaar trades corporation
bâzi	game, play
bâzi-ye javânmardâneh	[equivalent phrase] fair play
bed'at	innovation
bedard-e mardom residan	receiving people's grievances; paying attention to the people
Behesht-e Zahra	Paradise of Zahra, the name of the cemetery in the south-west of Tehran
behzisti	well-being
beyt	house or place where people of the same entourage meet; household
beyt-e rahbari	household of the Leader of the Revolution
beytol-mâl	treasury belonging to the people
birun	appearance
boresh dâshtan	to be efficient, decisive
bumi	indigenous, native, authentic
châdor	garment covering the body from head to feet with an opening at the front
châqu kesh	knife wielder

chelo-kabâb	dish, said to be traditional, made from rice and meat grilled over a coal fire
cheshm-o del pâk	to have pure looks and a pure heart, without frivolity in relation to the sex instinct
cheshm-o del sir	a fulfilled person
cinemâ-ye jang	war films
daftar	office
dafter-e rahbari	office of the Leader of the Revolution; other term used for *beyt-e rahbari*
dallâl	middleman
dânesh âmuz	pupil
dârâ	rich, with possessions
darun	interior being, internal
dâsh-mashdi	term used for a 'roughneck' (*gardan koloft*) or *javânmard*
dast-e bedeh	the giving hand; generosity
dast-e begir	the taking hand; meanness
dast-o del bâz	to be generous
degar andish	someone who thinks differently
delsuz	to have a good heart
dieh	blood price
din	religion
do'âye nodbeh	reading of a chapter (*nodbeh*) of the Book of prayers on Friday morning
dolat	the state
dolati	of (relating to) the state
donyâ	the social field
dowreh	circle, meetings (held in participants' homes in turn)
duq	yoghurt-based drink
dust	friend
eftâr	breaking the fast
eftekâr	pride
ejtemâ'i	social
ejtemâ'i shodan	the process by which one becomes a 'social being'
ekhlâlgar	disturber
'elm	science, knowledge
emâmzâdeh	descendant of an Imam
ensân-dust	philanthropist
enzebât	discipline
'erfâni	esoteric, gnostic
e'temâd	trust
faqih	person of religious learning

faqr	poverty
farang-sarâ	foreigners' dwelling
farhang-sarâ	cultural centre
farizeh	duty
farrâsh	caretaker
faryâd-ras	helping one's kin
fati	(lit.) young; *javânmard*
fesâd	corruption
fetriyeh	Islamic tax at the end of Ramadan
fiqh (Arabic) or	
feqh (Persian)	the corpus of Islamic law
firuzeh	turquoise, precious stone especially favoured by men of religion
fotowwat	the existential ethic of the *fati* or *javânmard*
frâksion-e varzesh	'sports faction' in parliament
gardan koloft	roughneck, strong man, local bullyboy
gedâ-khuneh	house of the beggars
golhâye junemun	the flowers of our soul
gorg	wolf
guyandeh	female speaker or TV presenter
Hadis	record of the words and acts of the Prophet, as relayed by various sources and testimony
hafteh nikukâri	good deeds week
hamegani	public, for the use of everyone
hamshahri	fellow citizen
haq	justice, truth
harâm	unlawful
hedyeh	gift
hejâb	state of mind or value system, reflected in ways of behaviour, notably regarding dress
hejâb-e zâher	clothing, more particularly the *chador* or standard Islamic dress
herfehi shodan	acquisition of a professional skill
hesâb	arithmetic
hesâb-o ketâb	(lit.) arithmetic and book; norms of good behaviour
hey'at	religious meeting for men
hey'at modireh	management board
hey'at-e omanâ	founder members
hezb	party
Hezbollâh	the Party of God
Hojjatiyeh	pious society created in 1953 and suspended in 1983
hojjatoleslam	proof of Islam
hojreh	places for trade within the bazaar

hojrehi	cellular
hoseynieh	religious centres dedicated to Imam Hussein, used for celebrations, especially religious ones
hozeh	religious schools; by extension, the clergy generally
imam jom'eh	the Imam of Friday prayers
irân-e âbâd	fertile Iran
jadvali	multiplying (with reference to loans)
jaleseh	religious meeting especially for women
jam'iyat	group
jâme'eh	society
jang-e zargari	a jewellers' war; a discussion too remote to be understood by ordinary people.
javânmard	the man of integrity
javânzan	(neologism) woman who shows proof of selflessness, woman of integrity
jib chon bânk	to have a pocket the size of a bank
jigar dâshtan	to have heart or courage; to dare
joz'	one of the thirty more or less equal parts into which the Koran is subdivided
kaftar-bâz	pigeon-fancier
kalâm ol-lâh	the Word of God, the Koran
kâr	work
kâr-o bâresh gerefteh	his business has got ahead, is solid
kârâi	efficiency
kas nakhârad posht-e man, joz nâkhon-e angosht-e man	assertion of man's independence, but also of his loneliness
khâb-e zan chapeh	women's dreams are reality back to front
khâneh Sabzevar	Sabzevar House (called after Sabzevar in Khorassan)
khânum	lady
kharâb kardand	to have ruined
kharâbeh	ruin
khâreji	foreigner
khâsiyat-e 'erfani	mystical virtue
khayyer	benefactor
kheyrieh	benevolent or public generosity institution
khod-yâri	to help oneself
khodâ posht-o panâhet	may God be your support and protection
khodi	intimates
khoms	one of the Islamic taxes
khosh hesâb	to be a good account/customer

khoshki	dryness
kolâh bardâr	hat snatcher, i.e. swindler
komiteh	originally, armed protection groups set up during the Revolution to protect civilians; later they, with the police and gendarmerie, formed the Forces of Order (1992)
luti	term for 'roughnecks' *(gardan koloft)*; another term for *javânmard*
ma'âd	man's spiritual dimension
ma'âsh	material things
maddâh	reciter, singer of praises of the saints
madreseh	school
maghna'eh	a sort of hood coming down over the shoulders
mahalleh	district
Majles	the Iranian parliament
maktabi	doctrinaire (in respect of the Republic's Islamic ideology)
mâlek	possessing property or financial capital
mamlekat	the country
marâje'(pl. *marja*)-*e shakhsi*	personal interests
mardânegi	the quality of a man of integrity
mardom	the people
marja'-e taqlid	Source of Emulation
mashdi	term for 'roughnecks' *(gardan koloft)*; another term for *javânmard*
mellat	the nation
melli	national
meydun	market place (variant pronunciation, especially in Tehran, of *meydân*)
meydun-dâr	market manager
meyduni	market middleman
mo'âfiyat-e mâliyâti	tax exemption
mo'allem	teacher
mo'ammem	turbaned man, cleric, as opposed to *mokalla*
mo'tamed	person to be trusted
mofsed-e felarz	the corrupt man on earth; by extension, anti-revolutionary
mohandes	engineer
Moharram	one of the lunar calendar months
mokalla	man with a hat, layman
mollâh	learned man of religion; also, in some contexts, a man of religion belonging to the lower rank of the clerical hierarchy
momayezzi	censorship

mosâbeqeh	competition
mostaz'af (pl. *mostaz'afin*)	disinherited, deprived person
mote'ahhed	a man of conviction, a committed man
mote'âraf	according to norms laid down
motekhasses	expert
mozâreb	the party with capacity to work, in the contract called *mozârebeh*
mozârebeh	limited partnerships
nâ-haq	falsehood, injustice
na-javânmard	non-*javânmard*
nahâd	institution
nâmahram	any man over 15 who is outside the circle of intimates of a woman, i.e. her husband, father, father-in-law, brothers, grandfathers, legitimate sons (natural and fostered) and grandsons
namâz	daily prayer
nesf-e jahân	half of the world
nikukâri	doing a good deed
no'dust	philanthropist
nocheh	'small boys' who help the 'roughnecks' (*gardan koloft*); disciple, novice
noruz	the Iranian new year, right at the beginning of spring, on 20 or 21 March according to the year
nozul	interest; another term for *rebâ*
nozulkhâr	eater of *rebâ* (interest)
obâsh	delinquents, street boys
okhtâpus	octopus
omid	hope
orupâ'i	European
osul	principle
pahlavân	hero
pârti	string-pulling, using contacts to get favours
pârti bâzi	interplay of relationships; clientelism
pedâr sâlâr	patriarch
pishkesvat	precursors
pishraft	progress
porsesh-o pâsokh	question and answer
posht	back
posht be posht	back to back (close to others)
posht dâshtan	'to have back', i.e. backing
posht garmi dashtan	to have backing
posht-e ham budan	to be one behind the other, to show solidarity
posht-e ham râ dâshtan	to show solidarity
puldar	rich

qahramân	champion
qânun	laws
qâri	reciter of the Koran
qarz ol-hasaneh	a good loan, loan without interest
qeyr-e entefâ'i	non-profit-making
qodrat-e qom-o khish	the power of the families
qoldor	bully
qowm	tribute
râbeteh	the order of personal connections
raft-o âmad	reciprocal visits
Ramazân	Ramadan, one of the months of the lunar calendar
rebâ	interest, usury
rebâkar	eater of *rebâ*, usurer
regim	regime
resâleh	thesis
riba	see *rebâ*
ruhiyeh	morale, good spirits
sabz	green
Safar	a month of the lunar calendar
sahm-e emâm	the Imam's share
salâm sobh bekheyr	good morning greetings
salavâti	provided from benevolence (hence free)
saliqeh	taste
sandoq-e akhmâs	funds of the *khoms*, an Islamic tax
sandoq-e kheyrât va sadaqât	funds from almsgiving
sânsur	censorship
sarshenâs	to have a wide reputation
sâyeh-e sar	(lit.) shadow over the head; protectot
sekhâvat	generosity
sekkeh	coin
servatmand	rich
setâd-e tabliqâti	election propaganda front
shahr	city
shahro âbâd kardan	to have fertilised the city
shâl	cloth symbolising the presence of the deceased during mourning ceremonies
shâmi kabâb	cakes made from meat, eggs, chickpea flour and onions
shar'i	legal (in the Islamic sense)
shenâs	acquaintance
shenâs-e khânevâdeh	family acquaintance
sherkat	company (in the economic sense), enterprise

sho'ur	intelligence, reason
shojâ'at	courage
shorâ	council
shorâhâ-ye eslâmi-e shahr	Islamic municipal councils
shorâhâ-ye mahalli	local councils
shur	passion
siyâsat bâz	Machiavellian
sofreh	table cloth; by extension, the name of a religious ceremony
sofreh dâri	to be able to hold a table cloth, i.e. to receive guests
sokhanrân	female speaker
sonnati	traditional
ta'zieh	ceremony surrounding death, particularly the death of Imam Hussein
takhassos	competence
takiyeh	places arranged and reserved for commemoration of saints for a fixed period
taklif	duty
talabeh	religious student
tanzim-e khânevâdeh	family regulation/planning
tâquti	idolater; in revolutionary terminology, people linked with the Shah's regime
tar-dasti	practical skill
tavâshih	men's or women's Koranic choir
tejârat	trading activity
teroristhâ-ye eqtesadi	economic terrorists
umma/ (Persian) *ommat*	the community of Muslim believers
vâ'ez	preacher
va en yakâd	Koranic verse engraved on jewels in the form of a pendant or brooch
vakil	lawyer
vâm-dâr	debtor
vâm-e banki	bank credit
vaqf	Islamic religious property (Arabic *waqf*)
vâred budan	to have a business sense, to be skilful
varzesh	sport
varzesh-e bâstâni	ancient sport; sport played in a *zur-khâneh*
vâseteh	middleman
vaz'esh khubeh	he is well situated
vazifeh	duty
vekâlat	delegation
velâyat	region; mandate in accordance with the principle of transcendence

velâyat-e faqih	the guardianship of the Islamic jurist
virâneh	ruin
vojuhât	the portion of religious taxes reserved for the Sources of Emulation for the running of religious affairs
zâbeteh	the order of regulations
zâher	appearance
zakât	one of the religious taxes
zâlu-sefat	bloodsucker
zan	woman
zendegi-nâmeh	curriculum vitae
zeynabieh	places dedicated to Zeynab, the Prophet's granddaughter, and used especially for religious meetings
ziyârat	pilgrimage
ziyârat-o siyâhat	pilgrimage and tourism
ziyârat-o tejârat	pilgrimage and trade
zohur	coming, appearance (of the Twelfth Imam)
zoq	inspiration
zulbiyâ bâmiyeh	Ramadan pastries
zur-khâneh	(lit.) house of strength

INDEX